BEND,

OVERALL

a guide to Exploring the Area's Best!

by Scott Cook

Wall Street, circa 1910.

2nd Edition Copyright © 2010
1st edition 2004

All photography and text: Scott Cook

Design, layout and printing by Jody Conners and Gary Asher of Maverick Publications, Bend Oregon.

Email Scott: BendOverallGuidebook@yahoo.com
Scott Cook
PO Box 861
Hood River, OR 97031

Cover photo: Mt. Bachelor rising over Todd Lake (37)

*Don't Panic. A tribute to the late Douglas Adams for writing *Hitchhiker's Guide to the Galaxy*...the funniest guidebook **Ever!**

Warning: Hiking and exploring the Central Oregon and surroundings can be and is dangerous. All information in this book has been personally checked by the author to be accurate. Trail conditions do change though and unforeseen mishaps lurk around every corner. Don't do anything I'd do. The author can accept no responsibility for any injury, inconvenience, pregnancy, skullduggery...confusion, elation, or retaliation. If the beers you stashed in the ice-cold creek get swiped, ha-ha too bad. If you're driving round 'n' round the S-E-X roundabout laughing at the oddity and you get smashed by an in-a-hurry contractor...hmmm...you shoulda sped up! If you slip and fall to your death in a remote, gorgeous waterfall canyon and bigfoot scavenges your remains...well, sorry I guess. If you're skinny-dipping and some prankster sneaks up and steals your clothes... don't blame me.

   If, on the other hand, you find more outdoors happiness than you know what to do with...then please send me an email to brighten my day.

WHAT • WHERE • WHEN
Special things that happen in special places at special times

APRIL

Trout Creek Bluffs (89)
Prineville Res North Bank Rd re-opens (92)
Cougar Hot Spring (60)
Blue Basin/ Thomas Condon VisCtr (99)
Glass Buttes (9)
Badlands are good (7)

MAY

Gray Butte Trail (84)
South Ice Cave icicles (21)
Derrick Cave icicles (23)
Painted Hills wildflowers (98)
Billy Chinook – Tam-a-Lau Trail blooms (87)
McKenzie River trails open (63)
Pictograph Cave re-opens (12)

JUNE

Skylight Cave sunbeams (50)
Ochoco's Big Summit Prairie Blooms (97)
Hager Mtn wildflowers (mid) (24)
Deer Creek Hot Spring warms up (62)
Marion Lake's Falls FULL (71)
Lookout Mtn (Ochocos) bloom (late month) (94)
Salt Creek Falls Rhododendrons (last week)
    (27)
McKenzie Pass usually re-opens (late June) (52)

JULY

Cascade mosquitoes GALORE – bring DEET!
Wildflowers – First two weeks:
Canyon Creek Meadows wildflowers (75)
Iron Mtn wildflowers (67)
Coffin Mtn wildflowers (70)
Sunriver Nature Center – See The SUN! (16)
Sunriver Toads (last week) (16)

AUGUST

Time to swim! Cascade Lakes warm up,
    mosquitoes gone:
Lucky Lake (46)
Sisters Mirror Lakes (43)
Paulina/East Lakes (20)
Waldo Lakes (29)
Vivian Lake (28)
Benson/ Tenas Lakes (56,7)
Yapoah Lake (54)
Three Creek Lakes (48)

Warmish waterfalls:
Steelhead Falls (85)
Paulina Creek (19)
Marion Creek (71)

SEPTEMBER

Shevlin Park Aspens color (late) (4)
Deschutes River Trail colors (late) (6)
Broken Top Glacier Lake (38)
North Sister Thayer Lake (49)
Paulina Hot Springs – nice (20)
Crater Lake for locals (less crowds) (25)

NOVEMBER

Odell Lake Kokanee spawn (26)

OCTOBER

McKenzie Hwy/126 COLORS! (late) (52, 66)
Cougar/Deer Creek Hot Springs (60,62)

Larch Colors:
Metolius River (77-79)
Shevlin Park (4)
Round Mtn (96)
Kokanee Spawn (App 2)

BEND, OVERALL

35 Hikes and Explorations in Central Oregon

Scott Cook

Check BendOverallBlog!

BEND,
OVERALL

WHAT • WHERE • WHEN
Special things that happen in special places at special times

APRIL

Trout Creek Bluffs (89)
Prineville Res North Bank Rd re-opens (92)
Cougar Hot Spring (60)
Blue Basin/ Thomas Condon VisCtr (99)
Glass Buttes (9)
Badlands are good (7)

MAY

Gray Butte Trail (84)
South Ice Cave icicles (21)
Derrick Cave icicles (23)
Painted Hills wildflowers (98)
Billy Chinook – Tam-a-Lau Trail blooms (87)
McKenzie River trails open (63)
Pictograph Cave re-opens (12)

JUNE

Skylight Cave sunbeams (50)
Ochoco's Big Summit Prairie Blooms (97)
Hager Mtn wildflowers (mid) (24)
Deer Creek Hot Spring warms up (62)
Marion Lake's Falls FULL (71)
Lookout Mtn (Ochocos) bloom (late month) (94)
Salt Creek Falls Rhododendrons (last week) (27)
McKenzie Pass usually re-opens (late June) (52)

JULY

Cascade mosquitoes GALORE – bring DEET!
Wildflowers – First two weeks:
Canyon Creek Meadows wildflowers (75)
Iron Mtn wildflowers (67)
Coffin Mtn wildflowers (70)
Sunriver Nature Center – See The SUN! (16)
Sunriver Toads (last week) (16)

AUGUST

Time to swim! Cascade Lakes warm up,
    mosquitoes gone:
Lucky Lake (46)
Sisters Mirror Lakes (43)
Paulina/East Lakes (20)
Waldo Lakes (29)
Vivian Lake (28)
Benson/ Tenas Lakes (56,7)
Yapoah Lake (54)
Three Creek Lakes (48)

Warmish waterfalls:
Steelhead Falls (85)
Paulina Creek (19)
Marion Creek (71)

SEPTEMBER

Shevlin Park Aspens color (late) (4)
Deschutes River Trail colors (late) (6)
Broken Top Glacier Lake (38)
North Sister Thayer Lake (49)
Paulina Hot Springs – nice (20)
Crater Lake for locals (less crowds) (25)

OCTOBER

McKenzie Hwy/126 COLORS! (late) (52, 66)
Cougar/Deer Creek Hot Springs (60,62)

Larch Colors:
Metolius River (77-79)
Shevlin Park (4)
Round Mtn (96)
Kokanee Spawn (App 2)

NOVEMBER

Odell Lake Kokanee spawn (26)

Check BendOverallBlog!

TABLE OF CONTENTS

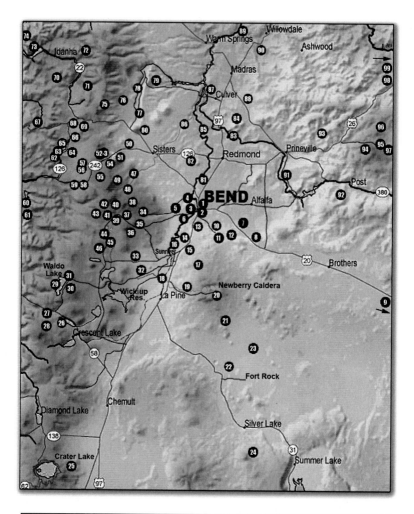

7

DEDICATION

"Come visit us again and again. This is a state of excitement. But, for heaven's sake, don't come here to live."

– Governor Tom McCall, 1971

Bend, Overall is dedicated to Tom McCall, the Governor of Oregon 1967-1975. Governor McCall was the rarest of politicians...one who put passion, courage and actions ahead of political maneuverings. Governor McCall had the rare vision, will, and charisma to attempt to shape the Oregon around him, and he succeeded in grand fashion. The Oregon we have today...a land of unspoiled beauty, public beaches, non-sprawling towns...owes a large debt of gratitude to Tom McCall's governance.

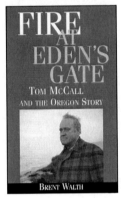

If you love Oregon today, then please read the Tom McCall biography *Fire at Eden's Gate* by Brent Walth. This biography details how a great man molded a great state to become even greater. This biography will make you appreciate Oregon like few other books will. Read it!

If you are already a long-time fan of Tom McCall, then here's a little extra bit of local insight. Tom, who was born near Prineville, is buried at the Redmond Memorial Cemetery.

Make a trip to honor a friend! The cemetery is located just 2 minutes off Hwy 97 at the south end of Redmond.

On Hwy 97 exit west at Yew Ave (the airport exit). Go west past Comfort Suites one block to Canal, then left at the stop for 100 yards to the signed entrance for Redmond Memorial Cemetery. The unassuming gravestone is in section D in row 980—the SE area of the cemetery.

Long live the memory of Tom McCall!

GOVERNOR
TOM McCALL
1913 — 1983

GOVERNOR OF OREGON
1967 — 1975
HE CARED

AUTHOR'S NOTE

Bend, Overall is a guidebook for people who want to HAVE FUN in the outdoors. *Bend, Overall* is primarily a hiking guidebook, but my intent is to also make it an EXPLORER'S guidebook…a guidebook highlighting what's fun and exciting to explore in Central Oregon. *Bend, Overall* has all the <u>Must-Do</u> Forest Service trails such as Green Lakes, Proxy Falls, Smith Rock, Black Butte, etc etc…but it also is chock full o' hidden waterfalls, swimmable lakes, off-trail bushwhack excursions, drivable viewpoint peaks, and strange historic/geologic oddities.

If you want a "HIKING" guidebook that's short on details and long on dull, then look to a Falcon guide. If you want a brilliant comprehensive guidebook that describes EVERY hiking option in Central Oregon, then please get William Sullivan's superb "100 Hikes in Oregon's Central Cascades". **Bend, Overall is meant to be a different offering.** I haven't written this guide to simply regurgitate the "same old, same old" in different words just to try to make a buck. I've revised and expanded *Bend, Overall* because the singularly remarkable landscape of Central Oregon deserves it. I don't think that the "hiking" guides go far enough in helping people explore and discover the staggering variety of outdoor options we have around here.

Overall, this 2nd edition of *Bend, Overall* isn't nearly as sexy, nor quite as off-the-cuff as the first. I'm sorry to those that rejoiced at how sexy and playful my original edition was. I still poke fun at ATV'ers and gun-folks, still show skinny-dippers, but just not as often. The realities of retailing "to the masses" have smacked me down a bit. To those who mourn the shrouding of the boob, hold tight to your 1st edition…and check in with page 133 to see what happened to the forest pixie.

Overall overall, I think this edition's BETTER…way better. I've attempted to add nuance to EVERY entry…a li'l nugget of insight, history, movie trivia, or extra exploration options. In **<u>EVERY</u>** entry I've tried to go beyond the norm of what a typical guidebook or website would give you. I re-hiked <u>every</u> trail, took <u>every</u> picture, watched *every* Bend movie and read ~~every~~ lots of local history books. Give the new *Bend, Overall* a good read-thru. Re-read the excursions you've already done—I bet you'll learn of some new stuff, even at places you've been more than once. I've learned a lot about guidebook writing in the past 6 years, and I've also learned a lot more explorable nooks and crannies in our own neighborhood. I've tried to pack almost everything I know into this edition.

I've also learned as a guidebook author that even if people buy my book, they rarely go out and explore the obscure places in any significant numbers. In my original book I was leery of telling "the secrets" for fear that masses would rush out and ruin the very spots I love. But now, 8 years and 4 books into my guidebook "career", I've realized that most people don't make a mad rush to the obscure spots. Only a few gung-ho explorers will really dig deep and seek out the super-obscure. Most folks just don't have the time or gusto to ferret-out "the secrets"… they're just happy to have good directions to the highlight spots they've heard about. I truly hope that I motivate <u>YOU</u> to find the obscure gems of Central Oregon. I hope my directions and exaltations lead you to wonders you've never heard of…places to take your breath away…places that will inspire you to love and protect our outdoors.

Thanks for buying my book,

USING THIS GUIDE

WhatWhereWhen. This is a new feature of this guide attempting synopsize 20 years or Central Oregon exploring into one succinct reminder-chart. **WhatWhereWhen** is based in the notion that plenty of stuff in Central Oregon is seasonal and if you don't "catch it" at the right time, then you COMPLETELY miss out. You can't see a wildflower, a cave sun-beam, a spawning salmon, or an icicle when they're not there!! It's not fun to see a waterfall that's already dried up, nor is it fun to be at a swimming hole/lake when it's too cold to swim. Thus, this chart is a reminder of those special seasonal spots that you'll want to plan for. I put two of the charts in an easy-to-reference spot so that you won't miss them…and one is meant to cut out and be magneted onto your fridge. I actually want you to catch our wonderland at its best!!

BendOverallBlog. This is a blog meant to enhance each entry of Bend, Overall with "the rest of the story" as well as additional Google maps, pix, updates, changes, etc etc. A check-in with the blog will improve any excursion you take, especially the obscure ones. The Google maps can really help clarify and simplify the excursion more so than a photo of a Topo map.

And, since it's a blog, you can comment on the entry and add feedback as to whether the wildflowers are blooming, fish jumping, icicles dripping, Kokanees spawning etc etc. The blog also will allow me to link to other sites and info spots to add flavor to an entry. Personally I've yet to see a guidebook with a companion blog…but I think it'll be a wave of the future. I'm not attempting to create one of those semi-worthless books mass-produced by the big publishers. *Bend, Overall* attempts to nudge the paradigm a bit to make a better guidebook. Please chime in on the blog and lemme know what you think.

I haven't included a definitive Blog address because I'm not sure where the blog may be hosted or if it'll change with popularity…but if you Google "BendOverallBlog" I think you'll find it.

Obscure-o-Meter. The Obscure-o-Meter is an odd attempt to relate the entry's relative popularity vs. obscurity. I've included this li'l meter to try to help out two different sorts of people: long-time locals vs. first-time visitors. My notion is that first-timers mostly want Bend's popular highlights, whereas locals are often interested in places they maybe haven't heard of—the obscurest stuff. Visitors may not want to spend the day chasing after an obscure 100-foot waterfall like Linton or a lake as hidden as Hidden Lake when there are plenty of spectacular excursions with much easier access. But to a local who has "seen it all", then an hour's drive to see something rarely-seen and obscure is totally worth it. I believe that most first-time visitors should stick with the entries on the more-popular half of the meter because these attractions are popular for good reason—they're both easy-to-find and spectacular. Still though, most visitors often want to see some lesser-known spots instead of solely the highlight spots written up in every promo article. I believe that seeing Crater Lake's obscure *Lady of the Woods* definitely makes a trip to Crater Lake more memorable, mostly just because most of the millions never know it's there.

The Obscure-o-Meter let's you in on "secrets" few locals even know about, especially locals who aren't savvy enough to buy *Bend, Overall*! On the other hand, this book isn't written with only tourists in mind...and when long-time locals see entries for places they've never heard of with obscurity ratings pinned to the left...then they'll know that it's time to bust out the maps and plan some ventures!!

Dogs. Central Oregon has more dog restrictions and leash laws than anywhere else I've ever visited. Listed on every entry is a "head's up" whether there are restrictions on Fido at that particular location. The most restrictive areas—the Deschutes River Trail and the near-in Cascade Lakes areas—have summertime restrictions and actual enforcement. There are plenty of places with no restrictions—you're holding an entire book full of ideas...go fetch some.

Drive time. The "Drivetime from Bend" is a guess as to a reasonable expectation for the one-way drive time. Of course there are variables, but at least it's a suggestion to help you plan.

Trail Fees. Each entry lists the applicable fee. If you hike a lot just buy the annual NW Forest Pass—check online for locations. If you are a visitor, then each Central Oregon town usually has one spot that sells the passes, or they're available at the popular trailheads for $5 per day. These passes are PARKING PASSES only—using the trail itself is free. If you don't have a pass, then find some farther away spot to park and walk extra rather that risking a ticket. Google "NW Forest Pass".

Google Maps. Google Earth is simply REMARKABLE!!! If you tried it a year ago...then you ain't seen nothing yet! It has vastly improved since just 2009. The maps included in *Bend, Overall* are screen-grabs. Hopefully they do not violate Google's Fair-Use policies. My intent with including them is to use Google's fabulous resource to help people better enjoy our outdoors...and to introduce people to Google Earth who may not already know about it.

FYI, in all my Google-Earthing, all over the globe, I've found NOWHERE as interesting to look at as Central Oregon! Seeing the lava terrains from above is nothing less than WOW. The local geology comes alive like I'd never experienced it before. Learn to use the tilt feature! Thanks Google!

KIDS LOVE

Mirror Pond for its space and chance to feed and harrass the geese.

4) **Shevlin Park:** Fish at Aspen Hall or picnic at Tumalo Creek.

10) **Boyd Cave:** fun if everyone is dressed warmly and has their own flashlight.

13) **High Desert Museum:** kids go crazy for all the wildlife, the puppet room, and the chance to ask questions and participate at the presentations.

14) **Lava Butte:** interesting short hikes. Check out the fire lookout and feed the squirrels at the summit picnic tables.

15) **Lava River Cave:** Lanterns for rent. The cave is pretty long—warm clothes and their own flashlights keep kids excited.

17) **Lava Cast Forest:** they like to climb and crawl in the tree casts, and the one-mile length and map keep things moving.

16) **Sunriver Nature Center:** lots of hands-on kids displays, plus the popular telescopes and raptors.

19) **Paulina Creek Falls:** First waterfalls are about 1.5m up from McKay, or just play and picnic at McKay Campground and its waterfall.

21) **South Ice Cave:** May icicle exploration.

32) **Fall River:** Shallow, mellow...and near Sunriver.

36) **Mt. Bachelor Chairlift:** kids love it! The ride and restaurant make for a great family outing.

37) **Todd Lake:** a bit chilly for adults, but shallow for all-ages wading. Independent kids may be able to hike the lakeshore trail by themselves.

39) **Sparks Lake:** Shallow and warm for all kinds of splashing, wading or rafting. Maybe a first canoe or kayak trip.

45) **Cascade Lakes Resorts:** Swimming...ice cream!!

52) **Dee Wright Observatory:** they love the weirdness of the castle and its view windows for a short stop.

59) **Proxy Falls:** Short enough with a variety of trees, lava, and waterfalls to keep kids excited.

65) **Sahalie/Koosah Falls:** a short path between two big falls.

66) **Clear Lake:** kids love paddling rowboats and eating in the homey café.

76) **Head of the Jack:** run and play and splash across the creek on the logs...the creek's not deep enough to worry about if they fall in.

78) **Wizard Falls Hatchery:** fish-feeding frenzy for a buck, plus some bonus curiosities and lunkers.

81) **Petersen Rock Gardens:** picnic and play hide 'n' seek while pestering the roosters and peacocks.

85) **Steelhead Falls:** mostly for older teens who can drive to it.

90) **Richardson's Rock Ranch:** Every kid loves Thundereggs. Happiness is digging their own and having it cut—only for a couple of bucks.

STROLLER FRIENDLY PLACES (R means rugged)			
1)	Pilot Butte	39)	Sparks Lake trail (R)
2)	Shevlin Park (R)	52)	Dee Wright Obs.
3)	Deschutes South Canyon	66)	Clear Lake (R)
6)	Deschutes River Trail (R)	77)	Head of the Metolius
13)	High Desert Museum	81)	Petersen Rock Gardens
14)	Lava Butte	83)	Smith Rock
17)	Lava Cast Forest	88)	Rimrock Springs (R)
18)	LaPine State Park		

LIST-O-MANIA

Public hot-tub soaking pool:
McMenamins Old St Francis School (2)

Public Showers – Fee:
McMenamins (2), Smith Rock State Park (83), Tumalo State Park (Bend), Lava Lakes Resort (45)

Drive-to viewpoints:
Pilot Butte (1), Cline/ Three Creek Buttes (82), Paulina Peak (20), Smith Rock (83), Dee Wright Observatory (52), Round Mtn (96), Painted Hills (98)

Worth-it Waterfalls:
Tumalo (34), Sahalie/Koosah (65), Proxy (59), Whychus Creek (47), Paulina (19), Marion Creek trio (71), Linton Lake Falls (58), Benham/ Dillon (6), Steelhead (85)

Collectible Rocks:
Richardson's Thundereggs (90), Camp Abbott cinders (17), Glass Buttes obsidian (9), Hager Mtn obsidian (24)

Blue waters:
Crater Lake (25), Waldo Lake (29), Tamolitch Falls (63), Clear Lake (66)

Historic interest:
Museums (13, App 3), McKenzie Wagon Rd (53), Arnold Ice Cave (11), Petersen Rock Gardens (81), Ochoco Mines (95), Lookout Tree (97), Black Butte (80), Condon Visitor Center (99), Fort Rock (22)

Bizarre Rock Forms:
Balanced Rocks, palisades (87), Stein's Pillar (93), Lava Cast Forest (17), Monkey Face (83), Alder Springs hoodoos, Rainbow Rock (86), Fort Rock (22), Wake Butte (33), Trout Creek basalt bluffs (89), Painted Hills/ Blue Basin (98,99)

Get Naked!
Cougar Hot Spring (60), Deer Creek Hot Spring (62), Hidden Lake (61), Sparks Lake (39), Paulina Lake Hot Springs (20), Alder Springs (86), Kuitan Lake (64)

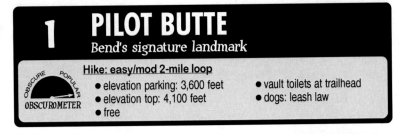

1 PILOT BUTTE
Bend's signature landmark

Hike: easy/mod 2-mile loop

OBSCUROMETER

- elevation parking: 3,600 feet
- elevation top: 4,100 feet
- free
- vault toilets at trailhead
- dogs: leash law

Paris has a tower, Seattle's got a needle, Frisco sports a bridge, Baby's got back, and Bend's got butte! Seems fitting that such an outdoorsy town would have a hike-able volcano as its landmark rather than some fabricated structure.

There are two routes spiraling to the top of Pilot Butte—either drive up via the mile-long paved road or hike up via the mile-long dirt trail. Each delivers you to the top of the 480-foot butte and its newish sightseeing plaza. By far most people hike up for a little exercise with their views, then loop back down using part of the road and then a different trail. All day long the butte is popular with moms and strollers, retirees, and Bend sightseers.

The view from the top is, of course, Bend Overall. There's now a nice mountain-identifier plaque that points out the 360° of mountains and hills which surround Bend. The fabulous scenery comes with consequences though; 100-year-old Bend has gone from range town to lumber mill town to recreation/tourism/retirement town. From atop Pilot Butte everybody ponders the pros and cons of present-day, population-boom/bust Bend. Instead of spewing some additional guidebook-speak about "magnificent panorama" or "ubiquitous Hi-Desert flora", here's some population and Bend/USA history to mull over on our "town hike".

Deschutes County 2000-2025 Coordinated Population Forecast					
Year	Bend	Redmond	Sisters	Unincorporated County	Total County
2000	52,800	15,505	975	47,320	116,600
2005	69,004	21,838	1,777	53,032	145,651
2010	81,155	28,171	2,405	59,127	170,858
2015	91,462	34,503	3,003	65,924	194,892
2020	102,625	40,836	3,776	73,502	220,739
2025	111,925	47,169	4,688	81,951	245,733

The butte is located on Greenwood/Hwy 20 a mile east of Third St. The road up the butte is on the western side off Greenwood whereas the trailhead parking area is accessed via the first left turn east of the butte (follow the signs).

➤ **Drivetime from Bend:** 1 min.

YEAR	POP.	HISTORY	
1904	300	1903:	Wright Bros. fly at Kitty Hawk
		1904:	Crater Lake becomes Nat'l Park
		1908:	Ford Model-T rolls nationwide
		1909:	Power Dam built, electrifying Bend, creating MirrorPond
1910	536	1911:	Railroad arrives in Bend
		1916:	Brooks-Scanlon, Shevlin-Hixon Lumber Mills open. First population boom!
		1914-19:	World War One (USA enters 1917)
1920	5,415	1919-33:	Prohibition
		1922:	Road built up Pilot Butte promoting tourism
1930	8,848	1929-33:	Great Depression
		1938:	Santiam Pass opens – *Bulletin* declares "Bend moves closer to ocean"
1940	10,021	1939-45:	World War Two (USA enters 12/7/41 – Pearl Harbor)
1950	11,409	1950:	Brooks-Scanlon buys out Shevlin-Hixon, closes S-H mill
		1958:	Mount Bachelor Ski Area opens
1960	11,936	1962:	Hwy 97 moved from Wall St. to Third St.
		1964-65:	Astronauts train in lavalands near Bend
		1965-73:	Vietnam War
		1967-75:	Governor Tom McCall shapes modern Ore.
		1969:	Woodstock. Neil Armstrong, first man on moon
1970	13,710	1977:	Elvis dies
		1978:	Sun Country runs first commercial raft trip on Deschutes
1980	17,200	1981-85:	Bhagwan Shree Rajneesh turns Antelope into Rajneeshpuram and poisons The Dalles
1990	20,469	1990:	Newberry Caldera becomes Nat'l. Monument
		1994:	Brooks-Scanlon (Crown-Pacific) mill closes permanently
		1997:	*The Source Weekly* debuts
2000	52,800	1999:	Bend's first roundabout is built at Century Dr. & Colorado Ave.
2001	55,080	2001:	Bend Parkway opens 8/22/01
2002	57,750		
2003	62,900		Old Mill re-development
2004	65,210		*Bend, Overall* released 7/15/04
2005	70,328		REI opens
2006	75,290		Real Estate bubble bursts
2007	77,780		
2008	80,995		Redmond Bypass opens
			Obama creates Badlands Wilderness
2009	82,280		

Whimsical hotel/bar/theater complex with a fabulous open-to-the public soaking pool

OBSCUROMETER

- public soaking/shower fee: $5
- pool open 10am to 10pm
- room reservations: 541-382-5174
- 700 NW Bond (Bond & Louisiana)

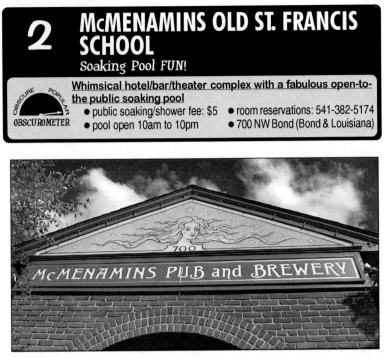

The McMenamins chain of bars, restaurants, hotels, theaters, etc etc needs little introduction for any Oregonian. But for visitors and travelers, McMenamins Old St Francis School Hotel/Bar/Restaurant harbors a surprising little nugget—a public soaking pool!

The McMenamins geniuses, when they bought and renovated the school in 2004, added a Turkish bath-style soaking pool in its own little quaint room. Best yet, it's open to the public for just a $5 fee!! Thus, if you're one of the many visitors who come to Bend to buy guidebooks and go out and play and camp....then the Old St Francis School provides the perfect venue to shower off the fun grime and have a pleasant social soak at the same time. All this AND you'll be already inside a complex of fun pubs where the happy hours can then continue for your now-clean group...Wooohooooo!

The Turkish-style bath is a work of art in its own right. First off, it has an open-air skylight in the ceiling where you can watch the stars shine as you wallow. A bonus of this skylight is that in mid-winter, when the thermometer bottoms out, the skylight lets the cold air in and it condenses the warmer air into a thick steamy mist—so much so

DRIVE

The Old St Francis School is located at the south end of downtown on Bond St. It's the first real downtown building if you're coming in on the one-way north-only Bond St from the Old Mill direction.

that you can't even see across half the pool—it's SO neat. You can hear other people, but you and your snuggly will be enshrouded in your own "girls in the mist" scenario! Then, once again expounding on the genius of this room…there is a sprinkly fountain in the middle of the pool with spouting lions around the edge. The genius here is that all this sprinkling drowns out the sound of everyone else's conversations, so you don't need to hear the mortgage travails or Phil's Trail tales of your neighbors. And lastly, the decorations include funky stained glass windows and hanging lights which cast a mellow ambiance onto the nighttime soakers. And, lastly lastly, the four walls are decorated with tile mosaics depicting the life 'n' times of ol' St Francis himself—he was known as the patron saint of animals.

Hike: easy 3-mile or 4.3-mile loops

OBSCUROMETER

- elevation: 3,625 feet
- free
- flush toilets (Farewell Bend Park)
- dogs: leash only

The new (2009) South Canyon Trail along the Deschutes River is a true gem of a trail located just minutes from downtown. Huge Huge kudos to Bend Park & Rec for cadging together the necessary private-land easements to make this trail a reality! The South Canyon Loop is a major new feather in Bend's "outdoorsy" cap—how many other towns can you walk from a shopping mall into a wilderness-like river canyon? What a great town!

These loops are very popular already and soon will be even more so. Visitors are gonna love the novelty of shopping their hearts out one minute in the Old Mill, then getting some exercise and nature the next minute up the fabled Deschutes. This trail is a trail for everyone—from toddlers to ancients, from hand-in-hand strollers to sprinting athletes, from moms with kids to dads with dogs. No longer do you have to drive 15 minutes to get to a forested trail for an after-work trail run/walk. Yup, expect plenty of company on this trail.

The trail has two different loops which can be connected to form one longer loop. For the upstream South Canyon loop park at either Farewell Bend or River Bend parks and head upstream under the Bill

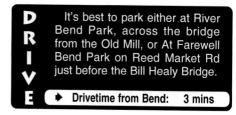

DRIVE It's best to park either at River Bend Park, across the bridge from the Old Mill, or At Farewell Bend Park on Reed Market Rd just before the Bill Healy Bridge.

➜ **Drivetime from Bend:** 3 mins

Healy Bridge for 1.5 miles (30 minutes) along the banks of the rapids-filled Ponderosa-lined Deschutes River. You'll cross the South Canyon footbridge and then return 1.5 miles back along the opposite bank.

The Centennial Loop is the portion of the trail that runs along either side of the river to the Old Mill's footbridge, making a 1.3-mile loop. This loop is paved and has a kid's park on one side, a dog park on the other…and lots of Deschutes paddlers/floaters in the river in between. Thus, everything connects up, so you could make a 1.3-mile downstream loop, a 3.0-mile upstream loop, or 4.3-mile combo loop. There are no dead-ends or wrong ways, so just walk to your heart's content.

For visitors the trail could be a fabulous option for the part of the family who'd prefer to walk 'til they drop rather than shop. Everyone can park at the Old Mill, say REI, and the shoppers can take to the stores and the walkers can take to the river. Give yourself 1.5 hours to do the long loop from Old Mill if you walk at a brisk pace.

South Canyon Bridge

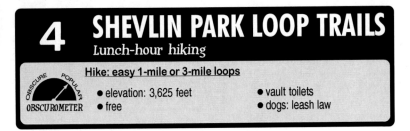

4 SHEVLIN PARK LOOP TRAILS
Lunch-hour hiking

Hike: easy 1-mile or 3-mile loops

OBSCURE POPULAR
OBSCUROMETER

- elevation: 3,625 feet
- free
- vault toilets
- dogs: leash law

Shevlin Park is one of the parks that make Bend such a great town. It's so great to have parks nearby that you can quickly access for a nice dose of nature without having to see any signs of civilization-sprawl. Unlike Pilot Butte (1) or Deschutes' South Canyon (3), in Shevlin Park you can do any number of loop hikes without seeing any homes and uttering the phrase, "I remember back when Bend…" Nope…a walk in Shevlin will remind you how great Bend still is rather than how much it's changed. Nice!

Forgive me for writing this one in the 1st person, but I want to help people enjoy their first visit to Shevlin, so I'm gonna state some opinions: There are other guidebooks that recommend longer hikes in and around Shevlin's canyon…but sometimes I think those author's miss the point. I like rushing creeks, interesting rocks, historical spots…and some neat nooks to explore. Other guidebooks may send you on a longer loop around the top of each side of the canyon, but I feel that route misses the point…at least for a first-time visitor. Shevlin Park is basically a 2-mile canyon with Tumalo Creek rushing down its center. So, you've got a pretty canyon filled with regal Ponderosas with ready access to the rushing creek. Nice!

So instead of describing a long hike which tours some canyon-top sprawl and wildfire-burnt trees, with only a brief crossing of the creek…I'll tell you about two loops that can be easily combined, where you'll get to hike a bit of the rim, a bit of the creek, a bit of history, and a mile-long signposted interpretive loop…no sign of sprawl or devastation. But wait, not only do you get all that, but as an extra bonus, if you call right now, I'll throw in my favorite parking nook for free. Now is that worth your $16.95?? Call now, operators are standing by!

Hixon covered bridge

Most locals simply park at the entrance...but this makes the park seem busy. For either of these hiking loops head up the park road. In 1.0 miles you'll pass the Hixon covered bridge which will be the northern (far) end

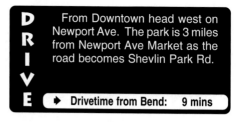

D
R
I
V
E

From Downtown head west on Newport Ave. The park is 3 miles from Newport Ave Market as the road becomes Shevlin Park Rd.

➦ **Drivetime from Bend: 9 mins**

of the longer loop. The BEST place to park is .5-miles past the bridge at an unsigned left-side dirt road that heads quickly to a private picnic spot

Frémont Meadow

In the spring of 1843, John C. Frémont an official explorer for the U.S. Govt. left St Louis with a select group which included some of the most noted mountain men, Kit Carson, Joe Walker, and Brokenhand Fitzgerald. This area was a campsite for the explorers.

along the creek. This is the best place to park for the longer loop because you can stash some bevvies in the icy creek to chill for your return, or at least when you're done you're at a nice creekside hang-out rather than some busy parking lot. However, if you're only going to do the one-mile loop, keep going another half-mile to the road-end Fremont Meadows parking.

A bonus surprise at Shevlin is that the Hixon Bridge makes a guest appearance in *Homeward Bound* at minutes 60 and 66 (see Appendix 5).

HIKE: The one-mile interpretive loop begins at Fremont Meadows where you'll find the brochures.

If you park at the picnic spot for a 3-mile loop, then begin upstream on the trail that crosses the access road. In .5 miles you'll pick up the Fremont loop. Follow the markers and make sure to side-track at #8 to see the bridge. The trail loops around and after a mile you can descend back to the Fremont parking if you want a shorter loop. Otherwise keep heading north on the Ponderosa'd ridge. A mile north of Fremont you'll see the Hixon bridge down below, but don't bushwhack—keep going another 2 minutes and go right at the junction to descend Red Tuff Gulch and see its semi-

balanced rock. Go right on the road and immediately zig left across the Larch Grove bridge (the Larches all turn vibrant yellow here in Oct), go 1 minute then zag right to cross the Hixon covered bridge. Go left after the bridge for .5 miles back to the picnic parking.

Balanced rock ➤

RED TUFF GULCH

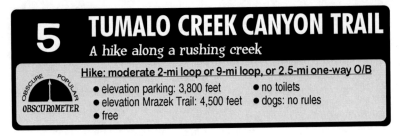

5 TUMALO CREEK CANYON TRAIL
A hike along a rushing creek

Hike: moderate 2-mi loop or 9-mi loop, or 2.5-mi one-way O/B

OBSCUROMETER

- elevation parking: 3,800 feet
- elevation Mrazek Trail: 4,500 feet
- free
- no toilets
- dogs: no rules

In Tumalo Creek Canyon, between Tumalo Falls and Shevlin Park, you'll find a rough trail fashioned by Bend Parks & Rec that parallels the rushing creek. Tumalo Creek, after leaping 97 feet off its namesake falls,

meanders through the Bridge Creek Burn before entering this steeper and deeper portion of its canyon. This section of Tumalo's canyon isn't waterfall-filled like above Tumalo Falls, but it is non-stop whitewater...much more so than in its lower Shevlin Park section. The trail follows the creek upstream for 4 miles and then ends at a junction with the Mrazek Trail. You could then loop back down via the Mrazek Mtn-biking trail to make an 8.5-mile loop. The problem with this idea is that the Mrazek is dull and viewless as it winds 4 miles back (great for biking, lousy for hiking). Thus, the question becomes, "should you do the trail as an Out/Back?" This depends on you. Some people just love loop hikes, even if half the loop is lousy. But the best

Out/Back on this trail is probably to go 2.5 miles upstream and then turn back. This is a good choice because the first mile of trail is along the stream, then the trail climbs the canyon slope and stays up there for the next 1.5 miles before the trail and the creek angle together once again at the 2.5-mile mark. Thus, when you get to the 2.5-mile mark turn-around, you can have a snack and maybe a splash on the riverside rocks and then head back, for a 5-mile total. (Above the 2.5-mile mark the canyon is still nice, but nothing remarkable—the reason to keep going is to make the loop).

D R I V E From downtown Bend take the Franklin/ Galveston/ Skyliners roads that head past Mirror Pond, the Flaming Chicken Roundabout, and then head towards Tumalo Falls. In a few miles, as you leave the outskirts of town and pass the last left-side houses, look for MP 3 just past the Phil's Trailhead road. You want to turn right at MP 3.5 onto gravel FS 4606. Go 100 yards and turn left and descend 1.5 miles to the bridge and park on the far shoulder at the trailhead signs.

➡ Drivetime from Bend: 10 mins

There is one other option. One mile into the trail, as you first climb away from the creek up the steep canyon slope, you'll come to a minor junction. If you go right here the trail heads back downstream but stays immediately under the rocky bluffs—this is the rock-climber's trail. This path goes a mile "downstream" then intersects the final bit of the Mrazek/ Tumalo trail, where then you'll descend steeply back to your car. Thus you could do this trail as a short 2-mile loop, or on the 5-mile O/B you could veer onto the climber's trail for a little extra variety on the way back.

HIKE: Check the blog to see Google maps. Begin upstream on the lower of the 2 trails (the upper is the climber's). At one-mile you'll ascend the canyon slope to the climber-trail junction. The creek trail stays high for 1.5 miles until descending back to the creek. If you continue on to do the loop, go 1.5 miles more until angling upwards to meet the Mrazek under a power line. Go right and up for 2 minutes and at the Happy Valley trail junction go right to begin the descent. You'll meander thru forest for 4 miles before crossing a major dirt road—keep straight for a few more minutes until a signed junction where you'll turn right to emerge onto road 4606. The quick/easy way back is to take the road .5 miles to the car, but there's also an extension of the creek trail (across 4606) that makes a much more arduous 1.0-mile back to the car with lots of up/downs (it tours the hardcore climbing area).

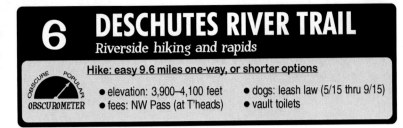

6 DESCHUTES RIVER TRAIL
Riverside hiking and rapids

Hike: easy 9.6 miles one-way, or shorter options

OBSCUROMETER

- elevation: 3,900–4,100 feet
- fees: NW Pass (at T'heads)
- dogs: leash law (5/15 thru 9/15)
- vault toilets

The Deschutes River Trail is the nearest-to-downtown section of the river without visible development or roads. A great trail parallels the west side of the fabled Deschutes. This trail is easy-walking for people who want great riverside scenery without too much effort. Across the river for most of the trail you'll see the Lava Butte lava flow which nudged the Deschutes into its present course of rapids and drops. Beginning at the Meadow Picnic area, a 9.6-mile hike/ bike trail hugs the river while passing popular "waterfalls" Lava Island, Dillon, and Benham. Besides the Meadow trailhead, there are spur roads off FS 41 leading to three popular spots. You can hike up or downriver from any of the access points. The movie *Rooster Cogburn* filmed many scenes along the Deschutes ...see Appendix 5 for details.

Lava Island Falls. This is where most commercial raft trips take out. From the boat ramp parking you can head downstream 150 yards to check-out an ancient Indian rock shelter and info panels. Rugged and curious folk may find a scramble trail down to a hidden falls just past the trio of info signs. Hiking upriver is popular, heading .75 miles to the class-III Big Eddy rapids where the commercial rafts get everyone wet. In summertime there's always plenty of action around Lava Island.

Geologically Lava Island is interesting because it marks the farthest lobe of the Lava Butte lava flow. On Google Earth you can really see how the lava filled up the river channel, causing the river to split around the "island". This is the only spot where the Deschutes flows over the Lava Butte lavas.

Lava Island Falls rafting take-out

D R I V E

From Bend take the Cascade Lakes Hwy for 4.7 miles. The Meadow Picnic area is signed before the Widgi Creek golf course. To access the falls, pass the Seventh Mtn Resort and turn left onto FS 41 at a sign for Deschutes River Rec. sites. The Lava Island turn is .3 miles (then .7 gravel), Dillon is 2.5 miles (then .8 gravel), and Benham is 3.8 miles (then 2.2 gravel). Benham Falls can also be accessed from Lava Butte on Hwy 97 (14).

➡ **Drivetime from Bend: 5-15 mins**

Big Eddy Rapids

Dillon Falls. A two-minute walk downstream brings you to Dillon's frothing chasm of certain death! This is much more of a waterfall than at Lava Island. There are picnic tables, BBQs, and bathrooms. In *Up the Creek* a raft goes over Dillon Falls (see Appendix 5).

Benham Falls. This is the most scenic and geologically interesting place on the trail. A short path overlooks the Deschutes churning thru a narrow rhyolite defile. Here's the geologic story: about 6,000 years ago Lava Butte erupted (over by Hwy 97), forming a cinder cone and discharging a huge lava flow. The fluid lavas flowed west and blocked the bed of the ancient Deschutes with a 100-foot lava dam. A lake backed up, extending south to LaPine and covering Sunriver. Eventually the rising lake found a path around the new lava dam and flowed over a low spot in much-older rhyolite rock. Since that time the re-routed river has been eroding its way downward in this channel, creating present-day Benham Falls.

Upriver from the falls you can take a stroll on a flat, easy half-mile railbed trail. Lava Butte is across river in the distance. Cross the bridge and check-out the logging history park—the whole deal takes about 45 minutes.

Benham Falls

PBR

25

7 THE BADLANDS

Bend's new home-grown Wilderness Area

OBSCURE POPULAR OBSCUROMETER

Hike: easy loops, short and long

- elevation: 3,700 feet
- free
- no toilets
- dogs: no rules

The Badlands are Bend's new local wilderness as of 2008. The Oregon Natural Desert Association (ONDA) fought for years, with the help of a legion of volunteers, conservation groups, and local businesses to move the Badlands from the nebulous "Wilderness Study Area" to an actual politically protected Wilderness Area. Bravo ONDA, bravo volunteers, bravo supportive businesses!!

The Badlands are hardly new, as Indians, homesteaders and desert-lovers have been rambling around the area for centuries. What is new is the attention and publicity that the Wilderness designation has prompted. Now, more than ever, Bendites are heading out to examine this odd little corner of our back yard. Other than a few signs and some newer close-to-town trails, nothing has really changed in the Badlands...except now there are regulations so that the Quad-yahoos can't run amok over the land in a Friday night shoot-'em-up frenzy. Thank ONDA! The most poignant change in the Badlands may be that the "Wilderness Study Area" sign now has a dash of brown paint over the word "Study"...one small swipe of paint for the Badlands, one giant step for Conservation-kind!

Atop Flatiron Rock

Any trip into the Badlands improves if you read a little about its geologic history and about the ancient old-growth Junipers that cover its Mazama-ash covered spaces. The Badlands brochure available at the trailheads (or the blog) details how the Badlands lavas are theorized to have flowed out of a lava tunnel up onto the surface.

HIKE: The Badlands map shows plenty of options, but most are aimed for horses. Here are a couple of recommended hiking loops. See the blog for Google maps.

Head east from Bend on Hwy 20. In 16 miles, at MP 16, is the signed Flatiron Rock trailhead. One mile farther turn left for a mile to the Badlands Rock trailhead. For extra interest drive a couple miles farther on Hwy 20 up to the overlook of the Dry River Gorge and its info-sign (8). Coming back down the Hwy you'll have a view over all the Badlands and the wee little bumps out there (like desert whales) are Flat Iron and Badlands Rocks.

➡ **Drivetime from Bend: 18 mins**

Flatiron Rock semi-loop. Beginning at the Flatiron Rock trailhead there's a 2.6-mile loop with an add-on 1.5-mile foray out to Flatiron Rock, for a total 5.6-mile outing. The initial loop may seem like it'd be just fine by itself, but doing it lacks the satisfaction of "getting somewhere". The short loop simply makes a circle within the Junipers with no views or destination. Thus, adding the 1.5-miles (one-way) out to Flatiron helps you feel like you "went somewhere". Don't expect any ooohs and aaahs at Flat Iron Rock, cuz it's not that Wow. It's like a poor-man's Fort Rock, only elevated about 50 feet of the desert floor. There is a neat loop trail within the fort-like enclosure with some small arches to see. It does have an elevated picnic spot with a Cascades view—notice how nicely Pilot, Aubrey, and pointy Three Creek Buttes all line up (82).

Little Dry Canyon pictograph cave loop. From the Badlands Rock trailhead this 2.5-mile loop follows an old road over to an Ice-Age mini-canyon where you can walk through the canyon to see some super-faded Indian pictographs on a cave overhang that was blackened by many an ancient fire. This short gorge is like a mini version of the Dry River Gorge (a few miles "upstream" [8]). The cave overhang was probably the best shelter available in all the surrounding badlands…and it had the advantage of having some water-collecting "tinaja" rock depressions that were carved into the basalt by the Ice-Age river. From the Badlands Rock trailhead go .3 miles then right at the fork for another 1 mile on the sandy road. When you see 3 boulders blocking a road on the right, go right here, then right again to enter the Dry Canyon. To make a loop out of this walk, simply continue

upstream and out of the gorge and follow the faint waterway SE until you bonk into a fence around the quarry site's dirt berm. Follow the fence to the right and you'll soon intersect the road just beyond where you parked. Surprisingly, this gorge was featured prominently in the 1958 Disney movie *Tonka* (see Appendix 5).

Little Dry River's Tonka *Cave*

8 DRY RIVER GORGE
An Ice-Age remnant

OBSCUROMETER

<u>Hike: easy/mod 2 miles one-way</u>
- elevation: 3,700 feet
- closed: 3/1 thru 9/1
- free
- no toilets
- dogs: no rules

Spiro-glyphs

(NOTE:) The BLM closes this gorge each spring to protect nesting Prairie falcons from human disturbance. Once the falcons have fledged their young the gorge is re-opened for exploring. Please respect the closure dates from March thru August. Call the BLM at 541-416-6700 for info or dates.

Dry River Gorge is the extinct waterway that emptied the Ice Age "Lake Millican". This lake filled the expansive basin SE of Horse Ridge, surrounding the Millican area. Within the two million year Ice Age there were many cycles of warming which caused this pluvial lake to rise and overspill Horse Ridge, eroding a deep canyon on its way to the Crooked River.

Nowadays you can explore this dry gorge via a 2-mile trail that meanders gently "upstream" on the canyon floor. This trail weaves among boulders and ancient junipers until being blocked by tumbled-down basalt. Many small surprises await; colorful wildflowers, striped banding on the steep walls, and, at the turn back point, a couple of very out-of-place Ponderosas. Sharp eyes may even spy raptors, snakes, or even feral sheep.

The strangest thing of all in this canyon is a vast array of modern petroglyphs that adorn the boulders near the canyon mouth. Most (of the few) write-ups that this gorge receives never mention these oddities, but in a way they spice-up the excursion with their puzzling presence. They're sort of like Geocaches, in that they give you something to look for. And, believe me, once you start finding these puzzling spiro-glyphs, you'll be hooked!

D R I V E

(Note: as you drive from Bend look for Ponderosas. See any among the Badlands junipers? Nope.) From Bend take Hwy 20 east for 17 miles. Just past MP 17 turn left onto the quarry road, then immediately right towards the gravel piles. Pass gravel piles towards canyon mouth and follow the rough dirt road for about .75 miles to the road-end trailhead.

→ **Drivetime from Bend:**   17 mins

Look for these about a five-minute walk upstream from the road-end trailhead. Scan the basalt boulders on either side of the trail—the huge glyphs are easy to spot if you're looking. At one rock you'll find a 1988/89 date. It's kinda neat to see what 20 years of lichen

Feral sheep

looks like as it covers over some of the "art". Hmmm… is this rock art or defacement? Will these be considered art 1,000 years from now? Go take a look. (Check Appendix 4 too).

(Author's note: I find these glyphs ever-intriguing. Since I first found them a decade ago, I've been fascinated to watch how the lichen is coming back to almost completely obscure some etchings. The one that's been most memorable to me says, "A mouse in the mouth of a cat is in no more danger than a man in the hand of a lawyer." Not only is this phrase-in-rock ODD, it's also now almost 100% lichened-over. There are at least 4 other "sentence-rocks"…go find 'em! I visit this gorge a lot, but never make it beyond the grove of glyphs.)

HIKE: First off, if you arrive when the canyon's closed for peregrine nesting, then head over to the Badlands Trailhead instead and leave the birds in peace.

The trail begins as double-track and soon narrows to a single-track path. At the 2-mile mark there are two huge Ponderosas marking the turnaround point (Ponderosas generally need 14 inches of rain to grow – this canyon gets less than 10 inches… hmmm, odd…sort of like Christmas Valley's "lost forest").

9 GLASS BUTTES
Public obsidian collecting hills

Hike: no official trails—just wander and look

OBSCUROMETER
OBSCURE · POPULAR

- elevation: 4,600 feet
- free
- no toilets
- dogs: no rules

The Glass Buttes have been synonymous with obsidian collection since humans arrived in Central Oregon. Native Americans collected and shaped obsidian here for thousands of years, then traded it to peoples throughout the West via trading center in The Dalles. Archeologists have traced obsidian originating at the Glass Buttes all over the western states.

Surprisingly, you can still visit the Glass Buttes and pick up heaps of obsidian right off the ground! There's literally black glass almost everywhere…all easy pickin's! There are flakes, razor-sharp shards, hunks of rough grey with red streaks, and shiny bits strewn hither and yon. Previous rock hounds have left an endless array of pits and piles, all free for the collecting!!

Snip of Ochoco Rockhounding map

Mahogany Obsidian hunk

Good fun is bringing a hammer to break open larger hunks into shiny shards. Inside these dull hunks you'll find a shiny dazzle of swirly colorful streaks. Each hunk is like a treasure chest, just waiting for the hammer to "crack" the lock! Everyone who's visited the Glass Buttes has some hunks of obsidian decorating their garden or windowsill, reminding them of a fun day of easy rock-hounding. The most prevalent kind of obsidian is Mahogany, identified by the swirls of reddish streaks that

D R I V E

BRING: sunglasses, hammer, old rag/towel, first aid kit.
From Bend head east on Hwy 20 for 77 miles to MP 77. Turn right onto the possibly-unsigned dirt road and go a rough 2.2 miles. At a campsite (on the right) you'll need to turn sharply left and uphill to the next road junction. Park the car somewhere near here and start scrounging around—there'll be no shortage of obsidian hunks scattered about!

➡ **Drivetime from Bend: 70 mins**

decorate the cracked-open faces of the obsidian hunks. The map delineates collection areas by type of obsidian, but most of the varieties, other than Mahogany, take some serious scouting and rock-hounding. Don't ex-

Cracked open!

pect a dazzling rainbow piece just laying about...but do keep your eyes peeled.

Before you make the long drive, spend some a moment on the blog to find a link to a geologists summation of all things obsidian. Then go...drive east young man...you'll love it! Walk in the footsteps of the ancients and claim a souvenir of your own. Dream arrowhead dreams and ponder a society where the sharpest knife came from a glassy rock from a peculiar hill in the middle of nowhere.

Hammertime. Bring a hammer, eye glasses, gloves, and a crappy rag to cover up the obsidian hunks as you bash them. **BE SUPER CAREFUL!!** The shards of obsidian glass <u>are</u> the sharpest things you'll ever touch and a flying shard will slice you faster than a Ginsu knife! Obsidian flakes can be the sharpest blade known to man at just a molecule thick—way way way sharper than a Ginsu even! If you're too stupid to wear glasses of some sort, then don't even make the drive. Nobody wants to slip in your pool of blood or stumble over the slimy remnants of your eyeball that got sliced off by a flying shard! Be warned, don't bleed... WEAR GLASSES and GLOVES!!

FYI: As I type this I can look down and see the scar on my right thumb where a flying shard cut me deep. Stupid me only had one glove on...the one holding the hunk. The shard flew up and basically went right thru half of my thumb. If it had been my face...yikes. Be warned... be smarter than I was... please.)

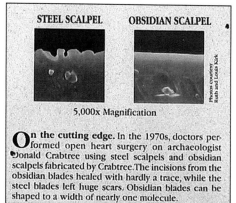

STEEL SCALPEL   OBSIDIAN SCALPEL

Photos courtesy Ruth and Louis Kirk

5,000x Magnification

On the cutting edge. In the 1970s, doctors performed open heart surgery on archaeologist Donald Crabtree using steel scalpels and obsidian scalpels fabricated by Crabtree. The incisions from the obsidian blades healed with hardly a trace, while the steel blades left huge scars. Obsidian blades can be shaped to a width of nearly one molecule.

Bend's most easily-accessed unregulated cave

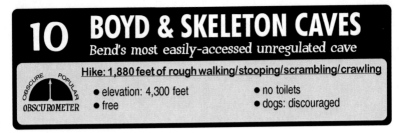

Hike: 1,880 feet of rough walking/stooping/scrambling/crawling

OBSCURE / POPULAR

OBSCUROMETER

- elevation: 4,300 feet
- free
- no toilets
- dogs: discouraged

Boyd and Skeleton Caves used to be the two most easily-accessed unregulated caves open to the public for exploring. As of 2006 Skeleton Cave was closed and gated for the nebulous "protection of resources" reasons, thus leaving Boyd Cave as the only easily-accessed underground adventure besides the overly-popular/touristy Lava River Cave.

Why mention Skeleton at all in this new edition? It seems to this author that the closing of Skeleton is a tad capricious, since commercialized tours are let into the cave. If the closing was for bat protection—a worthy goal— then why allow commercial tours? If there are no bat issues during the summer months, then why not unlock the gate then and allow free public access? If vandalism is the issue, then why not issue free public entrance permits at the Forest Service office…like the permits needed to hike the Obsidian Trail or visit Pamelia Lake. This guidebook believes that if any access to the cave is to be had, it should be free access. Closing public lands and then charging for commercialized tours is a questionable practice, one which may merit public awareness.

Inside Boyd Cave

D From Bend head south on Hwy 97 for 2 miles to exit 143 – Knott
R Rd. After exiting go left at the stop for 1.4 miles to China Hat Rd.
I Go right on China Hat and set your odometer. Go 8 miles and at
V MP 9 look for the signed left turn to Boyd Cave, then .2 miles to the
E cave (if you get onto gravel you just passed the turn).

➡ **Drivetime from Bend: 12 mins**

Boyd Cave. This 2,000-foot lava tunnel has a bit of everything in its length, from easy sand-floor walking to difficult squirming and crawl passages. This cave's no "walk in the park"! You will feel as though you've had a good workout if you do the full out and back. If you just want a little look-see, then the first 5 minutes of cave are fairly easy-going with some neat lava guttering and break-down piles...but any further than that requires athletic navigation. Boyd Cave is ice-cold inside, so don't bother driving out without serious winter clothing and at least one light per person.

Boyd's 6-foot-long crawl

Once inside you'll first notice the flat sand floor. This sand, and farther along also, comes from contraction cracks in the ceiling that let the sand and Mt Mazama ash sift into the cave. Half way into the cave you come to a 6-foot crawl section (careful of the knee-breaker rock). Just before the crawl is a large contraction crack that has let in a hill of sand and if you look closely you'll often see roots from the plants above inside the crack. Through the dusty crawl the cave opens up again with plenty more explorable passage. Every obstacle in this cave offers further rewards—keep going!

Skeleton Cave

SKELETON CAVE IS CLOSED AND GATED TO PROTECT SENSITIVE CAVE RESOURCES. CALL 541-383-4000 (DESCHUTES NF) FOR PRIVATE TOUR MAY 2 – OCTOBER 14. VIOLATIONS PUNISHABLE.

Hike: short scramble explorations

OBSCURE POPULAR

OBSCUROMETER

- elevation: 4,500 feet
- free
- no toilets
- dogs discouraged

Arnold Ice Cave is pretty boring to visit if you don't know anything about its history. Nowadays the cave seems just an overhanging pit with an icy floor.

What you may not know is that there's a half-mile of cave behind that icy floor that nobody has seen for 30+ years! OK, before telling you about Arnold's secrets, let's start from the beginning with some history. Back in the early 1900's saloon keepers, meat packers, etc looked to the Deschutes River for ice. Pockets of the Deschutes and its canals froze solid every winter and ice harvesters dug out the ice, stored it in ice houses, and sold it throughout the summer. One particular year, a saloon-keeper/hotel owner named Hugh O'Kane (now of McMenamins bar fame) somehow "cornered the market" on ice during a bad year for the Deschutes ice crop. He raised the price to an unheard of

$50 per ton and the other two Bend saloon keepers were distraught. They decided to go into business harvesting ice from the Ice Cave. Thus, the famous era of Arnold ice mining began. Ice from the cave was cut into huge blocks and pulled up a chute to be delivered by cart to Bend. As the years went on the ice miners cut deeper and deeper.

By the 1950s the ice-mining was over, due to the advent of refrigeration. At that time two local cavers chipped a trench into the ice and found a half-mile of passage beyond the ice-choked entrance area. In 1963 the Forest Service built a staircase down into the entrance of the cave, which was then a dangerous frozen slope of ice—a so-called "ice cascade." The ice was advancing though, taking back the ground it had lost to the miners, and within 12 years the stairway had been enveloped by the advancing ice. By the late 1980s the entrance to the ice cave had become completely choked with ice…and that's how we see it today. Few present-day visitors know that there is an entire stairway entombed within the thick ice

D
R
I
V
E

Head south from Bend on Hwy 97 for 1.5 miles and exit at Knott Road exit 143. Stop for supplies at Riverwoods Country Store then go east on Knott for 1.4 miles then turn right onto China Hat Road. **SET YOUR ODOMETER HERE!** In 8 miles (near MP 9), just before the pavement ends, you'll see the turn for Boyd Cave (10). To continue to Arnold/Hidden, check odometer again and go 3.1 miles more on gravel to FS 300 (just past the more-obvious FS 1820). Turn right onto 300 and go .5 miles to the road-end parking in front of Arnold's pit.

➤ **Drivetime from Bend: 15 mins**

and a long passage of "ice cascade" cave hidden below.

1963 Ice Cave

HIKE: The cave pit is a direct one-minute scramble down from the parking area.

Hidden Forest Cave. This huge collapsed lava tube has a band-shell type cave overhang and a forest of huge Ponderosas growing from its expansive floor. The neatest part of the cave is the hidden portal deep in the dark overhang. If you squeeze through this body-sized portal you'll emerge into the Land of the Lost!! (I won't spoil your surprise…the climb out isn't bad. Have fun!!)

Historic Photos Courtesy of Bowman Museum

Surprisingly, Hidden Forest Cave made an appearance in *Even Cowgirls get the Blues*—Uma partied in the cave! (See Appendix 5.)

HIKE: To find Hidden Forest Cave take the sand road from Arnold heading up and south. It's about a 5 minute walk (.25 miles) to the cave. In a minute you'll see a pit off to the right—keep straight. In 3 more minutes is another pit on the right and you'll need to keep to the narrowing trail that skirts its left side. Soon cross a sand road and Hidden Forest Cave will be directly ahead in 60 feet. At the lip you'll see the cave overhang… and to

get down to the floor keep heading along the left side until the easy way down becomes clear. to the floor keep heading along the left side until the easy way down becomes clear.

Looking out of Hidden Forest Cave (the Uma Thurman view)

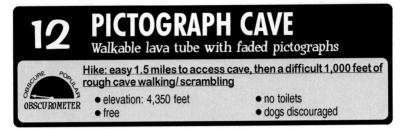

12 PICTOGRAPH CAVE
Walkable lava tube with faded pictographs

Hike: easy 1.5 miles to access cave, then a difficult 1,000 feet of rough cave walking/scrambling

OBSCUROMETER

- elevation: 4,350 feet
- free
- no toilets
- dogs discouraged

Cave closed from Oct 15th to May 1st every year for bat protection!

Pictograph Cave is remarkable in three ways. The first is that it is still open to the public after most of the nearby caves in the Arnold tube system have been gated for various protective reasons. The second reason is that there a number a faded Indian pictographs painted on the rocks at the very entrance to the cave—very neat! And, the thirdly, the circular portions of the tube display some of the most symmetric shaping of all the local lava tubes.

Pictograph Cave skylight pit

This cave requires a substantial walk to get to it since its one-time 4WD access road has been decommissioned. Thus, Pictograph is mostly interesting to die-hard cave junkies— Boyd Cave is an easier option if you want something less touristy than Lava River Cave. Once at Pictograph Cave you'll find two openings, the SW one just a skylight having no way down. The NE pit requires an easy rock-climb down into it where you'll then find two tube sections. The lefthand one is rough-going for the 150-ish yards to go see the SW pit opening from below. The faded red pictographs are nearer to the righthand tunnel. This righthand tunnel is the more interesting one, as it goes about 1,000 feet. The walking is fairly rough the entire way and there are two massive breakdown piles that you'll have to negotiate over and down.

Historically, Charlie Larson's *Central Oregon Caves* booklet states that at the time of this cave's 1957 public "discovery", the cave "housed a complete but rusty distillery." The front cover photo of his booklet is Pictograph Cave. Interestingly, Larson doesn't mention the pictographs. The 1976 edition of Oregon Grotto's *The Speleograph* states, "Of the seven named segments of the Arnold cave system, Pictograph Cave is the most interesting."

**D
R
I
V
E**

Follow the directions as to Boyd Cave (10), but continue past Boyd for 2.5 miles on the gravel and turn left onto FS 200 (signed "Wind Cave closed year-round"). Go the 1,000 feet to the end of this road and park.

Note: at Wind Cave look NW for the "gated" skylight opening.

➡ **Drivetime from Bend: 20 mins**

Skylight opening

HIKE: **Bring lots of lights and <u>warm</u> clothing! It's best to visit this cave when it's cold out so you'll already be dressed warmly for the hike.**

From the now-closed end of Wind Cave's road walk .5 miles to Wind Cave's entrance turnaround. Continue NE on the sandy double-track road and go about .7 miles to a railroad-tie gate. Pass through the open gate and veer left, soon stepping through a newer barb-wire fence. From this fence the cave is just a few hundred more yards. The path passes between the two cave openings, with each hole marked with restrictive signs. If you crest the hill and see the Cascades (Bachelor to Hood!), then you're too far.

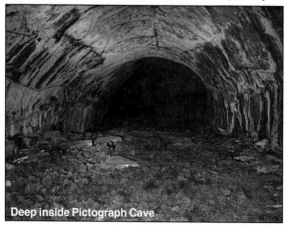

Deep inside Pictograph Cave

37

OBSCUROMETER

- open 362 days, 9am–5pm
- phone: 541-382-4754
- flush toilets
- fees: $15 adults, $9 kids (less in winter!)
- dogs: no

The High Desert Museum is a local treasure born out of a passion to preserve the natural and cultural landscapes of our High Desert. This non-profit museum has thrived since 1982 on the enthusiasm it creates in kids and adults alike! Typical of a museum, there are displays, photos, and artifacts... but unlike most museums this place is alive with all kinds of High Desert wildlife. The Otter antics are always a huge crowd-pleaser. All kind of eagles, hawks, and owls inhabit the Birds of Prey wing—wow, at least 5 different types of owls and a PAIR of Bald eagles! Just inside the front door are separate habitats for both a lynx and a bobcat—it's super neat when they're active. Porcupine feeding always draws a crowd to see the cute buggers munch, especially if they have uber-cute porcu-babies. Snakes, lizards, Gila monsters, and even a fat little fox round out this marvelous Great Basin showcase.

Otter

Baby porcupine

DRIVE

From Bend head south on Hwy 97 for 4 miles. Just past MP 145 turn left into signed entrance.

➡ **Drivetime from Bend: 5 mins**

Because the intent of this museum is to interpret the High Desert environment, there are show-and-tell presentations given by passionate volunteers scheduled throughout every day. These talks are no dull lectures—they're super-interesting and engaging, so plan your visit around them! Also, various exhibits detail the lives and history of the Plateau Indians and they're clashes with the encroaching settlers. As of 2010 a wing is devoted to "Sin in the Sagebrush"...bringing alive the life and times of the pioneers with all the attendant whorin', drinkin', and gamblin' that typified the frontier lifestyle.

Overall, kids adore the High Desert Museum for all its wildlife, while adults marvel at the terrific job the museum does of informing without too much dull reading—quite a feat!

Screech Owl

Details:
- 3 hrs. are recommended.
- Little known fact—the admission price is good for two days. Stop in for a sample then return the next day with more time.
- The Rimrock Café offers good variety for great prices.
- The Silver Sage Trading gift shop is excellent—leave time for it.

14 LAVA BUTTE
Highway-side volcano and volcanic info center

Hike: easy short trails

OBSCUROMETER

- elevation parking: 4,500 feet
- elevation top: 5,000 feet
- fees: NW Pass (at entrance booth)

- open 9-5pm 5/1 to 10/15
- flush toilets
- dogs: on leash

Lava Butte is the impressive red and black cinder cone "volcano" rising directly above Hwy 97 ten miles south of Bend. The butte is the home of the Lava Lands Visitor Center—the informational hub of the Newberry Volcanic Monument. Its friendly staff can answer all questions concerning Lava River Cave, Lava Cast Forest, and Newberry Caldera. The center now houses a fabulous mini-museum depicting all things lava-like! Besides fascinating displays and photos there are also short movies which play throughout the day—the Lava Flows/Lava Tubes one is spectacular. Make time...the Lava Lands VisCtr is the best all-things-lava showcase between Hawaii and Iceland!

The must-do trail at the Center is the Trail of Molten Land—you'll "lava" it! It swerves through the lava flow on a paved pathway and has signs explaining all the surrounding weirdness, even detailing the 1966 astronaut training on the lava field. The other must-see is the Top-o'-the-Butte. A 1.5-mile drivable road spirals up to its 500-foot height. The rim has killer views, picnic tables, a crater filled with Ponderosas. Also, don't miss the fire lookout's lower public room with its brilliant mountain-identifying panels. For a butte-top stroll an easy .3-mile trail tours the rim. Summertime can be crazy atop the butte—tons of kids happily feeding the swarm of hungry squirrels.

For people looking for a bit more serenity, try hiking up to the butte (on the road) after the Center closes at 5pm. Simply park outside the front gate and walk through the parking lot and up to the top. A Cascade sunset, fiery sky bathing the red cinders in warm light, only gets better by adding a boyfriend and a bottle of red wine! There's no mob like atop Pilot Butte and the walk down in the dark is a breeze. A full-moonrise is double deluxe!

D
R
I
V
E

Note: as of spring 2010 there's a massive Hwy 97 re-route planned for access to both Lava Butte and Lava River Cave, but during construction and afterwards there will be clear roadside signage indicating how to access both. Basically you drive south from Bend on Hwy 97 for 9 miles. Near MP 150 Lava Butte should get a new exit which will also access Lava River Cave....just watch for signs.

➡ **Drivetime from Bend: 9 mins**

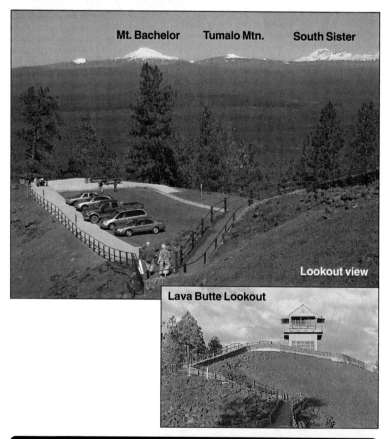

Mt. Bachelor   Tumalo Mtn.   South Sister

Lookout view

Lava Butte Lookout

WHATEVER WHATEVER WHATEVER WHATEVER WHATEVER WHATEVER WHATEVER WHATEVER WHATEVER WHATEVER

There are four common types of lava, each identified by its percentage of silica. Basalt has less than 54% silica, Andesite has 54%-62%, Dactite has 63%-72%, and Rhyolite has more than 72%. The silica content determines the viscosity of the lava. Low silica basalt is very fluid and can flow far from its vent (Lava Butte or Belknap Crater). The other lavas are too thick to flow far, so they build up steeper "composite" cones (the major Cascade peaks).

WHATEVER WHATEVER WHATEVER WHATEVER WHATEVER WHATEVER WHATEVER WHATEVER WHATEVER WHATEVER

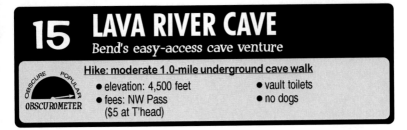

15 LAVA RIVER CAVE
Bend's easy-access cave venture

Hike: moderate 1.0-mile underground cave walk

OBSCUROMETER

OBSCURE · POPULAR

- elevation: 4,500 feet
- fees: NW Pass ($5 at T'head)
- vault toilets
- no dogs

Ever spelunked for a mile? Bend's famous Lava River Cave is the place to begin your explorations of Central OR's many lava tubes. Why? Because this cave is Oregon's longest <u>walkable</u> tube and its features are unique and intriguing. This cave is user-friendly—at the Ranger's entrance booth there are specialized lanterns to rent, signage, map, warnings etc etc.

Don't expect a sanitized "walk-in-the-park" in the Lava River Cave. While you can walk the entire length (no stooping, climbing, or crawling) the underground terrain is still rough and sometimes steep and slippery. The entrance is a long stairway descending over tumbled-down lava. Immediately inside you'll notice the 40° chill—whoa, you better have solid shoes, pants, jacket, and maybe even hat and gloves if you plan to walk the bowels of the earth! As your eyes adjust to the pitch black the rough terrain will get easier to navigate but at first it'll seem that the cave is just swallowing the beam of

your lamp/flashlights. **<u>Everyone should carry some kind of light.</u>** It's way more fun shining your own beam wherever your curiosity dictates than it is to stumble after your friend's/dad's beam. Progressing into the depths, the brochure details the glories of this cave; Hwy 97 passing overhead, the rare tube-in-the-tube, the 'sand garden', and other lavacicle weirdities. This cave is amazing—an easy, must-see family adventure!

Entrance walkway

D R I V E

Note, as of spring 2010 there's a massive Hwy 97 re-route planned for access to both Lava Butte and Lava River Cave, but during construction and afterwards there will be clear roadside signage indicating how to access both. Basically you drive south from Bend on Hwy 97 for 9 miles. Near MP 150 Lava Butte should get a new exit which will also access Lava River Cave....just watch for signs.

Coming from the south, most likely you'll exit onto Cottonwood Rd (MP 151) to access cave.

➡ **Drivetime from Bend: 10 mins**

DETAILS:

- To the end and back is a slow 2.2 miles—usually about 1.5 hours.
- No dogs, food, drinks, or smoking.
- Lantern rent is $3 (until 4PM). No personal GLASS lanterns allowed.
- Use toilets outside—there's no toilet inside the cave. Don't pee in cave—it causes a gross white fungus to grow.
- **Warm clothing is a must** to be comfortable past 100 yards.
- Bring extra lights. People are always needing help because they stumble and break/put-out the lanterns. Bring a flashlight and also a lighter as backup. Being a mile underground with a dead flashlight sucks!

Tube-within-the-tube

16 SUNRIVER NATURE CENTER
Totally worth a visit!

OBSCUROMETER

- phone: 541-593-4394
- hours: 9-5 daily
- fees: $4 adults, $3 kids
- solar view 10 am-2pm
- night program 9-11 pm ($6)
- dogs: on leash

The Sunriver Nature Center is all about telescopes, eagles/owls, meteorites, and critters…and educational programs to try to wean kids off the Xbox. It doesn't have the budget or get the hoopla as its more famous neighbor up the highway, but if you're looking for some family fun that doesn't cost a bunch, then c'mon down—you will enjoy this place! I'm going to "break the mold" a bit here and talk about my personal feelings about this center because I feel that it just doesn't get its due. It's like a mini museum combined with a mini Pine Mtn Observatory….but the Nature Center is more

Great horned owl

personable and fun than either. The great staff here has the time and enthusiasm to answer questions and go beyond the norm for curious kids-of-all-ages. Personally I think it's a shame that more people don't pop by for at least a quick 45 minutes, especially on a sunny summer day. Why a sunny day?? Because that's when the solar telescope is pointed at the sun! Putting my eye to that telescope is something I've never forgotten…this photo of the sun is mine—all you have to do is put your camera on macro and put it up to the lens. Of all the things I've photographed in Central Oregon…from lavas to lakes to Mtns to cave-beams to Kokanees to two-headed fish….my photo of our sun and prominences may be my favorite, and it's the one that friends gawk at the most in my home. Nobody else I know has their own close-up of the sun…and the

Prominence

The Sun!

chance to see and do this yourself is just a few minutes away at the under-appreciated Sunriver Nature Center.

The Starport Observatory. Stare at the Sun—close-up! A research-grade telescope is fitted with special filters to enable this unforgettable experience. Available 10-2pm daily in the summer, included with admission price. The Observatory also has a little-known, yet excellent, nighttime star program. In summer it runs 9-11pm every night except Monday ($6/adult, $4/kid). Included is a fun slide presentation on astronomy while the numerous telescopes are focused on different nebulae, clusters, binaries, etc. The volunteers who run the program are fun-loving and engaging—no boring lectures here! If you ever wondered about Subaru's star-constellation logo,

D
R
I
V
E

From Bend take Hwy 97 south for 12 miles. At exit 153 turn right towards Sunriver then 1.5 miles and right at the roundabout. Pass the Sunriver entrance at the Country Store and <u>follow Nature Center signs</u> through three traffic circles—turn at 3 o'clock in the first circle, 11 o'clock in the second, and 9 o'clock in the third. The only way you'll find the Center is to follow the signs, and there's a sign at each turn.

➡ **Drivetime from Bend: 18 mins**

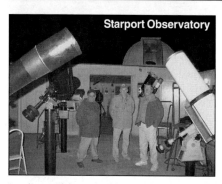

Starport Observatory

then this is the place you'll learn the quirky answer. Personally I've been to both Pine Mtn and here, and I much preferred Sunriver's Starport program.

The Nature Center. Displays contain local history, animals such as snakes, lizards, salamanders, and frogs, plus kids' hands-on exhibits. The meteorite nook is outta this world—it's a fabulous display of everything Chicken Little was afraid of!

Outside the center there are a number of Birds-of-Prey rooms, each with its own raptor. There's a new nearly-blind Golden eagle who perches just a few feet away from his window—maybe the nearest you'll ever be to an 8-foot wingspan eagle! You'll get a great look at the eagle's feathery legs and his treacherous talons…and the staff will tell you fun stuff like that if you had the grip strength of this eagle, you could crush a baseball with your bare hand—yikes! The owls are cute and easily photographed and the one-winged goshawk often puts on quite a show.

Be sure to ask about Sunriver's annual (last week of July) **toad migration** when volunteers gather up the toads by the bucket-full off the

area roads so they don't get squashed by all the weekend visitors. Not a few toads…but a half-million toads…all in one week! It begs the question, "Why did the toad cross the road"…and the answer may be, "to get eaten by another critter". Ask about the toads—you'll love the story and the pictures! (Check blog for a link to an OPB segment.)

Hike: easy 1-mile loop

OBSCURE / POPULAR

OBSCUROMETER

- elevation: 5,700 feet
- fees: NW Pass ($5 at T'head)
- vault toilets
- dogs: leash only

Red-hot lava pours down the hillsides, engulfing the living forest in a molten embrace. Fires dot a blackened landscape embroiled in a hellish inferno. ~~God flees as Satan dances on the corpse of Mother Nature~~ (oops, scratch that, got carried away). Fires dot the landscape as molten lava surrounds and ignites the standing trees. The sluggish lava cools around the tree trunks before they fully burn…leaving…a Lava Cast Forest!

At the trailhead you'll pick up an interpretive map to tour the easy one-mile paved pathway as it snakes between numerous well-like "casts" and a collection of twisted trees. The likenesses of the long-gone trees are now cast in stone while their younger siblings live and die in a tortured tango atop the lava.

Tree Casts

As you stroll imagine Bend's cataclysmic landscape 7,000-8,000 years ago…Mt. Mazama (Crater Lake) has blown its top and covered everything in feet of ash. Soon after, Newberry's 400 cinder cones sprout up and spew ash, cinder, and lava… the hillsides burn…Satan dances. Lava Butte belches cinders and a huge lava flow which dams the Deschutes into a 20-mile lake. Whoa, bad times for the locals.

Overall, the Lava Cast Forest is a pretty neat outing for the entire family. The kids like climbing around into the casts and the adults like the views and interpretation. Note the re-melted drippy casts near sign #12. After the tree had burned away, or in the process, the heat re-melted the hardening lava causing it to smooth-over and drip. At Petersen Rock Garden (81) there are numerous examples of this re-melt on display from when Rasmus and his cohorts chiseled-out keepsakes before the park existed. FYI, if you have a chance to look at this area on Google Earth before you visit, then do so…it's completely impressive to see the flow patterns from above.

Note: By mid-summer the dirt road is very dusty and washboardy for the entire 9 miles to Lava Cast.

From Bend speed south on Hwy 97 for 11 miles. At Sunriver take exit #153 and turn left to head back under the highway on FS 9720. Follow signs on this gravel washboard for 9 miles to trailhead.

➡ **Drivetime from Bend: 30 mins**

EXTRA: An extra interesting place to visit on the access road to Lava Cast is the Camp Abbott cinder cone just .8 miles from the Hwy (where the road turns to dirt). This pit has been extensively quarried and has a 1.0-mile 2WD road to its top, where a sweeping Cascades vista awaits…but that's not all. Here's a li'l secret about this butte: just before the final 50-foot left-turn, if you look down the scoria slope, you may notice that most all the cinders have a rare iridescent rainbow sheen. Yup, Roy

Well, well, well

G Biv himself glimmers on the cinders! Grab a souvenir—ODOT just grinds up the stuff to sprinkle on the winter roads anyhow. Do the Central Oregon wonders never cease??

Lava re-melt

Exploring a tree cast

18 LAPINE STATE PARK
A mellow place along the Deschutes

Hike: easy, short hikes to Tree or 5-mile loop

OBSCUROMETER

- elevation: 4,200 feet
- free
- vault toilets
- dogs: no rules

Tranquility defines this sprawling park hemmed-in by both the Deschutes and the spring-fed Fall River. Numerous trails meandering over very gentle terrain make for easy strolling or family-style Mtn-biking. There are 3 popular reasons to visit this park: 1) The Big Tree, 2) Fishing and camping on the Deschutes, 3) Trails to the crystalline waters of Fall River.

The Big Tree: "Big Red" is the biggest Ponderosa in Oregon, now that a taller one has been found in California. But the Cali tree is only about 8-feet wide compared to Big Red's 8.6-foot width. If the top of Big Red hadn't toppled, then surely this giant would win all the honors. Regardless, this massive "yellow-bellied punkin" lives a contented life just steps from a lazy bend in the Deschutes. At close to 500 years old, this tree has seen everything...except you. Go visit, he'll love your company.

Fall River Trail: A couple miles past the Big Tree, after crossing the Deschutes, turn right for the McGregor Memorial overlook. The scenery from the viewpoint bench is ubiquitous Central Oregon serenity. Looking past an orange-barked Ponderosa, your gaze will take in a tranquil bend of the Deschutes before settling on Paulina Peak on the far horizon. This

**D
R
I
V
E**

From Bend take Hwy 97 south for 20 miles. At MP 160 turn right at State Park signs. The Big Tree is 4.5 miles then right at a sign onto gravel for .7 miles more. For McGregor Viewpoint, pass Tree and Day Use, cross the river, then turn right at sign. Camping is farther along, past the Ranger Station.

➧ **Drivetime from Bend: 26 mins**

is such a nice contemplative spot! Notice the thick layer of white Mazama ash along the river's wall.

From the memorial a 4.75-mile trail makes a loop over to see Fall Creek's 10-foot falls. This hike is flat the entire way as it winds through Lodgepole pines. It makes for a great family Mtn-bike outing. A signboard at the trailhead details the route.

Paulina Peak

Deschutes River

McGregor Viewpoint

Camping: Extensive RV-type sites. Plenty of prime riverside sites.
Fishing: Can't tell ya or the good spots wouldn't be good anymore.

Fall River Falls

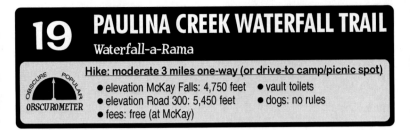

Hike: moderate 3 miles one-way (or drive-to camp/picnic spot)

OBSCURE / POPULAR
OBSCUROMETER

- elevation McKay Falls: 4,750 feet
- elevation Road 300: 5,450 feet
- fees: free (at McKay)
- vault toilets
- dogs: no rules

Paulina Creek is hot-day nirvana! In the Newberry Caldera, East Lake percolates into Paulina Lake which then spills over to form Paulina Creek. The creek then tumbles 2,200 feet in about 8 miles down to Hwy 97 (and eventually the Little Deschutes). What makes this creek so happy and fun is the sun-drenched top waters of Paulina Lake filling the creek rather than the typical local ice-cold snow/spring-fed waters, thus making the bounty of waterfalls warm enough for splashing and dipping! To access the waterfalls along the creek, the Peter Skene Ogden Trail (named for Paulina Lake's 1826 discoverer) parallels the creek as it descends from Paulina Lodge.

McKay Falls

The trail can be hiked, biked, or horsed the whole 8-mile length, but a 3-mile stretch in the middle gives the most bang for the hiking buck. This stretch, beginning at the McKay Camp waterfall, starts upstream with an easy-going 1.5 miles through a 1988 burn. Then the next 1.5 miles steepen, as does the creek. Steep creek means waterfalls, waterfalls mean smiles ☺! You'll pass a variety of beauties (listen and bushwhack to find some really secret ones) until you reach the Road 300 junction trail. It goes right to a bridge and it's got some great waterfalls just downstream. This bridge marks the turnaround point for this hike. After exploring the nearby gems, head back to bask in a favorite or, for a longer outing, continue upstream 4 more miles to Paulina Lodge.

From Bend take Hwy 97 south for 20 miles. At MP 161 turn left at signs for Newberry Caldera. Go 3 miles and turn left onto gravel at sign for McKay Campground. Go 2.2 miles, cross the creek bridge, and park at trailhead sign on the right.

➡ **Drivetime from Bend: 28 mins**

Twin Falls

FYI: The McKay Campground is one of the nicest anywhere in Central Oregon!

HIKE: This hike should not be attempted without cold beers stashed in the insulated pocket of your Camelback. From the riverside campground/parking area, McKay Falls is just downstream. Otherwise, head upstream on the trail and let your ears dictate your off-trail explorations. The Road 300 junction is about 3 miles.

Road 300 Bridge

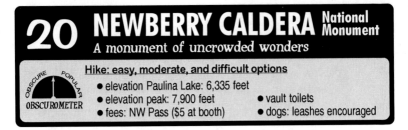

Hike: easy, moderate, and difficult options

OBSCUROMETER

OBSCURE — POPULAR

- elevation Paulina Lake: 6,335 feet
- elevation peak: 7,900 feet
- fees: NW Pass ($5 at booth)
- vault toilets
- dogs: leashes encouraged

The debate over where to site Oregon's National Park raged all through the late 1800's—Crater Lake or Newberry Caldera?? Crater Lake won, Newberry lost. Newberry Caldera has the qualities of a National Park but politicians have only granted it Monument status. All the better—their loss, our gain! Been to a National Park lately? High fees, crowds, rules, regulations, and RVs. No bikes, no dogs, no boats, no access blah blah blah. Crowd together on Old Faithful's bleachers, wait in line at Half Dome's ladder, frame the Grand Canyon between RVs and helicopters…whatever. The National Parks may be "America's Best Idea", but for lots of folks all the crowds, fees and hassles taint the experience.

Rejoice—here in our backyard we've got the joys without the hordes! Newberry Caldera is both an embarrassment of natural riches and a playground for "doers", rather than just picture-takers. You can bike, hike or snowmobile, rent a boat, catch a big fish, drive or hike to spectacular viewpoints, or watch osprey dive while basking in clothing-optional hot springs. You can marvel at the unique Obsidian flow, splash in Paulina Creek's many waterfalls, or watch a majestic sunset from either of two rustic Resorts. All this for only $5…compared to Crater's $10 and Yellowstone/Yosemite's $25/$20! National Park neighbor, Crater, certainly offers un-

Hot Springs

East Lake

Paulina Lake

Obsidian flow

Paulina Peak view

Paulina Lake Resort

real beauty and a quick refresher in foreign languages, but it seems crowded and RV-touristy compared to Newberry's laid-back user-friendliness. Few things make you happier to be in Central Oregon than a full day of Newberry's charms followed by an amazing Cascade sunset as you head home. Tell all your friends…no wait, don't tell anyone.

Note: when paying the NW pass fee at the entrance booth on the access road, you get a detailed caldera map pointing out all the options (except the hot springs).

Paulina Peak. **A Must-Must See!** Without a doubt, this is Oregon's finest viewpoint. As your gaze sweeps the 360° words may fail you…but the Carpenters wrote a song to fill in the gap. "Sitting on top of the world", this 7,984-foot peak looks down on some amazing creations—twin caldera lakes and a frozen flow of black glass. Clear morning air reveals WA's Mt. Adams (168 miles distant, just to the right of Mt. Hood). To the south peaks California's Mt. Shasta (165 miles) while to the SE Steen's Mtn. is a hump in the hazy distance—Wow! Nearby, to the SE, look for tiny Fort Rock looking like a black whale breaching in the flat desert.

While you could hike a trail to the peak, it's much better to do the 4-mile drive and save your energies for elsewhere. It's sort of frustrating to do a hard hike only to realize everyone did an easy drive. Other than Steen's Mtn, this is the highest point in OR that you can easily drive…and NOWHERE else sports a view this incredible—Don't Miss It!!

Paulina Creek Falls. Just before arriving at Paulina Lake you can pull into a signed parking lot for the short walk to overlook this double waterfall.

Paulina Falls

Big Obsidian Flow Trail. A moderate .75-mile (30-minute) trail begins up 80 stairs then loops into the heart of this uniquely young obsidian wonderland—it's just 1,300 years old. Surrounding the path are crazy swirls and zigzagged bands of pumice and glass. Excellent interpretive signs enlighten and enliven the route. Tree sleuths should examine the dwarfed pines; 5-needle, 3-needle, and 2-needle also (see Appendix 1 to ID them). Don't miss this trail, as there are few places anywhere in America this unique!

The trail is signed on the caldera road between the lakes. (Don't take

continued ➡

Paulina Lakeshore Trail

any obsidian—you will be frisked as you leave the park. See entries 9 and 24 to find your own free and legal obsidian).

Paulina Lakeshore Trail. A fairly easy 7-mile trail circles the lake. The NE 3.5 miles between Paulina Lodge and Little Crater campground are the best for serenity, views, obsidian, and hot springs. The south section along the lake passes lots of summer houses and campgrounds – only worth it to make the loop. The best short out 'n' back hike is the 1.5 miles going north from Little Crater Camp to the red cinder hill/ hot spring beach area—awesome scenery, no development, epic views!

Big Obsidian Flow   Paulina Peak

Hot Spring pool

D
R
I
V
E

From Bend take Hwy 97 south for 20 miles. At MP 161 turn left at signs for Newberry. It's 13 miles to Paulina Lake. After paying at the booth you'll see the signs for the waterfall, or continue on to the lake, Lodge, and info center. East Lake is just a few miles farther.

➡ **Drivetime from Bend: 36 mins**

Paulina Hot Springs. Shoreline springs hotly seep up through the pumice gravel "beach" just right (east) of the red cinder hill (NE corner of lake). Every spring helpful fishermen-folk dig pools into the pebbly beach and line them with downed trees…and the hot water seeps in to fill the pools. Pools vary widely in temperature/depth, but the outstanding sight of the Paulina Peak and the Big Obsidian Flow never fails. And where else can you sit in a natural hot spring and toss floaty pumice pebbles into a caldera lake? Just imagine how mobbed and regulated this place would be if it were in a Natl Park! Fishing boats cruise the area so suit (or not) to your

fancy—whichever feels right—there's no rules (Yay!). Soak, swim, soak, and smile!

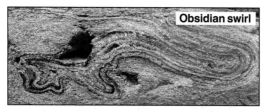

Obsidian swirl

Find the springs about 1.25-mile hike from Little Crater or 2.25 miles from Paulina Lodge (on the lakeshore trail). The springs aren't "easy" to find, as there are no signs or obvious trails. Faint paths lead down to the hot spring "beach" on the immediate east side of the red cinder hill.

East Lake. Cabins, restaurant, store, boat rentals, boat ramp, nice people! Not only is the Lodge's beach the best in the caldera, but the sand is mostly black obsidian—weirdly unique! Ask owners about "secret" hot springs on the shore of East Lake.

Fun at East Lake Resort

SOUTH ICE CAVE
A better ice cave than Arnold

Explore: difficult .25-mile rough, rocky cave walk

OBSCUROMETER
OBSCURE POPULAR

- elevation: 5,000 feet
- free
- vault toilet
- dogs: discouraged

Ice, indeed…especially in the springtime! This is no Arnold Ice Cave…no wee patch of floor ice in an overhang masking as a cave. No, the South Ice Cave is a real cave with a whole lotta ice—bring the skates! Ok, well maybe not the skates, but there is an ice floor in this cave stretching 80 feet long—plenty of room to slide a bit and revel in the oddity of a large boulder-strewn underground ice rink. Every spring the ice in the cave is different…some years it's jaw-drop city, other years just blah. The month of May is the prime month to visit…still cold at night, but warm enough to melt the snow on the road to the cave. Wait until mid-June though and you'll just see the drippings and a wet icy floor. **(If you want to see the ice formations at their best, make sure you plan an excursion in May!)**

Entering the cave is fairly easy down a not-too-steep boulder heap into the vast room with the large ice floor—cool, yes, but no stalactites. But, once you climb over the first (of many) rock piles you'll emerge into another chamber with a ceiling of stalactite chandeliers (in good years). From this vantage it looks like "this is all she wrote" for exploration potential…but wait, climb the far jumble and you'll duck through to more space, more icicles, more ice floor…plus the bonus crystallized ceiling. Sweet!

The South Ice Cave delivers some fun explo-

Cave entrance

Ice floor

D R I V E

From Bend head south on Hwy 97 for 27 miles to LaPine. In LaPine turn left (east) onto Finley Butte Rd (FS 22, next to Sugar Pine Café). Follow this paved forest road 25 fast miles to the signed cave entrance. If you get to a stop sign at FS 18, then you're a mile too far.

To get to Fort Rock from South Ice Cave go 1 mile beyond the cave then turn right onto dirt FS 18 (signed to Fort Rock). This is a high-speed dirt road which leads 15 miles to Fort Rock's entrance road.

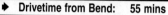

➡ **Drivetime from Bend: 55 mins**

Icicle array

ration. It's never easy going—the surface under foot is a continuous jumble of breakdown necessitating careful hands 'n' feet negotiation. But if you're scramble-ready and bring enough light, i.e., both lantern and headlamps, warm winter-type clothing, gloves and hat…you'll have a fun hour exploring and photographing the icy wonders of this cave until you reach the end and curse the "1966" assholes.

Given that exploring the Ice cave may only be an hour's fun, think about combining it with an outing to Fort Rock (22), Hager Mtn (24) or Derrick Cave (23).

Ceiling crystals

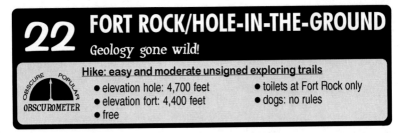

Hike: easy and moderate unsigned exploring trails

OBSCUROMETER

OBSCURE   POPULAR

- elevation hole: 4,700 feet
- elevation fort: 4,400 feet
- free
- toilets at Fort Rock only
- dogs: no rules

Fort Rock and Hole-in-the-Ground are two examples of a rare geologic phenomenon. Both are explosion craters caused by red-hot magma surging upwards under the earth's crust until contacting groundwater. If the magma doesn't hit groundwater on its surge to the surface, then a regular cinder cone forms—like Lava Butte or Pilot Butte. But, in the case of these two spots the magma hit groundwater each time, but with very different results. The Hole formed by the rising magma encountering an underground aquifer, resulting in a huge explosion that blew rock and ash into a perfect circle around the vent—called a tuff ring. The Hole-in-the-Ground is a mile across, 425 feet deep, and was often mistaken for a meteor crater by pioneer scientists!

To contrast, Fort Rock formed similarly but its magma came up underneath a surface of an Ice-Age lake that once filled this basin 12,000 years ago to a depth of 200 feet. Fort Rock's explosion also built up a 300-500 foot tuff ring, but under water. Over time the water and waves of the lake washed away all ash and left a circle of solidified tuff. Thus, the Fort looks like a steep-walled rock enclosure, while the hole resembles a crater.

Both these quirks of geology are fun to explore together as an outing, especially Fall thru Spring when the Cascades are snowed-in.

Fort Rock

Parking/
Trailhead

D
R
I
V
E

From Bend take Hwy 97 south for 28 miles. Pass LaPine and near MP 169 turn left onto Hwy 31. Take this 22 miles and turn left onto gravel at signs for Hole. Set odometer here and go 3 miles. You need to turn right onto dirt FS 3130—sometimes there's a sign, but often it seems to disappear. Go one mile on 3130 to the rim access road.

Leaving the Hole, go left on 3130 for 1.5 miles. Turn right and go another mile back to Hwy 31. Go left and at MP 29 turn left again at Fort Rock signs. Go 6 miles to the town of Fort Rock, then left at Fort Rock park signs and 1.8 miles more to parking.

➡ **Drivetime from Bend: 70 mins**

HIKE: **Hole-in-the-Ground.** From the drive-up west rim a path plummets steeply to the crater floor. There's a gentler .75-mile path that descends from the south rim. You can make a loop out of both in about an hour's walk. Check out the trees on the floor—they may surprise tree-knowledgeable folks (Appendix 1). While the rim is all Ponderosa, the crater is too cold for Pondo seeds to germinate. Also, a rough road circles the rim. Since the diameter of the hole is 1 mile, that makes the road π-miles long (*Circumference = π x diameter*). Woohoo—where else can you hike a perfect circle π-miles long?? If you hike to the east rim you'll get good views of the Cascades and Paulina Peak, as well as Fort Rock.

Hole-in-the-Ground   *Meteor Crater, Arizona*

Fort Rock. Picnic tables, bathrooms, and multiple info-boards surround the parking area. You can tour the interior of the Fort via an old roadbed and various scramble paths. The western edge has bizarre rock shapes, easy-to-explore wave cuts, and a view over to the cave where Dr. Luther Cressman found the famous 9,000+ year-old sandals in 1938 (some of the oldest human relics ever found in the USA!)

Luther in the Fort Rock Cave, 1938

Photo courtesy of Bowman Museum

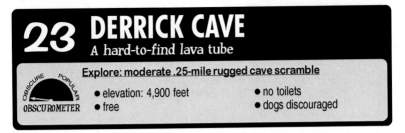

Explore: moderate .25-mile rugged cave scramble

OBSCUROMETER (OBSCURE ◦ POPULAR)

- elevation: 4,900 feet
- free
- no toilets
- dogs discouraged

Once upon a time Bend had a number of caves close to town that were unregulated to visit and explore. Sadly, the past decade has seen local favorites such as Skeleton, Wind, and Bat caves closed-off and gated. Lavacicle Cave was closed long ago when vandals broke and stole the famed lavacicles. Never heard of these caves? Some folks think it better that way. Not **Bend, Overall.**

2nd skylight

Derrick Cave is still there, still free, still unregulated...but a pain-in-the-ass to get to no matter which way (of the many) you drive. The highlights of this quarter-mile tunnel are many, including two fabulous skylight openings. Rock-hopping and scrambling is a must here—bring solid shoes, lights and lanterns, and winter clothes (hats, gloves, coats, pants). Descending into the opening, the first thing you'll see to the right is a metal door frame left over from a 1963 Civil Defense Agency scheme to fortify the cave as a nuclear war shelter. Beyond the door the lower level was stocked with food, water and facilities for an estimated 1,200 people. The plan was to further stock and fortify the site, but funds ran dry and the

Ice nubbin

plan was abandoned. Vandals broke open the door and soon removed everything, including the doors. Now all that remains of this one-time nuclear shelter is the door frame.

To the left of the opening is the cave proper. First up are the two skylights, then another 15-minute rocky walk/clamber to the tunnel's end. Derrick's got a lot of neat cave features for such a short tube. The best time is definitely in May when icicles may be dripping from the ceiling's mini lavacicles—whoa! The cave floor is somewhat jumbly, but walking with a lantern in

D
R
I
V
E

Derrick Cave is a long bumpy arduous drive no matter which way you approach it. Don't try to drive to Derrick Cave without having a Fort Rock Ranger District map in hand. The map gives you options in case whatever directions you have aren't working out for some reason. A Gazetteer is sketchy, but it <u>might</u> get you there.

The most straightforward route is taking Hwy 20 for 21 miles east of Bend, then 32 miles of washboardy gravel/dirt forest road on FS 23/2325 (75 minutes from Bend at high-speed). This route requires that you haul-ass on the straight-ish forest roads to smooth-out the bad washboard. If you're not comfortable going 30-50mph on gravel, then this route will be a slow torture. Check the map! From Bend head east on Hwy 20 and at MP 21.5 turn south on paved FS 23 (to China Hat). In 6 miles stay left on FS 23 onto gravel. Head 13 miles to the FS 22 fork— stay left towards Sand Sprgs/Fox. Head 7 miles to the FS 23 fork and now stay left onto FS 2320. In just .6 miles turn right onto FS 2325 at the Aspen Flat fork with "Derrick Cave 7 miles" sign). From here it is 6 more miles underneath the powerlines. In 5.4 miles you'll cross the forest boundary at a cattle guard…and the cave is just .6 miles more, staying straight at the next intersection. The cave is unsigned, but the parking area has an obvious man-made rock border.

From Fort Rock it's a 45 min, 22-mile drive (4WD rec'd). From Fort Rock town head east 5.6 miles and stay straight at the junction. Zigzag for another 4 miles and turn left on Derrick Cave Rd (10miles so far). Go 5 miles more of pavement (14.8m), then onto dirt road. In 2.5 miles (17.3m) skirt around cabins, then 3.8 miles more to splatter cones camp spot (21m). From here it's a rough .5 miles more to cave parking (22m).

From South Ice Cave it's a 35-minute, 14.5 mile drive…via FS 22, then FS 23, then FS 700, then FS 820/800...then a final right onto FS 2325 for the 2 miles.

➮ **Drivetime from Bend: 75-100 mins**

hand isn't too tough. In between icicle groves the floor is often a maze of ropey "pahoehoe" lava flows—you really get the feeling of "lava-FLOW" in this cave. At the very end of the cave you'll need to crouch a bit to see a lavacicle-laden roof.

After your exploration, back above ground, try to find the skylights—it's much trickier than you'd think.

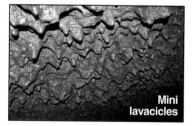

Mini lavacicles

Ropey pahoehoe lava

The best time to visit Derrick Cave is in the early spring when most of Bend's fun is still under snow…and also the icicles will be at their finest. Primitive car or tent camping is available at the parking lot or .7 miles south at the splatter cones. Camping is extra good because the best skylight cave-beams are before 10am (throw dust into the air).

24 HAGER MOUNTAIN TRAIL
A good springtime/early summer wildflower peak

Hike: moderate 2.3 miles one-way or 4-mile one-way

OBSCUROMETER

- elevation road: 5,200 feet
- elevation trailhead: 5,600 feet
- elevation top: 7,200 feet
- free
- no toilets
- dogs: no rules

Hager Mtn is the distinctive conical volcano topped with a lookout building poking skyward 25 miles south of Fort Rock. A steady trail traverses thick stands of Ponderosa and wildflower-cloaked slopes on its way up to the mountain-top staffed lookout building.

Hager Mtn.   Fort Rock

Approaching from the north (from South Ice Cave)

Much like the Ochocos, springtime is the best time to visit Hager Mtn…think June….the Cascades are still snowed in and inaccessible, yet Hager is a-bloom with wildflowers and wonderful springtime scents.

At the peak you'll find a rest-stop picnic table with the lookout cabin looming above. If you're nice, and maybe bring a little bag of candy orange slices as a gift (wink wink), Kathy, the long-time lookout may invite you up for a look-see and chat. Ask her about her twin loves—knitting and lightning! Enticed by your thoughtfulness, she may point out the sights to see, from Fort Rock and China Hat to Mt Theilsen and Crater Lake's Mt Scott. You may even see way down to Mt Shasta on a clear day! In June Thompson Reservoir glimmers directly below Hager Mtn, but it dries up by summer. Also, while you're spinning around taking in the 360° view, notice that Hager

is the easternmost volcano before the landscape turns to Basin-and-Range faulting. The eastern Oregon Basin-and-Range landscape begins just east of Hager at Picture Rock Pass on Hwy 31 as it descends to Summer Lake—no more volcanoes, but rather tilted/sunken ridges with lakes in the low spots.

Kathy the lookout says she only sees about 200-250 visitors a summer and everyone seems delighted to have made the hike. Hope she's still there when you go.

D R I V E

Drive as to Fort Rock (22), but don't turn for Fort Rock but rather go straight for 17 more miles to Silver Lake town. On the west side of Silver Lake town turn south onto East Bay Rd (FS 28) and go 9 paved miles to the signed roadside trailhead.

To get to Hager Mtn from Fort Rock, go into Fort Rock "town" (gas and snacks) then turn left (south) onto Pitcher Rd for 16 high-speed dirt miles, then right at the T one mile into Silver Lake. Just west of Silver Lake turn south onto East Bay Rd and go 9 miles to trailhead.

➤ **Drivetime from Bend: 90 mins**

Hager Mtn. Lookout

HIKE: For a longer (4 mile one-way) hike, begin at the "official" trailhead on FS 28. To shorten the hike by half drive past the FS 28 roadside trailhead a few hundred yards and turn left onto FS 012 and drive 2 miles to the road-end upper trailhead. At this upper parking area, notice the obsidian that litters the roadway, revealing Hager's volcanic origins. At Newberry Caldera you'd be arrested for pocketing a hunk of ebony obsidian, but here at Hager you can grab a guilt-free chunk for the kitchen window sill! The trail from the road-end to the lookout is straightforward, but make sure to look around at the junction with the trail coming up from FS 28 so you won't be confused on your way back down.

Hager Obsidian

25 CRATER LAKE
Oregon's sole National Park

OBSCUROMETER

- elevation lake: 6,180 feet
- elevation lodge/rim: 7,100 feet
- elevation Scott parking: 7,700 ft
  elevation Scott peak: 8,900 feet
- fees: $10 Day Pass
- toilets everywhere
- dogs: leash law
- On-line reservations: **www.CraterLakeLodges.com**

Oregon's sole National Park needs little introduction—everyone has heard of Crater Lake. 'Tis the country's deepest and clearest lake at 1,943 feet deep with a record-setting visibility of 144 feet. The Rangers will tell you, "go ahead and have a drink of it—there's none purer!"

Crater Lake is a perfect park for sightseers because there isn't much to actually <u>DO</u> except drive around the 33-mile Rim Drive and stop at the plentiful overlooks. You'll find plenty of company on this Rim Drive since Crater Lake sees an estimated 500,000 annual visitors, most all of them in the short snow-free period July-Sept (4,000-ish people per day).

1903 photo from Mt. Scott

If the Rim drive and rustic Lodge were all there was to Crater Lake, then it wouldn't need to be in this book. What I want to tell you about are the three best things to "DO" at the park.

The first is to hike to the top of Mt Scott, the 8,900-ft peak directly east of the crater rim. This is the only place in the park where you can get a photo of the entire lake (if your lens is a bit wide). Everywhere else on the rim will only allow you a slice of the blue-blue lake, but Mt Scott delivers the entire WOW. The best time to ascend Mt Scott and see the lake at its bluest is EARLY in the DAY, near 10am to noon.

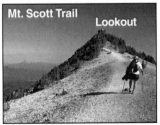

Mt. Scott Trail
Lookout

HIKE: The trail is 2.5 miles one-way, at a fairly easy grade, but at altitude! You'll hike from 7,700 ft to 8,900 ft to the lookout building at the top. Mt Scott trailhead is clearly signed midway round the rim drive on the east side.

The **BEST-best** thing to do at Crater Lake is the boat tour. Hands down! There are seven tours daily from 10am to 3pm. Each boat holds 48 people for a total of about 340 people per day. These tours (at $27pp) are deservedly popular…and since only about 10% of the daily visitors can squeeze onto the boats, you better be prepared with some inside tips if you want to get aboard.

The highlight of the boat tours is Wizard Island. Wizard Island is one of the most unique places on the Earth. Where else can you climb a volcano within a volcano, all the while surrounded by the clearest and bluest waters on the planet?? Good answer… NOWHERE! Being on Wizard Island is both the neatest and least touristy place in the Park. **The trick is that only two of the daily boat tours**

DRIVE

Head south on Hwy 97 for 72 miles to Diamond Lake Junction and signs for the park's north entrance. Turn right and go 15 miles to the park entrance road. Go left and the entrance booth is up ahead.

➤ **Drivetime from Bend: 90 mins**

will let you off on Wizard Island—the 10am and 1pm boats. This means only 96 people per day can venture onto this wonderland of jagged lava rock rising out of the bluest lake ever—it's quite an experience (and totally memorable since every time you see a photo of Crater Lake you'll nod and think "been there!")

Here's the deal: as of 2010 half the seats on the boat tours can be reserved online up to 5 days in advance. This leaves only 170 walk-in seats available per day. The boat box office opens at 8am and there's a line every day awaiting the opening. Thus, if you want to visit Wizard (or just go on any regular boat tour) without a previous reservation, you better be in line at 7am to get one of the 48 daily Wizard Island Drop-off tickets.

Off to see the Wizard

The tour boat drops you off at Wizard for a 3-hour stop, making for a 5-hour total boat tour. Here's how to get the most out of Wizard: debarking the boat, everyone heads up the 1-mile cinder cone trail…but this is less fun because the trail is narrow and people are out-of shape and breathless…all making for a pain-in-the-ass hike. Instead, head a half-mile to Fumarole Bay, work your way down to the shore and go for a dip!! Yes the water is chilly—probably about 60° in the shallow coves, but where else are you going to find an opportunity to strip and plunge into the purest waters on Earth!! Open your mouth, take a gulp—it's PURE! The rangers guess that only one outta a hundred people go for a swim. Be one of those people…one of the few who suckle the sweet nectar of nature! Afterwards, up the cinder cone you go to join the other 47 people milling around the rim…no waiting behind all the slow-pokes. Wizard's rim is, of course, fabulous! Dead whitened snags and red scoria slopes contrast the bluuue while friendly squirrels scurry and beg. Hope you get a sunny day—you'll love it!

The 3rd thing is to find at Crater Lake is the hidden *Lady of the Woods*.

Cleetwood Cove

She's a nude figure sculpted into a boulder back in 1917, secretly hiding out sorta behind the Lodge. That's all I'll say here—see my blog for her story and have fun scouting her out! (See Appendix 4.)

Holding a special Wizard On/Off ticket at Cleetwood Cove

Hike: easy walks

OBSCUROMETER
OBSCURE — POPULAR

- elevation lake: 4,791 feet
- free
- vault toilets
- dogs: no rules

Just before Thanksgiving every autumn Odell lake hosts one of the most amazing wildlife spectacles anywhere in Central Oregon. In late Oct. and Nov. Odell Lake's abundant Kokanee salmon spawn along the western shoreline of the lake and in tributary Trapper Creek. Bright red and green 12-inch spawners color every nook and cranny of Trapper Creek. Few people know this happens, but plenty of Bald eagles do. In Oregon, most Kokanee are spawned out and dead by Nov. 1st, but not at Odell Lake. The spawning here lasts longer, attracting eagles from afar for a final frenzied feast.

Shelter Cove Resort

The owners of the Shelter Cove Resort, Jim and Trula, report hundreds of eagle sightings most years. Their resort is the center of the action as eagles perch on the trees above their waterfront. Every so often eagles swoop down among the docks and grab flapping Kokanee to fly to the treetops to feed. Beware—the eagles love to drop their leftovers on unsuspecting tourists! Even if the eagles aren't around or very active when you show up, the sight of the brightly colored Kokanee swarming the streams is still magnificent. It's pretty incredible though to be standing beside the gurgling creek watching the fish doing "battle' for spawning rights when an eagle swoops and wooshes by your head mid-zoom to a new tree-top. Jaw-drop to say the least!

For further Kokanee spawn info see Appendix 2.

D R I V E

There are two ways to get to the resort, depending on early snow-fall—each takes about 1.5 hours. If it's open, the best route by far is the Cascade Lakes Hwy. From Bend it's a gorgeous 70-mile drive, past Wickiup and Davis, to the Crescent Cutoff Rd. Go right on the Cutoff for 4 miles then right again onto Hwy 58 for 10 miles to Odell West access, turning left for 2 miles to the resort.

If it's snowy, take Hwy 97 south 45 miles to Crescent then turn right (in the middle of town) onto the Cutoff. Follow it, then Hwy 58, for 22 miles to Odell West access.

➡ **Drivetime from Bend: 90 mins**

DETAILS: Shelter Cove Resort is busy with fishermen all summer. There is plentiful camping and a bunch of rustic rental cabins. The spawning time is quiet at the resort—few except bird-watchers are in the know. Call 1-800-647-2729 for details, reservations, road/weather conditions. The eagles feed primarily at dawn and dusk, but midday you'll see plenty soaring and cavorting. Staying at the Shelter Cove Resort is best. Get there by 3PM for the dusk feeding and wake early to witness the morning frenzy.

Trapper Creek Kokanee (Nov.)

Spend the day looking for Kokanee or visiting nearby Salt Creek Falls (27). If your timing is right and the eagles are putting on a show, this experience is one you'll be telling your friends about for a long time!

Photo by Jim Kielblock

WHATEVER WHATEVER WHATEVER WHATEVER WHATEVER WHATEVER WHATEVER WHATEVER WHATEVER WHATEVER

Biologists guess that there were approximately 1,000 pairs of bald eagles in Oregon around 1800. By the 1960's only about 400 pairs existed in the entire lower 48 states (due to both hunting and DDT). Nowadays the estimate is about 6,000 pairs in the lower 48, thanks to the Endangered Species Act.

WHATEVER WHATEVER WHATEVER WHATEVER WHATEVER WHATEVER WHATEVER WHATEVER WHATEVER WHATEVER

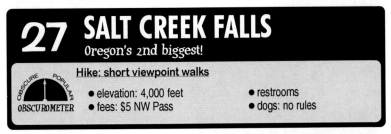

Hike: short viewpoint walks

OBSCURE — POPULAR
OBSCUROMETER

- elevation: 4,000 feet
- fees: $5 NW Pass
- restrooms
- dogs: no rules

Salt Creek Falls is a doozy! Come see it for just a quick look, or take one of two longer hikes to make a day out of it…either way is sure to please (see next entry). Salt Creek Falls is Oregon's 2nd highest at 286 feet (behind Multnomah's 612 feet)….but the

comparisons stop there. Multnomah gets two million yearly visitors, clogging its dedicated highway exit as well as its concession stands. Salt Creek Falls sees few visitors, has no commercialized tourist junk…and, more importantly, Salt Creek Falls is just as breathtaking. Yup. This is 286 feet of sheer MESMERIZE! A basalt amphitheatre corrals the waterfall with viewpoints studding the rim. The basalt walls are dazzling in their own right, showcasing a mish-mash of crazy-angled columnar jointing. But of course you've come to see the mammoth waterfall, and it doesn't disappoint! You can easily watch this waterfall for a half hour without tiring of its ever-changing combination of gush and wisp. For some trippy fun fix your gaze on the cascading delicacy for a minute, then move your eyes to the neighboring basalt wall—Whoa—it's as if the wall throbs...bizarre!

D R I V E

Salt Creek Falls is on Hwy 58 just west of Willamette Pass. From Bend there are two ways to get to Hwy 58—either by taking Hwy 97 south 47 miles to Crescent and turning right on to the Crescent Cut-off…or by taking the Cascade Lakes Hwy all the way past Wickiup and Davis to its end at the Crescent Cut-off (then right to Hwy 58). On Hwy 58 at MP 57 (between the Hwy tunnel and Willamette Pass), turn into the well-signed Salt Creek Falls entrance and go down the road a half mile to the parking area.

➧ **Drivetime from Bend:** **70 mins**

The fenced cliff-edge viewpoints are just 30 seconds from the parking lot. There's also a trail that descends about 150 feet via a bunch of easy switchbacks to a lower viewpoint. This lower view is totally worth the small effort—your eyes will process the water's movement differently from this lower level—don't miss it.

If Salt Creek Falls seems a long drive as an out/back, consider making a loop if you're up for the Waldo Lake backroads route (see entry 29).

Hike: easy/mod 3-mi waterfalls loop, or mod 4.25-mi one way (to lake)

OBSCURE • POPULAR
OBSCUROMETER

- elevation trailhead: 4,000 feet
- elevation lake: 5,400 feet
- fees: NW Pass (at trailhead)
- vault toilets
- dogs: no rules

Map page 214

Do this hike either in June or August—skip the mosquito-mobbed July! In late June the Rhododendrons' explosion of pink jazzes-up the entire trail, but Vivian Lake will be too chilly to swim. In July you'd need DEET[2] to deal with the mosquito plague. By August the mosquitoes have abated and Vivian Lake is invitingly bath-like!

Beginning at Salt Creek Falls' gargantuan cascade, there are two trail options here that feature an embarrassment of Central Cascades riches. First you've got Salt Creek's must-see waterfall (probably Oregon's least-seen must-see). Then you

Diamond Creek Falls

quickly get a look at Too Much Bare Lake (can there be too much?), and a bunch of cliff-edge viewpoints of the Diamond/Salt Creek canyon confluence and obscured views of Lower Diamond's huge yet mostly-invisible falls. Soon thereafter comes a side trail down to Diamond Creek Falls via charming log staircase and bridge...where you'll find a mossy Eden decorated by Diamond Creek's 100-foot waterfall veil. After this waterfall you can shorten the hike by looping back to the car on the Vivian Lake trail, making for a 3-mile outing. Better yet is to continue another 2.5 miles to Vivian Lake, passing Falls Creek Falls along the way. Vivian

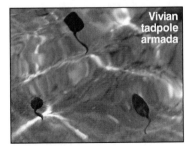

Vivian tadpole armada

Lake, like many others, is the perfect Cascade lake. But Vivian is different than many in its perfection. It's shaped like a figure-8 with a shallow area between the deeper halves. These shallows are divine when the lake is warm—you can walk crosswise between the shores and there are lots of rocks to perch and sun on. Mt Yoran looms above the idyllic setting and there are shoreline campspots—how much more could you ask for? A perfect Cascade lake at the end of a waterfall and rhododendron festooned trail—gotta love Central Oregon!

If you visit in July, skip the mosquito-y lake and do the shorter loop…but in August/Sept the longer outing is the best.

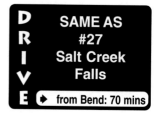

HIKE: Begin at the picnic area to the left of Salt Creek Falls' parking lot. Cross the bridge, soon cross another bridge, then go right at the signs for Diamond Creek Falls. The next 1.5 miles to the falls is peppered with highlights—Too Much Bare Lake at .25 miles, then cliff-edge canyon viewpoints, the June rhododendron pink-a-rama, and finally a mandatory 3-minute side trip down to the Diamond Creek Falls.

After the falls head uphill for a couple of minutes to the signed junction—heading left is the short loop back to the car, either now or retuning from the longer hike (it's a mile back to the car from here, mostly downhill after the first steep uphill).

Vivian Lake

Shallows

For Vivian Lake stay straight and soon cross the creek bridge and then the railroad tracks (2-mile mark). Across the tracks the trail steepens and enters the wilderness. In .75 miles you'll get some obscured views of the lower bits of Falls Creek's namesake cascade and then after a rock-hop across a stream you'll ascend a cursedly steep .5 miles to the top of Falls Creek Falls and its sunny overlook perch. After a rest it's just one mile more uphill to Vivian Lake's signed turn off…then a couple of minutes over to the refreshing blue. Shoreline footpaths circle the lake. Return the way you came.

71

29 WALDO LAKE
A Cascades stunner!

Hike: easy 2-mile one-way to South Beach

- elevation Waldo: 5,414 feet
- fees: NW Pass
  ($5 at lakeshore parking)
- vault toilets (at Waldo only)
- dogs: no rules

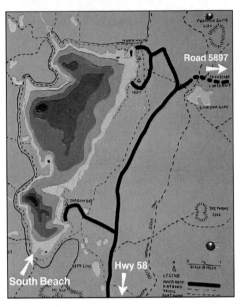

Waldo Lake is both Oregon's second biggest natural lake as well as one of the most pure and clear. Waldo has no in-flow streams—all its water comes from snow and underwater springs—and thus no stream-born sediments murk up its clarity. Signs around the lake tout 100-foot deep clarity! Waldo Lake also has a 10-MPH motor limit, so most people visit for much more a pristine experience than at the other big Cascade "resort-lakes". At Waldo the vast lakeside camp-grounds are sprinkled with canoes, kayaks, and swimmers…not fishing boats, wave-runners, or ATVs. Get it? Waldo is the only major Cascade Lake with drive-up access without a Resort or motor-ized-yahoo factor.

View from the north campground

Diamond Peak

D R I V E

The drive to Waldo seems super far from Bend via Hwy 58 past Odell Lake, over Willamette Pass, then up Waldo's access road. But, little-known is that a rough road cuts over from the Casc Lakes Hwy just past Crane Prairie reservoir (MP 53, at the FS 42 junction). This rough washboardy road (FS 5897) zips over to Waldo in just 8.6 miles, taking about 25 minutes. The road is signed "Unmaintained", but locals say that the road has been in the same washboardy-yet-OK condition for the past 30 years—it's the "local secret" access road. After the bumpy ride the road pops you out on the north end of Waldo Lake's road (MP 11) after passing Charlton Lake. This route saves you about 20 minutes and 36 extra miles rather than driving the Casc Lakes Hwy to Hwy 58. FS 5897 is unsigned on the Casc Lakes Hwy side (as if the Forest Service doesn't want you to know)…but at Waldo it's signed "Century Drive 8 miles—unmaintained road".

➤ **Drivetime from Bend: 80 mins**

Waldo Lake's famous cobalt waters are its main drawing card, but many people visit without experiencing the captivating hyper-blueness. You've GOT to go 100 yards or more out into the lake to really see the blue-blue cobalt/indigo blue of Waldo. The shoreline doesn't do it justice at all! Along the shore Waldo's water doesn't look any bluer than any other Cascade lake…but once you get out into the deep the blue become mesmerizing! Thus, you need to bring something to float on. As a bonus, Waldo is usually swimmably warm in August…and nowhere else in the USA can you swim in water both this warm and this clear. Crater Lake is inaccessible and chilly, Clear Lake is frigid. Waldo may be the clearest swimming ever!!

The BEST beach on the lake is on the south shore at the farther of the two little coves. This beach has sand, wade-able shallows, a camp spot…and views to the distant South/Middle Sisters. It's best to paddle over to it from Shadow Bay, but the shoreline trail heads over from Shadow Bay also, taking about 2 miles to get there.

For hiking and biking a 21-mile trail encircles the lake. The trail is popular with both Mtn bikers and backpackers. The trail isn't that good for day-hikes, except the 2-mile bit to the south beach. Better hiking is up the Twins Mtn (30) or over to Bobby Lake (31).

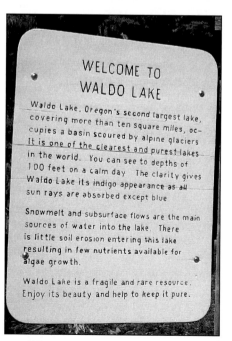

WELCOME TO
WALDO LAKE

Waldo Lake, Oregon's second largest lake, covering more than ten square miles, occupies a basin scoured by alpine glaciers. It is one of the clearest and purest lakes in the world. You can see to depths of 100 feet on a calm day. The clarity gives Waldo Lake its indigo appearance as all sun rays are absorbed except blue.

Snowmelt and subsurface flows are the main sources of water into the lake. There is little soil erosion entering this lake resulting in few nutrients available for algae growth.

Waldo Lake is a fragile and rare resource. Enjoy its beauty and help to keep it pure.

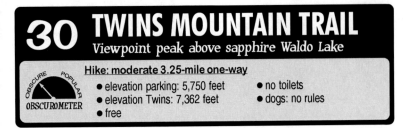

Hike: moderate 3.25-mile one-way

OBSCUROMETER

- elevation parking: 5,750 feet
- elevation Twins: 7,362 feet
- free
- no toilets
- dogs: no rules

The best viewpoint near Waldo is up the 7,362-foot Twins Mountain. This twin-tipped volcanic summit sports a view down over indigo Waldo Lake akin to Mt Scott's view of Crater Lake or Paulina Peak's overlook of Newberry's two lakes. The hike is a bit dull—a viewless 3.25-mile climb— but the view makes the trek more than WORTH IT! Seven-ish lakes are scattered in sight and the Cascade volcanoes put on a grand showing between Mt Hood and Mt Shasta—Whew! From the Twins' scoria-topped summit the intensity of Waldo Lake's cobalt blue contrasts nicely with the striking red/black/yellow scoria slopes. You <u>will</u> like this view—it's worth the effort!

Waldo Lake

Burn

North Waldo Campground

For fun look SE to see the black lava flow cradling Davis Lake. Also, note the ghastly 1996 Waldo Lake burn around the north side of Waldo Lake. Looking towards the Three Sisters, notice the Rock Mesa pumice flow below South Sister with little bump of LeConte Crater in front of it. Also notice on South Sister's right slope the first polyp of Devil's Garden lava and the pointy bump of Devil's Hill beside it.

On a sunny Cascades day the Twins viewpoint is sure to please. The only dilemma you'll face on top of Twins Mountain will be deciding exactly where you'll swim when you get down.

HIKE: The easy-to-overlook trailhead is barely signed at MP 6.5 on Waldo's road, between Betty/Bobby Lakes and Shadow Bay. The trail begins easily and after 1.5 miles you'll cross the PCT and continue a bit more steeply to the summit. Once on top of North Twin, make sure you go over to South Twin's peak to its higher and better viewpoint. (You know how twins are—they both like attention!) The scamper up South Twin only takes another 5 minutes and the sight of Waldo's blue peeking over North Twin's colored scoria makes the blue even more magnificent.

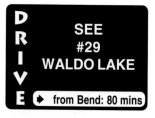

DRIVE

SEE #29 WALDO LAKE

▶ from Bend: 80 mins

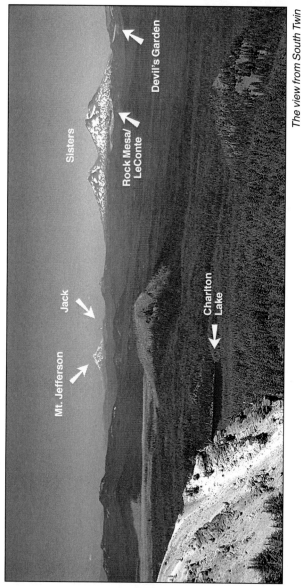

The view from South Twin

Mt. Jefferson

Jack

Sisters

Rock Mesa/ LeConte

Devil's Garden

Charlton Lake

31 CHARLTON, BOBBY & BETTY LAKES
3 smaller lakes near Waldo Lake

OBSCUROMETER

Hike: various
- elevation Charlton: 5,700 feet
- elevation Bobby: 5,400 feet
- elevation Betty: 5,575
- free
- no toilets at any
- dogs: no rules

Scattered near Waldo Lake are a myriad of other smaller lakes to explore. Waldo is the main draw of the area, but the only knock on Waldo is sometimes the lake is very windy. When it's windy the campground shoreline is rough with waves and a bit cold. So, head to one of these nearby smaller lakes to escape the wind or just to find some seclusion away from Waldo's shoreline. See map entry 29.

Betty Lake. Betty Lake is just a short .3-mile 5-minute walk from the Waldo access road. Betty is a fairly small lake without too much scenery…but it does have a small island/isthmus that makes a great picnic/campsite. The signed trail to the lake is on the left side of the access road at MP 5.5.

Betty Lake Campfire

Bobby Lake. Bobby is an easy 2-mile hike from the Waldo access road. Bobby is a much bigger and more scenic lake than Betty, situated between Twins Mtn and Maiden Peak. Arriving at the lake you'll find some camp spots and if you take the shoreline path to the right you'll find a nice sunning rock angling into the ever-so-swimmable waters.

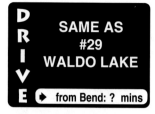

D
R
I
V
E

SAME AS
#29
WALDO LAKE

➤ from Bend: ? mins

The trailhead for Bobby is on the right side of Waldo access road at MP 5.5, just past Betty Lake…and a little hidden in the trees. Hike a meandering 1.5 miles to a T-junction with the PCT trail. Go left for just one minute then right at the next sign for the lake, then .3 more miles to the lakeshore.

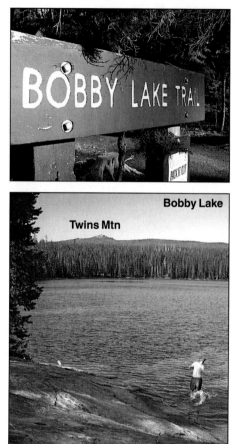

Twins Mtn

Bobby Lake

Charlton Lake. Charlton Lake is a fairly popular neighbor to Waldo. It's a big blue beauty! Most of Charlton's popularity stems from the fact that it's only a quick walk from the roadside parking, but just far enough away to feel remote. Long-time locals often bring a wheelbarrow to wheel their supplies in to the shoreline camp spots. To find Charlton drive to MP 11 on the Waldo road and turn right onto gravel road FS 5897 towards Century Drive and go just .3 miles to the signed pullout. The lake is visible through the trees.

32 FALL RIVER TRAIL
A gin-clear instant river

Hike: easy .5 miles one-way, with longer options

OBSCUROMETER

- elevation: 4,250 feet
- campground: $10 per site
- Guard Station rental: 541-383-4712
- free
- vault toilet
- dogs: no rules

Fall River Falls

The Fall River is Sunriver's answer to the famed Head of the Metolius. Just like over in Camp Sherman, this river springs to life seemingly out of nowhere, silent and freezing cold. From a pair of innocuous low points in a nondescript grove of pines, whammo, the full Fall River gushes forth and begins its short 7-mile (as the crow flies) or 12-mile (as the river winds) run down to its meeting with the Deschutes.

This river is tranquil[2]. If you're visiting Sunriver and a bit tired of all the summertime hoopla, then pop over for a stroll up the bank of this softly gurgling oddity and marvel at the quiet serenity of a river springing to life from "nowhere."

The best way to experience the Fall River is to park at the campground and walk the shoreline fishermen's path from the scenic foot bridge a half-mile up to the headwater springs. There is an official trail that leads from the campground up to the springs, but it stays about 100 yards up from the bank...so it makes a good return trail from the springs/Guard Station end point. Here's what to do: Park at the campground and, before hiking, stash a couple of drinks securely in the ice-cold stream near the footbridge, and then head upriver. The log-hopping riverside route takes about 15 minutes

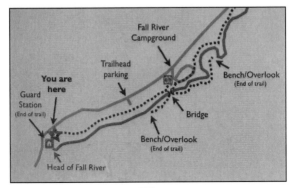

D R I V E

Head to Sunriver via exit 153 off Hwy 97. Go 2 miles, straight around the roundabout, then through the stoplight. Just past the stoplight turn left onto signed South Century Drive and go 2 miles then right onto the signed Cascade Lakes Hwy (MP 5). The falls are at MP 10.2 and the campground trailhead is signed at MP 15.

➧ **Drivetime from Bend: 30 mins**

Campground Bridge

until it contours around the first big gushing spring. At this point you'll see the former FS Guard Station through the trees (it's now rentable as an FS cabin, like a fire lookout). Walk a minute more and look sharp because the river seems to simply disappear! It's perplexing to fathom that the entire river that you've just walked all squirted out of these little holes.

The upper 10-minute return trail starts where the driveway meets the road. The return route will certainly pass quickly in anticipation of those drinks chillin' in Mother Nature's cooler ☺.

NOTE: The flat easy trails both up and downriver from the campground make for some easy family-style Mtn-biking. A signboard at the parking area shows the trails.

Fall River Falls. About 5 miles downriver from the campground the river spills over a 12-foot ledge. Fly fishermen love the spot! To find the un-

marked and unsigned waterfall head back towards Sunriver and at exactly MP 10.2 turn south onto the unsigned gravel road (with 15415 address marker) for .75 miles to the left-side parking lot. The falls are a 4-minute stroll downriver.

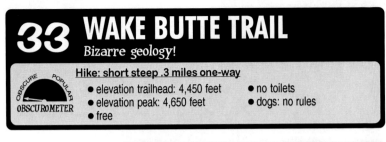

Hike: short steep .3 miles one-way

OBSCUROMETER

- elevation trailhead: 4,450 feet
- elevation peak: 4,650 feet
- free

- no toilets
- dogs: no rules

Wake Butte is bizarre. Bizarre in two different ways: geologically and recreationally. The geology is odd in that this butte differs from so many local buttes because it's neither a cinder cone nor Shield/ Strato volcano. Recreationally it's odd because it seems an unlikely place to maintain a signed short trail with a peculiarly large parking area.

OK, geology first: Wake Butte is a first cousin to Fort Rock in that it resulted from an upwelling of red-hot magma encountering groundwater on its underground surge towards the earth's surface, which caused a massive splatter explosion of cement-like lava goo. This goo then hardened into the peculiar layered striations that make up Wake Butte. This hardened volcanic goo is Palagonite Tuff—the same stuff Fort Rock is made of. For most of our local cinder cones, like Lava or Pilot Buttes, the rising magma reached

D R I V E

Head to Sunriver on Hwy 97. Exit at #153 and go right 2 miles to the Sunriver roundabout and go straight through it to the next stop-light. Set your odometer here. This is FS 40. Go straight 4 miles then turn left to stay with FS 40 towards Crane Prairie. From this junction go exactly 5 miles to the signed Wake Butte trailhead (at MP 11.5, if the MP signs are visible.)

➡ **Drivetime from Bend: 25 mins**

the surface, encountering air which caused an explosion sending the magma skyward to fall back down as bubble-riddled scoria. Only when rising magma encounters groundwater do you get an explosion of goo which plops back to the ground in stratified layers.

Thus, if you visit Wake Butte you'll find a large signed parking lot and a short trail to the top. It seems pretty odd that this trail even exists, since it sort of leads "nowhere." On the 7 to 11-minute ascent you'll see lots of lumpy yellow rocks with distinctly angled layering. This isn't a hike that'll "Wow" most folks, especially given that we live in a WOW landscape with a surprise around every corner. But for someone geologically inclined, or just someone who enjoys beating off the path a bit…then the oddity of Wake Butte will suffice. Don't expect a Cascades panorama from the top of the butte either, cuz there isn't one. Even if you bushwhack higher that the trail's-end knob…no dice…no great view. Geology is all you get, plus a view SE with Paulina Peak being the most distinctive sight. What a strange place for a signed trail with a large parking lot!

Sunset atop Wake Butte

Hike: drive-up view or moderate 4-miles one-way

OBSCUROMETER

- elevation falls: 5,000 feet
- elevation Happy: 6,000 feet
- fees: NW Pass ($5 at T'head)
- vault toilets
- dogs: no rules

Tumalo Falls is 97 feet of awesome! Tumalo Creek leaps off a basalt escarpment into a pretty rainbowed basin, all easily viewed from the parking lot's viewpoint. This viewpoint is mere steps from the parking lot or you can take a short trail to the top-o-the falls fenced view-platforms. The top is a must—it's totally worth the 5-minute walk! Surefooted adventurers might find a slippery path under the escarpment which leads to a groovy red-rocked nook behind the waterfall.

For hikers there are multiple trail options from the parking lot, all

are well-signed. The best option, by far, is the trail upstream along Tumalo Creek. Go just a mile to check out some more excellent falls or keep going a total of 4 miles up the waterfall-laden creek to find Happy Valley. The valley up there's happy with summertime wildflowers, so you'll be happy too. The creekside trail up to Happy Valley is fairly easy with plenty of big waterfalls to keep things interesting. The turn-around picnic point is the grassy meadows spangled with wildflowers. 'Tis possible to make a loop out of this hike via the signed Bridge Creek trail, but the Bend Watershed property is way less scenic than returning the way you came. The Bridge Creek trail makes a loop, but it mostly stays in viewless forest with no stream and waterfall punctuations—it's better to retrace your steps and enjoy all the sights and sounds of fantastic Tumalo Creek from the reverse angle.

D R I V E

In Bend you need to head west Franklin which becomes Galveston and go straight through the flaming chicken roundabout on 14th and Galveston. The road now becomes Skyliners—keep going straight west for 10 miles to the bridge over Tumalo Creek...then it's 2.4 washboardy gravel miles more to the road-end parking.

➤ **Drivetime from Bend: 15 mins**

Happy Valley

Twin Falls Viewpoint

HIKE: There's a map-board at the trailhead—take a photo of it. Begin up to the falls then past. The trail passes Twin Falls in one mile then Upper Falls a mile further. Cross a footbridge and pass more falls before intersecting with the Bridge Creek trail at mile 3.7. Go straight .3 miles more to Happy Valley and its sunny meadows—the mapboard is your turnaround point.

It's also possible to loop on the Farewell Trail, but this trail isn't scenic at all and caters mostly to downhill Mtn bikers. Once again, the best route down is the Creek trail. There are lots of trails to explore at Tumalo Falls, but for your first visit just stick with the out and back for the best bang-for-the-buck.

WHATEVER WHATEVER WHATEVER WHATEVER WHATEVER WHATEVER WHATEVER WHATEVER WHATEVER WHATEVER

Bend is a rare town that does not have to filter its drinking water. Bridge Creek Watershed (Bend's supply) is so pure that it is only treated with a small amount of chlorine to ensure its potability.

WHATEVER WHATEVER WHATEVER WHATEVER WHATEVER WHATEVER WHATEVER WHATEVER WHATEVER WHATEVER

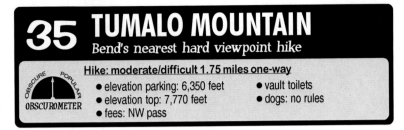

35 TUMALO MOUNTAIN
Bend's nearest hard viewpoint hike

OBSCUROMETER (OBSCURE — POPULAR)

__Hike: moderate/difficult 1.75 miles one-way__

- elevation parking: 6,350 feet
- elevation top: 7,770 feet
- fees: NW pass
- vault toilets
- dogs: no rules

Hurry up—a fast driver and a fit hiker can make it from Bend to the top of Tumalo Mountain in an hour! This trail, if you like steep and sweaty, is a joy. Hiked either for workout or pleasure, the views from the top are wicked good. Lots of Bendite fitness-nut/PPP racer-types charge up Tumalo Mtn as an after-work blast, but a slower pace will give your senses more time to dance. As the trail ascends, a dense hemlock/Lodgepole pine forest yields to spacious Whitebark pine/ Subalpine fir. Steepening to the top, wildflowers reign, then whoa, topping out the 360° vista that suddenly appears is whammo-pano fantastic! Aside from the obvious Cascade mountains, notice the recovering 1979 Bridge Creek Burn to the NE on Tumalo Creek (34). And hey, is that the tip of Jefferson poking over Tam McArthur Rim to the north? Also, trace the Deschutes from the backside of Bachelor (Little Lava Lake), past Crane Prairie and Wickiup reservoirs and then along the Lava Butte lava flows. Quite the view…and so close to Bend—wow! This trail kicks ass—the nearest trail to Bend where you get both stellar views and a healthy workout!

South Sister   Middle Sister   Broken Top

Atop Tumalo

From Bend take the Cascade Lakes Hwy 18 miles. Adjacent to Mt Bachelor, just past MP 21, turn right into Dutchman Sno-park and go to the far-end trailhead.

➧ **Drivetime from Bend: 21 mins**

The view of Mt. Bachelor

HIKE: The hike is as straightforward as it gets—no turns, no options, no surprises.

Hike: easy chairlift ride or difficult hikes

OBSCUROMETER (OBSCURE → POPULAR)

- elevation base: 6,300 feet
- elevation Pine Marten: 7,700 feet
- elevation peak: 9,056 feet
- free
- flush toilets
- dogs: no rules

Bachelor Butte is the youngest of the major Cascade strato-volcanoes— only about 15-20,000 years old. Bachelor's symmetric cone, being younger than all its neighbors, escaped 100,000 years of Ice-Age glaciations that gnawed-down the much-older Three Sisters and Broken Top. There **is** one glacial scar on Bachelor, but it's often mistaken for a high-up cinder cone…but nope, the "hill" west of the Summit chair is a moraine ridge left from a Mtn-top mini glacier. Interestingly, Bachelor Butte became a "Mt" when the Mt. Bachelor ski area began development in the late 50's and wanted a catchier name.

The original trail to the summit begins at the Sunrise lift and switchbacks arduously 2,500 feet in just 2.25 miles. The summit's 360° view is a delight worthy of the trudge though—there are Cascade lakes in every direction, Cascade mountains stretching north and south, Newberry Caldera and Pine Mtn to the east…and a whole lotta Bend overall!

Another popular, and less taxing, way to visit Bachelor (in July and August) is to take the chairlift from the west village to the Pine Marten Lodge. It costs $15 for adults and less for kids (your Mt Bachelor lift pass is good too for a free ride). The restaurant's views, while not as 360°-ish as the peak, are still a whole lotta Cascades. A bit of a secret is that there is **No Charge** to ride the lift down—Woohoo, free! Thus, if you hike up to the lodge or over from the summit trail, you save $15 and get a free lift ride down. Tired legs love cold beers, warm decks, and free lift rides!

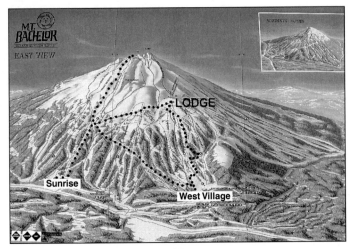

HIKE: Here are two options from the west village that include the free ride down—check the ski-area map to get your bearings. **First**, simply trudge up to the lodge via the below-the-lift service road—about 1.75

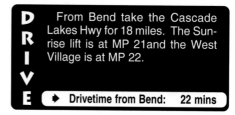

D R I V E

From Bend take the Cascade Lakes Hwy for 18 miles. The Sunrise lift is at MP 21and the West Village is at MP 22.

➤ **Drivetime from Bend: 22 mins**

miles and 1,400 feet. To do this walk uphill from the lift's base to the dirt road at the bottom of the Superpipe. Go right on the road and switchback up. At the red cinder hill stay sharp left. At "Thunderbird" sign go straight under lift then right and up. It's about 50 minutes for fit folk.

Happy September summit hikers

Second: For a unique route to the peak that'll take you over to the Lodge for a free ride down at the end, climb the "West Village Getback" ski run for one steep mile to the Summit chair (where you'll pick up the summit trail). Begin by heading up from the chairlift base and look for the Getback dirt road angling up and left, at about a 10 o'clock angle into the trees. Follow the Getback road to the Summit chair, pass the chairlift building, then continue up and left to find the Summit trail on the treed ridge. Now it's about 1.25 miles to the top. Coming down to this same point, take the "Summit Crossover" road left and up, passing the Skyliner lift (about .75 miles and a 500- foot gain to the lodge). Your legs won't like more uphill at this point, but making a loop that includes lunch, drinks, and a chairlift ride is worth it!

The NW Lift

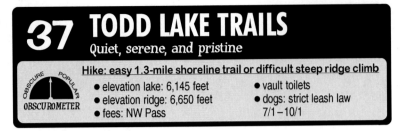

37 TODD LAKE TRAILS
Quiet, serene, and pristine

Hike: easy 1.3-mile shoreline trail or difficult steep ridge climb

OBSCUROMETER

- elevation lake: 6,145 feet
- elevation ridge: 6,650 feet
- fees: NW Pass
- vault toilets
- dogs: strict leash law
  7/1 – 10/1

Todd Lake is the nearest Cascade Lake to Bend along the Cascade Lakes Hwy. The lake is situated far enough off the highway and without drive-up access…so it stays quiet and serene. And, oh my, The Scenery!! The cover of this book was shot from the ridge in back of the lake with Bachelor presiding over the lake's tranquility. Arriving at the lake from the short access trail you'll first see the jagged crown of Broken Top poking up over the ridge. A trail circles the lakeshore, but Mt Bachelor hides its visage from those on the lakeshore trail—you gotta go up the ridge a bit for the Wow!

Todd Lake is super popular! Weekends make it tough to find one of the few parking spots in the all-too-few parking spaces…but this helps the

Bend Overall's cover photo

Mt. Bachelor

Todd Lake

The Ridge view

lake from being over-loved. That said, on weekends still expect a lakeshore busy with families, picnickers, campers, and people who drag a raft/canoe/kayak up the short access trail for a paddle. For more serenity

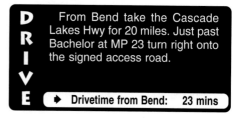

D R I V E

From Bend take the Cascade Lakes Hwy for 20 miles. Just past Bachelor at MP 23 turn right onto the signed access road.

➧ **Drivetime from Bend: 23 mins**

come weekdays or in the Fall…or just climb the ridge on a busy day and leave everyone behind.

Trail view

This same view is in Rooster Cogburn, *minute 50 (See Appendix 5)*

HIKE: A trailhead map details the hiking options. The most popular is the easy 1.3-mile shoreline trail circles the lake.

A more rugged option is an off-trail scramble up the steep 500-foot ridge in front of Broken Top. You'll be gasping for breath as you pick your way up the ridge, but it'll only take 10-15 minutes…and the view of Bachelor sweetens every time you stop for a breather. Once atop the ridge head left a bit to a clearing where a postcard-view of Broken Top and his 3 Sisters awaits. **Impressive[2]**!!

Niki was hot, so Mike got her wet

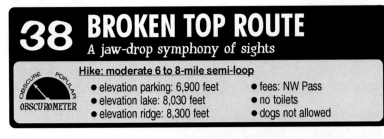

38 BROKEN TOP ROUTE
A jaw-drop symphony of sights

Hike: moderate 6 to 8-mile semi-loop

OBSCUROMETER

- elevation parking: 6,900 feet
- elevation lake: 8,030 feet
- elevation ridge: 8,300 feet
- fees: NW Pass
- no toilets
- dogs not allowed

An excursion to Broken Top's hidden backside yields some of the finest scenery, volcanic colorations, and sweeping vistas anywhere in the Cascades!

Inexplicably the Forest Service doesn't maintain an official trail to this scenic Shangri-la. But a century of beauty connoisseurs regularly make the trek in order to keep their jaw-drop muscles in shape, and thus there's an easy-to-follow path even though there are no signs. Given that there's no official path, feel free to wander wherever your curiosity calls—there are streamlets, mini-waterfalls, wildflower nooks and snowfields galore. The entire

Mid summer icebergs

route is above treeline, so it's pretty easy to ramble without getting lost.

The route described here heads up gurgle-riffic Soda Creek into a face-full of Broken Top's craggy 'n' colorful horseshoe shaped maw. Then you'll

Broken Top
Bachelor
Soooo green!

ascend Broken Top's righthand shoulder ridge to drop over into the "hidden" north side where you'll begin to see even more of BT's dramatic stratified innards that were scraped open by Ice-Age glaciers. Following Soda Creek the path approaches a large

Note: the route to the BT trailhead is a rough one, but USUALLY 2WD-OK, although slow-going.

From Bend take the Cascade Lakes Hwy 20 miles. Turn right at MP 23 to Todd Lake. Check odometer here. In .5 miles pass Todd as road roughens. Go 2.5 miles more, skirting some meadows then up to the pumice plains to the FS 378 junction. Don't turn left on FS 378 along Crater Ditch, but rather keep straight for a bumpy 1.5 miles more, making a left onto FS 380 (at BT sign) for more bump-bump to the road-end parking.

➧ **Drivetime from Bend: 45 mins**

moraine slope that cups a divine glacial lake in its palm. Scurry up the outflow channel in the moraine's notch and you'll soon be at the Oh-My-God lakeshore. From there you'll ascend the final western ridge where 8 volcanic exclamation points

4 sisters

line up all the way to WA's Mt Adams. The beauty here defies description…it's Bend, Overall's favorite overall spot.

HIKE: FYI, for photographers, the best light on BT's north-side colored innards is 9 to 10am, before the colored face goes into shadow.

From the BT parking head .5 miles to a sign post. Don't go left with the trail, but go straight on the unofficial path and soon rock-hop across Soda Creek and regain the obvious old-time road-grade path. Follow the path as it angles up BT's right shoulder…then across the stream-laden meadow slopes. You'll finally attain a low ridge where you'll see Soda Creek emerging from the moraine hill below the Bend Glacier. Follow the creek up the moraine notch to the lake, then around the lakeshore and up the final ridge. From the ridge it's possible to follow a faint tread that circles the Broken Hand outcropping. One way or the other traipse overland back to BT's shoulder to find the path back to the parking. Along the way maybe glissade down snow slopes...or find some glacial caves…or sing *Sound of Music* songs.

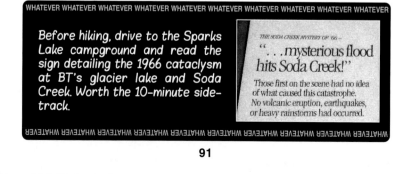

WHATEVER WHATEVER WHATEVER WHATEVER WHATEVER WHATEVER WHATEVER WHATEVER WHATEVER WHATEVER

Before hiking, drive to the Sparks Lake campground and read the sign detailing the 1966 cataclysm at BT's glacier lake and Soda Creek. Worth the 10-minute side-track.

THE SODA CREEK MYSTERY OF '66 –

"…mysterious flood hits Soda Creek!"

Those first on the scene had no idea of what caused this catastrophe. No volcanic eruption, earthquakes, or heavy rainstorms had occurred.

WHATEVER WHATEVER WHATEVER WHATEVER WHATEVER WHATEVER WHATEVER WHATEVER WHATEVER WHATEVER

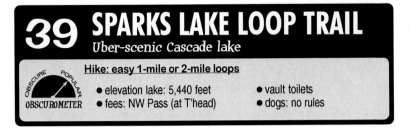

Hike: easy 1-mile or 2-mile loops

OBSCURE   POPULAR
OBSCUROMETER

- elevation lake: 5,440 feet
- fees: NW Pass (at T'head)
- vault toilets
- dogs: no rules

Sparks Lake is the most scenic of all the Cascade Lakes! The lake is a photographer's dream and it was a favorite of Ray Atkeson, Oregon's Photographer Laureate. You'll see scenes from this lake used in brochures, magazines, photos, and paintings all over Bend, as well as seeing it in movies such as *Rooster Cogburn* and *Homeward Bound*. (Appendix 5.)

The rugged lava-clad shoreline has flowering nooks and crannies that make perfect foreground framing for the South Sister/Devils Garden/Broken Top to-die-for panorama.

Sparks is a super shallow lake—about 8-feet at its deepest, but mostly much shallower. This makes it great for families with venturesome kids around the shorelines or explorers with kayaks or canoes. Nobody comes to fish at Sparks, so there's not much hubbub that way—Sparks is more a lake to play in and on, everybody having fun. The lake extends surpris-

Classic Sparks Lake

D R I V E

From Bend take the Cascade Lakes Hwy 22 miles. Pass Todd Lake and at MP 25 turn left at the Sparks sign. Stay left at the fork for 1.5 bumpy miles to the boat ramp/trailhead parking.

◆ **Drivetime from Bend: 27 mins**

ingly far to the south—about a mile. There's a nook, cove, island, or beach for everyone—even topless raft girls with one-eyed dogs! (Whew, guidebook photography is tough work!) See entry 44 for paddling info.

From the boat ramp a one-mile trail makes a figure-8 along the scenic shoreline and then through the lava field. The first .25 miles are paved and handicap accessible and this section features the uber-scenic mountain framing. If you're a Cascade Lakes Hwy visitor and were only to stop for one short walk, then this should be the one!

Mt. Bachelor

*Sparks'
rugged
lava
shoreline*

HIKE: The Atkeson Memorial Trail begins at the road-end boat ramp. A mapboard there details the route. The trail has two lobes, and if time is tight the first 1-mile loop is the much better one. Be sure to go through Davis Canyon's mini lava slot.

*Maybe the
dog is
winking*

93

40 GREEN LAKES TRAIL
Everyone's *favorite* trail

Hike: moderate 4-mi. one way to lakes, then 3-mi. optional loop

OBSCUROMETER

- elevation trailhead: 5,500 feet
- elevation lakes: 6,500 feet
- fees: NW Pass
- vault toilets
- dogs: leash law (July–Sept)

The Green Lakes trail is "everyone's favorite." It's pretty tough to beat a trail that follows a rushing waterfall-laden creek up a mellow grade for 4 miles before delivering you to at an incomparable alpine setting—a trio of crystal clear lakes nestled in a hyper-scenic valley between South Sister and Broken Top. Yup, everyone's favorite trail—huge bang-for-the-buck!!

Alas, the Green Lakes trail is also ultra-crowded on any mid-summer day. Expect to hear more than once, "Damn, I bet every family visiting Sunriver is up here today!" Go with an expectation of tourist hordes and you'll still enjoy the phenomenal scenery…but if you go expecting some sort of wilderness on this Three Sisters Wilderness hike, you best reckon ag'in pardner.

The only thing the least bit "wrong" with this trail, other than the crowding, is that the **Green Lakes are icy cold ALL SUMMER**. Too cold even for your dog, if you could let Fido legally off the leash (you can't). Ice-water literally pours off South Sister into the Green Lakes. There is NO WAY that you're going for a swim. Thus, if you like to swim or wade after a long summer hike, then give this too-crowded trail a pass. Maybe head farther on the Casc Lks Hwy to hike the loop to Sisters Mirror Lakes (43) or Lucky Lake (46), each a very swimmable yet way less crowded destination. Or

South Sister

Green Lakes backpackers

maybe head to Newberry Caldera for a hike/viewpoint/ swim/hot spring outing (20). Leave the Green Lakes for first-time visitors—our area has so many other excellent options…maybe give our "Wilderness" a break in the

D R I V E

Easy-peasy. From Bend take the Cascade Lakes Hwy 23 miles and just past Sparks Lake, at MP 26, turn right into the signed trailhead.

▶ **Drivetime from Bend:** 23 mins

mid-summer. If you live here, then visit the Green Lakes in the Fall when the leaves color and the tourists ebb—you'll like it better then anyhow.

Fall Creek's falls

Here are a couple of "secrets" to check out on the Green Lakes trail. If it's your first hike, then skip these… but if you've been many-a-time and you feel adventurous, then:

Miller lava flow springs. 2 miles up the trail you'll cross the first of two log bridges. The second is over Fall Creek, but the first is the mystery. If you follow either bank of this little creek upstream for 7 minutes you'll see the creek birthed at the base of the Miller flow.

Corral Lake. This is a little football-field-sized lake that's easy to spot on the map, but hard to find in person. Surprisingly, at 6,200 feet, this hidden nugget is often swimmably warm on hot summer days, unlike the icy Greenies. Once upon a time there was a trail to this lake, but the powers-that-be no longer want you to easily find it. Here's some help. After crossing the second log bridge (2-mile mark) and going about 300 yards more, you'll cross a wee micro-creek. The trail follows this creeklet for an-

other 300-400 yards (swinging away from Fall Creek). When this micro creek angles away from the trail and ascends the righthand hillside, look for the abandoned wood-strewn path just 20 feet past the creeklet. This path steeply climbs 200 feet in 5 minutes to the lake. Head right past the lake to spy Mt Bachelor.

Broken Top
Corral Lake

HIKE: Easy-peasy. 1.6 miles to the signed Moraine Lake junction, .5 miles more to the bridge crossings, then 2 more miles to the lakes. The main trail visits all three lakes in the next 1.5 miles, and a primitive path circles the west side of the big lake, making a 3-mile all-lakes loop. There is also another route back to the car, but it's way longer—the 7.5-mile one-way route via the signed Broken Top and Soda Creek trails.

41 DEVIL'S LAKE
The turquoise gem of the Cascade Lakes

Hike: various off-trail excursions
- elev. lake: 5,448 ft.
- elev. Devil's Garden Pass: 6,000 ft.
- elev. Tyee Spring: 5,100 ft.

OBSCUROMETER
OBSCURE · POPULAR

- fees: NW Pass ($5 at trailhead)
- vault toilets
- dogs: no rules

Devil's Lake is a heavenly spring-fed pool of mesmerizing green waters. All too often it's just a quick gawk-stop for tourists or a convenient parking lot for South Sister climbers. Too bad for them. Don't overlook the charms of this lake! An exquisite day can be had exploring this area—bring an empty memory card plus a bit of enthusiasm and you'll surely get plenty of exorcise!

Lakeshore trail "666" is an easy .5-mile stroll providing lots of eye candy. The short trail sports verdant forest and emerald waters framed by the roadside black lava flow called Devil's Garden.

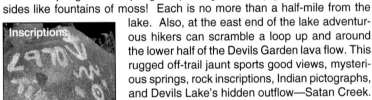
Idle hands at the Devil's sign
DEVILS LAKE TRAIL
NO. 6.66
HIGHWAY 46   1/2

Otherwise, there are also some little-known off-trail excursions leading to a handful of ~~film~~ pixel-devouringly beautiful spots. The lake's crystalline waters come from two sources: Tyee and Hell Springs. Both springs inspire sighs as they gush forth from hillsides like fountains of moss! Each is no more than a half-mile from the

Inscriptions

lake. Also, at the east end of the lake adventurous hikers can scramble a loop up and around the lower half of the Devils Garden lava flow. This rugged off-trail jaunt sports good views, mysterious springs, rock inscriptions, Indian pictographs, and Devils Lake's hidden outflow—Satan Creek. Overall it's a helluva trek!

Hell Spring. From the parking toilet, follow the S. Sis climbers trail. Cross the Hwy then up. You'll be near the creek for a few minutes and as the trail swings left, listen for gurgle and head off-trail to the right and follow the creek to its spring. It takes about 10 minutes.

Tyee Spring. Harder to find but, like a Mounds Bar, "indescribably delicious"! The spring is about .5 miles from the parking lot and there are two options to find it (to do both as a loop, go up Elk/Devils first). First, head up the Elk/Devils trail. In about 12 minutes listen for water softly gurgling

Tyee Spring

from your right. Head off-trail to the right here, hop a small stream and continue shortly to larger Tyee Creek. Scramble upwards to its gushing source. Or, from the parking, begin on the S. Sis trail, cross the log bridge, and

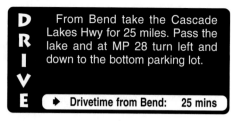

D R I V E

From Bend take the Cascade Lakes Hwy for 25 miles. Pass the lake and at MP 28 turn left and down to the bottom parking lot.

➤ **Drivetime from Bend: 25 mins**

turn left up Tyee Creek. Clamber over the Hwy and find the abandoned roadway heading up the right creek bank (this formerly was the 1960's pumice-mining road to Rock Mesa). Head upstream staying high on the bank as to not cause undue erosion. Enjoy the idyllic creek for about 10 minutes to its source.

Up Devil's Garden

Devil's Garden. About a 1.5-mile loop, including a tough 600-foot climb. From the base of the flow at the highway, begin climbing the slope left (west) of the lava. After a steep .5 miles (15 min), you'll descend into a gully then up to an obvious saddle—notice the banana-like Western white pine cones. This saddle is the top—trying to loop higher is possible, but a bitch. For killer views scurry up the lava at the saddle. Continuing, cross the saddle and head down. Springs and streams play hide 'n' seek with the chunky lava until you get to the flats where 50 years of inscriptions decorate/deface the boulders—WEIRD! Finally, hop Satan Creek to get back to the highway...but wait, do Bend's wonders never cease? On this last slope, curious eyes will find an array of faded red Indian pictographs. Needless to say, be respectful of these ancient and rare treasures!

FYI: John Wayne filmed among the inscriptions at Satan Creek! (Minutes 35 to 40 in *Rooster Cogburn*). (See Appendix 5)

Mt. Bachelor

Sparks Lake

View from atop Devil's Garden

Hike: moderate 4.5-mile loop with 2-3 miles of extras

OBSCUROMETER

- elevation parking: 5,480 feet
- elevation ridge: 6,700 feet
- elevation lake: 6,445 feet
- fees: NW Pass ($5 at T'head)
- vault toilets
- dogs: no rules

Map page 215

This loop begins at the Devil's Lake parking and combines bits of the Elk/Devils trail with some South Sister's climber trail to make an interesting loop. Along the route there are a few side-tracks to see some interesting spots—all adding a few miles to the overall total. The trail starts up to the Wickiup Plains where you can make an off-trail venture up to LeConte Crater's rim to see its early-summer dime-sized crater lake. Then it takes a

Pumice Mining Road into Rock Mesa

right and leaves the Plains to head for Moraine Lake… but along the way you can make another side track up into the Rock Mesa pumice flow via the 1960s pumice-mining road that snakes into the flow for about a mile—a neat, seldom-seen area!

Then, finally, before descending to complete the loop, you'll make a final foray over to very-popular Moraine Lake for a look-see and maybe a dip before backtracking and descending the steep S. Sis Cimbers trail back to the car. Overall, this loop packs a lot of sights and interest into one tight package!

HIKE: Begin by following directions to LeConte Crater in entry 43. After the crater backtrack to the Moraine Lake junction and begin a 1.5-mile climb to the next junction. Be alert—in about .75 miles there are a couple of level stretches with clear views of South Sister rising over Rock Mesa.

At the second of these clearings, notice the definite road-cut angling up and right in the distant lava wall. To check out this bizarre lavascape, head overland to the jumble, then up. The trail zigzags for a mile then abruptly ends—either backtrack or scramble down to the forest floor and back to the trail.

Happy Hood River backpackers

Now continue to the Moraine/ Sisters climber trail junction. A right turn here leads to the car, but first go straight .75 miles to Moraine Lake. Have a dip or venture along the shore to see the wildflower 'n' waterfalls outflow mini-canyon. Refreshed, backtrack to S. Sis. Climbers trail, go left and descend steeply 1.75 miles to Devils Lake. Towards the end listen for Hell Spring (41) gurgling to your left.

WHATEVER WHATEVER WHATEVER WHATEVER WHATEVER WHATEVER WHATEVER WHATEVER WHATEVER WHATEVER

The US Pumice Co. exploratory road history: They filed a mining claim in the early 60's to extract pumice—before the 1964 Wilderness Act passed. When the company pursued the claim in the 70's there was a public uproar about the devastation that a new road, big mining trucks, and heavy equipment would cause to the pristine surroundings. Courts upheld the valid mining claim though, and necessitated Senators Packwood and Hatfield intervening to enact a two million dollar buy-out, which Pres. Reagan Ok'd in 1982.

WHATEVER WHATEVER WHATEVER WHATEVER WHATEVER WHATEVER WHATEVER WHATEVER WHATEVER WHATEVER

43 SISTERS MIRROR LAKES LOOP
A loop of lavas and lakes

Hike: moderate 7-mile loop

OBSCUROMETER

- elevation parking: 5,480 feet
- elevation LeConte rim: 6,550 feet
- elevation lakes: 6,000 feet
- fees: NW Pass ($5 at T'head)
- vault toilets
- dogs: no rules

Map page 216

The Sisters Mirror Lakes loop is a scenic and fun 7-mile semi-loop. The highlights are many, but the most obvious are close-up views of South Sister and its pumice flow as well as a chance to frolic in a cluster of sun-warmed shallow lakes.

There are two things to note about this route: First is that it can be confusing as there are lots of junctions and options. Be sure to check the maps on the blog or have a Ranger District map with you—this route is confusing! The 2nd note is that July should be avoided, as the mosquitoes are often **SO** bad that you'll have to run while waving your hands around your ears…you've been warned!

The loop begins at Devil's Lake and only gains 600 feet the entire route to the lakes cluster (if you don't climb LeConte Crater). Most descriptions of this hike never mention venturing off-trail to climb LeConte Crater to see its dime-sized crater lake…but then most books aren't *Bend, Overall*. The view from atop LeConte is worth the extra effort because you'll get to see the entire ooze of the young Rock Mesa pumice flow from the crater's rim, as well as South Sister towering above it.

Then, after leaving LeConte and the Wickiup Plains behind, you'll ramble over to the Sister Mirror Lakes basin where a handful of warm lakes await your splashing. Sis Mirror Lake gets the fame because it's directly on the PCT, but it's only for folks who don't know that much-better lakes are just a quick walk farther. Denude Lake is bigger and has a better Sister-view, and Lancelot Lake has wonderful diving/sunning rocks. Bring whichever suit you prefer—bathing or birthday—because there's plenty of privacy and seclusion once you're off the beaten PCT path.

HIKE: Begin on the Elk/Devils trail. Head thru the underpass then .75 miles to the first junction. Go right towards Sis Mirror Lake. In another .75 miles comes the Wickiup Plains junction, where the loop portion of this

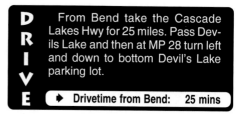

DRIVE

From Bend take the Cascade Lakes Hwy for 25 miles. Pass Devils Lake and then at MP 28 turn left and down to bottom Devil's Lake parking lot.

➧ **Drivetime from Bend: 25 mins**

hike begins. Go right and you'll soon emerge onto the Wickiup Plains—LeConte Crater is the grassy hill to the left of S. Sister. Go .5 miles across the plain to another junction and you need to stay left towards LeConte (right is to Moraine Lake [entry42]). As you near the crater scramble off-trail up to its rim.

In Denude

Now head down from the crater to pick up the trail angling NW…and soon it junctions with the PCT. Take a sharp left on the PCT to head back south. The next 1.5 miles cruises back thru the plains and into the forest again to the Nash Lake trail junction. This junction is important because a left here is how you'll go back to the car to finish the loop, AFTER an out/back venture over to the lakes (so, when all the trails near the lake inevitably confuse you, know that you need to head back here to complete the loop). In .75 miles the Nash Lake trail heads to the right, but you need to continue straight for Sis Mirror…and very quickly you'll come to yet another fork. To the left is the PCT traveling south along Sis Mirror and then beyond. This is where you'll leave the official trail and begin following the paths around and beyond Sis Mirror to explore the other lakes (at this point turn around and refresh your mind how your return route will look, because lots of people get confused in their rush to strip and swim! ☺)

For the return route to complete the loop back to Devil's Lake, the map shows another option to make a loop via the Nash/Mirror Lakes trail…but this loop is long and boring—heading back via the Wickiup Plains trail is better.

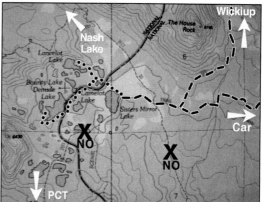

44 PADDLING CASCADE LAKES
Best lakes to paddle with drive-up access

OBSCUROMETER

- fees: NW Pass at all lakes ($5 at lakes)
- toilets at every lake
- check blog for lake maps

This page is aimed at kayakers and canoeists. There are a ton of options to choose from—every lake which has a boat ramp/drive-up shoreline is a possibility. The question is…which lakes are THE BEST? There are a number of factors to consider. Some of our big lakes are super-popular with motor-boaters—like Cultus Lake, Big Lake, Detroit, Billy Chinook, etc…but these big lakes are too popular to make them fun to paddle—too much traffic and wakes and noise. Then there are the numerous lakes that are popular with fishermen—Suttle, Twin, Elk, Lava, Paulina, Odell …these lakes also have a "crowded" feel, and they attract people for what's under the water rather than the scenic beauty of the surroundings.

What paddlers generally want is scenic beauty, peacefulness, and interestingness. Here are three top picks of our nearby Cascade Lakes which have drive-up access, peacefulness, and beauty.

Mt. Bachelor

Sparks

Sparks Lake: Far and away the best lake to paddle!! Sparks Lake is ridiculously scenic. The lava-jumbled shoreline of Sparks is every photographer's favorite—the image of South Sister, Broken Top and Devil's Garden above the lake may be the most captivating scene in all the Cascades. More so, once you begin a paddle southwards on this 1.5-mile-long lake the beauty boils over! Mt Bachelor towers in front of you…the lava-heaped shore offers innumerable nooks and crannies to poke your bow into…sunny beaches to pull over for a stretch and bite…finger-like coves and channels beckoning exploration. Way too much good stuff!

The south end of the lake also has at least 10 different popular paddle-in primitive campspots.

DRIVE: On the Casc Lakes Hwy, just past Mt Bachelor and Todd Lake, turn at the Sparks sign at MP 25 and drive 1.5 washboardy miles to the boat ramp parking.

Hosmer Lake: This is a lake which is super-popular with both paddlers and fishermen (electric motors only). Hosmer Lake is similar to Sparks in that it's long and narrow, icy cold, and surrounded by picture-perfect mountain views. The difference is that Hosmer has lily pads and reeds and ducks and abundant fish in its hyper-clear water, rather than Sparks' lava decorations. Like Sparks, Hosmer is an interesting paddle because it offers a JOURNEY! The lake is shaped like a dumbbell with a bulb on either end of a long narrow channel. Beginning at the south boat ramp Hosmer unfolds a secret at every twisty turn, becoming more beautiful

Sparks canoe camping

the further north you paddle. The lily pads give way to clear emerald shallows with abundant Atlantic salmon easy to spot swimming below…Bachelor towers above…and the north bulb sports nooks and islands to explore around. So nice!

DRIVE: Just south of Elk Lake, at MP 34 turn onto the signed "Elk Lake Loop" road and go 1.0 miles to the boat ramp sign.

Waldo Lake: Waldo is Oregon's second biggest lake as well as one of the clearest lakes in the world. Waldo was at one time more popular with boaters and fishermen, but the 10 MPH speed limit and lack of stocked fish has reduced popularity while increasing the peace and quiet. Waldo has a wilderness feel, but it's technically not a wilderness lake given its drive-up access.

The main reason to paddle Waldo is its BLUE-BLUE-BLUE. Waldo is a deep lake with no stream inflow…thus, no nutrients flow into the lake, and thus no algae or plants grow, and thus no fish thrive, and thus Waldo is astoundingly clear with visibility of up to 100 feet! Waldo sports some surreal cobalt blue waters that you can only witness once you are a couple hundred yards off shore out into the deep lake. From the shore Waldo seems no clearer or bluer than any other Cascades lake…but once you paddle out, the water will seriously WOW you! Think Crater Lake but more accessible, less crowded…and amazingly, Waldo gets swimmably warm!

Paddle-in campspots dot the shoreline. Be careful of Waldo though—it can be a windy lake, so a loaded canoe or kayak can get hard to handle as the wind and waves increase. The less-experienced would do well to stay near the shore until you get a feel for Waldo's windy moods. A great day-paddle is from Shadow Bay over to the south shore's nice beach coves. At the lake's north end a shoreline paddle displays the ravaged forest from the 1996 Waldo Burn.

South Sister

Hosmer Lake's far end

DRIVE: see entry 29.

Honorable mentions: Clear Lake (drowned forest, 66) Paulina Lake (to hot springs, 20), Scott Lake (56).

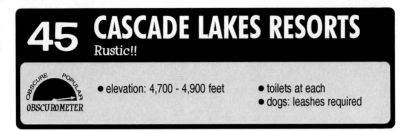

45 CASCADE LAKES RESORTS
Rustic!!

- elevation: 4,700 - 4,900 feet
- toilets at each
- dogs: leashes required

Three rustic lakeside resorts are located up the Cascade Lakes Highway past Mt Bachelor. Each resort is situated on the shore of one of our wonderfully scenic Cascade Lakes. All are worth a visit, as each has its charms, both in terms of scenery and amenities.

Elk Lake Lodge. This age-old Lodge and resort is the closest to Bend—at MP 32. Elk Lake has always been a family favorite for its scenic sailboating, paddling, and fishing...as well as the Cascades' best beach at the south end of the lake (MP 34). The resort has an ample rental fleet of watercraft of all sorts—canoes, kayaks, rowboats, sailboats, etc etc. Also, the Lodge has rustic restaurant and charming old-timey bar. Little-known is the fact that Elk Lake and this resort stood in for Mt St Helens and Spirit Lake in the 1981 movie *St. Helens*. *(See Appendix 5).*

Elk Lake Lodge

South Sister

Elk Lake Beach

Lava Lakes Resort. The Lava Lakes Resort and adjacent Forest Service campground at Little Lava Lake cater primarily to fishermen. The Resort, located at MP 38, has a small store with groceries, gasoline and fishing boat rentals. The scenic views from anywhere afloat on the Lava Lakes cannot be beat! Plenty of "bites" are surely missed as people gaze at the gorgeous mountain scenery rather than the tip of their fishing poles.

For sightseers, take the short drive over to the campground to see the silent headwaters of the Deschutes River beginning its legendary 252-mile flow just behind site #7.

Lava Lake

Cultus Lake Resort.

Cultus Lake, at MP 45, is the only natural lake in the area that allows EVERY kind of watercraft. Everything goes on this busy lake—jet skis, wave runners, Hobie Cats, fishing boats, speed boats... beers, bikinis and biceps. Cultus Lake is busy and FUN! The Cultus Lake Resort is a good-times rustic Lodge Resort with cabins, campground, restaurant (gorgeous lake view!), groceries, gas... and all kinds of boat rentals. Cultus Lake is action^2! Come for FUN, not for peace and quiet.

46 LUCKY LAKE TRAIL
The most swimmable Cascade Lake

Hike: easy 1.0-mile one-way

OBSCUROMETER

- elevation parking: 4,800 feet
- elevation lake: 5,200 feet
- fees: NW Pass (at Elk Lake)
- vault toilet
- dogs: no rules

Lucky Lake is a glimmeringly green 4-leaf clover. It's a pool of good fortune. Luckily it's located a mile west of the Cascade Lakes Hwy in the woods with no drive-up access—far enough that most people just don't get Lucky. After the "21" minutes it takes for the easy walk to Lucky, you'll feel like you've been dealt a blackjack when you first glimpse the pine-shrouded oasis. Head left at the junction and it'll be 7s all day when you spot Middle and South Sisters poking their heads above the lake on the far horizon. Jump into Lucky from these south shore campspots—the ones with the

Middle Sister

South Sister

Lucky Lake

best views—and the warm shallow water will make you feel like a leprechaun.

Every other Cascade Lake near here—Devils, Todd, Sparks, Lava, Elk, Cultus—are all packed with summertime families, camp-

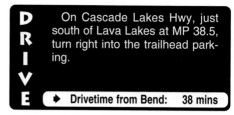

D
R
I
V
E

On Cascade Lakes Hwy, just south of Lava Lakes at MP 38.5, turn right into the trailhead parking.

▶ **Drivetime from Bend: 38 mins**

ers, and fishermen....but not Lucky. The 1-mile hike deters the hordes, as does the lack of roadside signage. Best yet is that Lucky is swimmably warm by mid-summer. Lucky doesn't have any ice-cold springs flowing into it, so the lake basks in the Cascade sunshine, heating up all the while

it awaits your plunge. Come to picnic, swim, sun, float...or just for an easy woodsy jaunt around a nice quiet lake. 777! Ya know who's really Lucky? Us...everyone who lives in the paradise of Central Oregon or comes here to visit. We've got an endless supply of nooks to explore around every corner... and each nook has its unique charms. We're Lucky! Come visit Lucky and celebrate our luck!

(HIKE:) From the trailhead parking lot it's 1.0 miles to the lake along the Senoj trail. At the lake a junction sign points both ways to further lakes, but both options are farther and less nice than Lucky. A rough path navigates the far shore of the lake making a 1.3-mile lakeshore loop.

An old Lucky Lager found at Lucky Lake

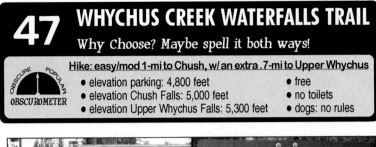

Hike: easy/mod 1-mi to Chush, w/ an extra .7-mi to Upper Whychus

OBSCUROMETER

- elevation parking: 4,800 feet
- elevation Chush Falls: 5,000 feet
- elevation Upper Whychus Falls: 5,300 feet
- free
- no toilets
- dogs: no rules

WHYCHUS CREEK 5 ➤

WYCHUS CREEK FALLS TR NO. 4080
END OF TRAIL

Note two spellings

Whychus Creek is the re-named "Squaw Creek" as of 2006 (turns out that "squaw" is a degrading slang term for female genitalia…who knew?)

Thus, Squaw has become Whychus and the popular waterfall has become Chush Falls. The drive from Sisters is still a washboardy and rocky chore…and then the official 1-mile trail disappointingly ends at a sub-par view-ledge.

But that's just the "official" trail—the fun begins beyond there. Whychus Creek and its neighboring South Fork Creek are an unrivaled waterfall playground…if you're athletic, adventurous, and playful enough to have a go at some gung-ho scrambling!!! (Yup, 3 exclamation points here!!!)

Chush Falls

First, at the obscured trail's end view-ledge above **Chush Falls**, head to the right of the Trail Ends sign and scramble down the path 200 feet to the creek. This is where Chush reveals its true glory as the 60-foot falls fans out in an ever-misty roar. Put on your water shoes here, cuz it's time to scamper over to get up close. Nearing the cascade the mist billows everywhere and on a hot sunny day you'll be circled by your own personal rainbow—a wondrous ROY G. BIV embrace! For the truly adventurous, skirting behind the falls to the dry-ish ledge is just more icing on this cake!

Now, back up atop the view-ledge, look for the path leading steeply upwards .7 miles to Whychus Creek's hidden upper spectacles. First comes li'l Middle Falls, then a bit of huffing more and voilà, **Whychus' Upper Cascade!** The path pretty much ends here at the first photo-op. But why turn back here when you've got 250-feet of Yosemitesque Cascades grandeur

D R I V E

(Bring: water shoes, swimsuit, towels, and optional long pants). In Sisters turn south onto Elm St. (FS 16) and head 7 miles. Turn right at signed FS 1514 and endure this washboard for 4.8 miles to the Whychus Creek bridge. Before the bridge turn left onto slowslowslow FS 600 and follow it 2.4 miles (staying left) to the trailhead.

➤ Drivetime from Bend: 1 hour

Upper Whychus Falls

in front of you? See the boulder a couple hundred feet up, directly in the streambed? Yup, it's The Place to Be. Scramble 3 minutes up the left side of the stream, splash across just below the boulder and then scamper up to the perfect viewpoint scoop—if you've brought a towel for padding this sunny perch makes a divine sunning spot!

OK, now for the extra-extra waterfall adventure... the bushwhacking "secret" that scarce few locals know. Chush Falls has a twin just 6 minutes away over the ridge (west) in the neighboring South Fork Creek canyon. If you study the map you'll see it marked, as well as another falls just upstream. Here's how to find Chush's twin: at the creek bed below Chush Falls, splash across the creek and bushwhack downstream for just one minute. As the trees pinch, at a many-burled tree, head straight up the steep hillside 150 feet and angle to the right. If you see two Ponderosas with a triangular rooftop gateway, scramble up and thru onto the level ground...and listen. Ah-ha, you can

South Fork Falls

hear the other falls now, so just pick your way through the trees and in a minute you'll be on the ledge overlooking 80 feet of "secret" waterfall. Scramble hounds can pick their way 10 minutes higher (and much rougher going) to find the less-spectacular but even more secret 45-footer.

Before you backtrack thru the root gateway, whack uphill a minute to see Chush from the "far" side—wow, it pours into its own rainbow ☺!

48 TAM MACARTHUR RIM TRAIL
A *DELUXE* viewpoint trail

Hike: difficult 2.5-mile one-way w/ 2.8-mile bonus option

OBSCURE • POPULAR
OBSCUROMETER

- elevation parking/lakes: 6,550 feet
- elevation rim: 7,732 feet
- elevation Broken Hand: 8,200 feet
- fees: NW Pass ($5 at T'head)
- vault toilets
- dogs: no rules

Map page 217

The 2.5-mile hike from Three Creeks Lake to Tam MacArthur Rim may be the Central Cascades' finest view-hike, especially for a hike so short! From the Rim, not only are you front-and-center to a 150-mile line-up of Cascade peaks from Bachelor to WA's Mt Adams...not only are you perched directly above the two emerald-hued Three Creek Lakes...but gazing eastward you'll also see <u>Everything</u> from Madras to the distant Glass Buttes (back behind Bend and Pine Mtn). And, as if that weren't enough, looking SE past Newberry's Paulina Peak oblong hump you can see pointy-topped Hager Mtn in the hazy distance. Wow, talk about eye-candy!

If you want a longer hike than just the rim 'n' back, the alpine landscape offers plenty more off-trail rambling with additional breath-taking vistas. The official trail ends at the jutting prow of rim that overlooks the lakes, but a fairly well-trodden path heads 1.3 miles to the west edge of the rim to an ooh-la-la overlook of the Three Sisters...and then an even rougher path contours southwards 1.5 miles along the rim edge, around the Broken Hand butte, and over to Broken Top's glacial lake overlook (38). Along the way to Broken Hand southern views will open up over Mt Bachelor, the headwaters of the Deschutes, Wickiup/Crane Prairie...and the peaks to the south; Diamond, Mt Theilsen, and Crater Lake's Mt Scott. The keen-est of eyes may even spot a wee slice of Waldo Lake. Needless to say, this is a helluva hike with heavenly views...what are ya waiting for? (Oh yeah, wait until late July for the snow to melt at this high altitude!)

After a long picnic or exploration at the top (where binocs and maps will sure help), then head down to one of the lakes for a dip before heading home. The big Three Creek Lake is the most popular with families be-

Smith Rock

Redmond

Tam MacArthur's Prow

3 Creeks Lake

cause of its rowboat rentals, drive-up shoreline, camp-sites, and beaches. For a bit more privacy pack your Camelbak cooler for the half-mile trek to the li'l Three Creek neighbor lake that you spied from above. The Au-

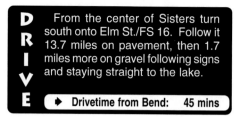

D R I V E

From the center of Sisters turn south onto Elm St./FS 16. Follow it 13.7 miles on pavement, then 1.7 miles more on gravel following signs and staying straight to the lake.

➤ **Drivetime from Bend: 45 mins**

gust-warmed waters and seclusion of this gem may invite a little skinny-dippin' in the shadow of the rim. No better day than a sunny hike with friends to a viewpoint of <u>Everything</u>...followed by some eat/drink/be-merrying at one of Little Three Creek's nooks....mmmm.

Sister Charity   Hope   Faith

The west rim viewpoint

HIKE: The Rim trailhead is opposite Driftwood Camp entrance, at the lake's outflow. Begin with a steep 1-mile gasp, then some flat before an-other steep .5-mile bit up to the first rim viewpoint. The jutting prow above the lake is your destination. The trail braids a bit, but all trails lead about a mile across the pumice slopes to the prow.

For the venturesome, continue west past the prow. The path skirts a snowfield and winds about a mile to the western rim and ooh-la- la Sisters views. From there the path heads up the obvious scoria slope and scrambles another rugged 1.5 miles around the west side of Broken Hand's outcropping to feast your eyes on Broken Top's watery treasure. Head back the way you came.

Once back down to the lake, to find Little Three Creeks Lake either take a 1-mile signed trail from the Driftwood entrance or take a .5-mile unsigned, but obvious, trail from the endpoint of the campground road.

The Prow

Li'l 3 Creeks Lake

49 NORTH SISTER'S THAYER GLACIER LAKE SCRAMBLE

A trail/off-trail route to a hidden lake

Hike: difficult 5-mile one-way

OBSCURE POPULAR
OBSCUROMETER

- elevation trailhead: 5,300 feet
- elevation lake: 7,700 feet
- fees: NW Pass ($5 at T'head)

- vault toilet
- dogs: no rules

Map page 218

This exploration hike begins at the Pole Creek trailhead and is dullsville for the first couple of miles through the beetle-killed pines, then also relatively dull also as you ascend a climber's path through the viewless forest up Soap Creek for 2 more miles. But then, all of a sudden… WOW, Cascades Magic! The trees give way and the NE flank of North Sister suddenly looms ahead. The rest of the way is now above-tree-line eye-candy. You'll leave the climber's path to go south cross-country to the creek that percolates from underneath the Thayer Glacier's moraine dam. Then you pick your way up the moraine slope until—sweet—you'll be looking down at the rarely-seen Thayer Glacier Lake and the incredibly striped Strato-volcano walls directly above the iceberg-riddled lake. (It's like Broken Top's lake, just way more secret.) After descending to the lake to explore, picnic, and make some snow angels…you can either turn back and retrace your steps or take the harder and WAY MORE SCENIC option of ascending to the southern ridge of North Sis…where the reward view of Sisters S & M is well worth the extra effort. To get down from this ridge you'll have to bushwhack and angle down and north to re-find Soap Creek and the route down.

BE WARNED, this is an off-trail route which will confuse and befuddle the direction-impaired. Before going you should get at least the Ranger District map, and better yet, the applicable 7.5 topo (Bend Map and Blueprint). If you don't know what a 7.5 topo is, or can't figure out which map

North Sister

Views

Moraine   Yellow Bulge

shows the east side of North Sister, then you don't belong on this excursion. Wandering off-trail in the Cascades at 7,500 feet without a map is dumb and potentially dangerous when the weather invariably turns sour. Check

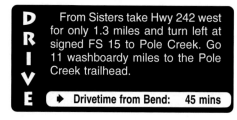

D R I V E

From Sisters take Hwy 242 west for only 1.3 miles and turn left at signed FS 15 to Pole Creek. Go 11 washboardy miles to the Pole Creek trailhead.

▶ **Drivetime from Bend: 45 mins**

the blog for a few overview Google maps and some pix showing the striking colors.

HIKE: Begin the Pole Creek trail for 1.25 dull miles then go left at the Green Lakes pointer for .8 miles more to the Soap Creek bridge. **At the bridge, backtrack 100 yards** and look for the definite spur path that heads uphill. This path heads uphill next to Soap Creek for 2-ish miles until you top a ridge and the sightlines clear. North Sis looms ahead and you'll now need to leave the path (which ascends the northern slope) and go overland a couple of gullies to the south until you find running water—there is no set route here. You now need to angle up towards the huge yellow bulge and then head to the slope of grey moraine rubble to its left. Picking your way up the moraine slope is the hardest part...but then, ahhh, below...the icy lake and colors to live for!

Head up the creek to climb the moraine

Before you descend to the lake to play and photo the cool colorations, look left for the ridge above and beyond to the south. It's the author-named "Ridge of Good Views" and you'll have to decide if it's worth it for you – but before you go, get a good eye-full of the terrain to come and how you'll make the descent afterwards. Descending, even if you get "lost" just know that the E-W Pole Creek trail is beneath you and keep working left and down.

Volcanic innards

Thayer snow angels

Hike: difficult, short, rugged scrambling

OBSCURE — POPULAR
OBSCUROMETER

- elevation butte: 4,000 feet
- elevation cave: 4,100
- free

- no toilets
- dogs discouraged

Cave is closed Nov 1st thru April 15th.

ATTENTION!
BIG-EARED BAT
HIBERNATING COLONY

CAVE CLOSED
NOVEMBER 1 through APRIL 15

Spend a late-May/June morning in this cave and you'll witness a glorious sunlight-show…inside the cave! Three skylight holes in the roof of this lava tube let three beams of sunlight shine down to the cave floor. In the springtime the moist cave floor steams where the sunbeams hit it. The steam, plus airborn dust, highlights the sun-streaks for an ethereal display! Wake up early though cuz our planet rotates fast—the spectacle only lasts from about 9am to 11am. Throughout the summer the beams still show up a little, but only in the spring does combination of the moisture and sun angle make for the best razzle-dazzle.

To get into Skylight Cave there's a short ladder descending into the opening. The skylights are left about 200 feet over rough scattered rocks. To the right the cave extends about 700 feet. This longer section has some breakdown and stoopways where you'll have to duckwalk a bit, but

June
9:45am
beams

the rewards are some great keyhole-shaped passages. The cave is closed *from Nov. 1 thru April 15* for bat habitat protection. Please honor this closure so that this cave isn't fenced (like too many others have been). The sunbeams don't work in the winter anyhow.

To explore the cave please use cave smarts: make sure you have at least <u>two lights,</u> solid shoes, warm clothes, and functioning brain. People whose brains don't function should wait outside and fiddle with their guns.

D R I V E

From Sisters head west on Hwy 242 for 7 miles. Just past MP 85 turn right onto red-cinder FS 1028. Follow 1028 3.8 miles until you see the Dry Creek Trailhead intersection. Go straight here, but almost immediately turn right onto red-cindered spur 260. Follow 260 for .7 miles and keep your eyes peeled for the often-unsigned cave opening/ parking/ turnaround on the righthand side.

To find Four-Mile Butte, follow the directions as to Skylight Cave, but just .7 miles along 1028 (from Hwy 126) turn right (east) onto FS 1008 and go .6 miles more, then angle right onto FS 600 and begin ascending. In .3 miles turn sharp left and take the left (2WD) road quickly up to the top.

➧ **Drivetime from Bend: 40 mins**

Skylight's entrance ladder

Four Mile Butte. Wanna see another neat place near this cave? The name sounds lame, but the view isn't!

Four-Mile is a classic red-cindered cinder cone volcano ...one of the many that have been quarried locally for the cinders covering the surface of the surrounding forest roads. Quarrying means quarry roads...and this one's got a road up to its top where you'll be greeted with a bizarre expanse of startling red Mars-scape...as well as a sumptuous 360° view! The up-close peaks range from Broken Top to Jefferson, with a look at Black Butte's perfect triangle and even Hoodoo's lift-top.

FYI: Don't expect Eden atop Four-mile...the gun folk and their Quad comrades make sure to keep the place liberally littered, apparently also making bonfires bigger than Dante's inferno.

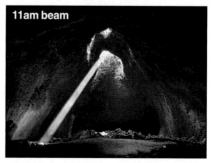

11am beam

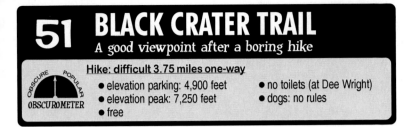

51 BLACK CRATER TRAIL
A good viewpoint after a boring hike

Hike: difficult 3.75 miles one-way

OBSCURE · POPULAR
OBSCUROMETER

- elevation parking: 4,900 feet
- elevation peak: 7,250 feet
- free
- no toilets (at Dee Wright)
- dogs: no rules

Author's note: *truth-be-told, this is one of my least-favorite trails because it lacks variety in an area that's chock full o' variety. I've left it in this edition so you don't stumble upon it and think... "wow, a hidden gem". It's a dull, overly long hike to a view that can be better had elsewhere. The trail is similar to Tumalo Mtn, but since you start so much lower, you have to climb that much higher. Leave this one for long-time locals who need to check it off their list. Try Matthieu Lakes (54), Tam MacArthur Rim (48), or Scott Mtn (57) instead.*

The Black Crater Trail is a strenuous and steep 3.75-mile trail that climbs 2,400 feet to a red-cindered peak. This is a great trail for someone looking for a sweaty workout, but a lousy choice for someone wanting a moderate jaunt. The trail climbs steadily through the thick forest with minimal glimpses of the views to come. As you near the peak an array of late-July wildflowers dots the slopes – blue Lupine, red Indian paintbrush, and orange-ish jester-hat Columbine. Finally, amidst the wind-tortured Whitebark pines, the trail gains the summit and a panorama of snowy peaks unfolds. You can reach out and touch Mt Washington, marvel at Belknap's extensive lava flows, and scope out some good-looking Sisters. Sharp eyes may spy little Dee Wright lava castle and even the tip of Bachelor.

Black Crater summit

EXTRA: For adventurous drivers, try to find the hidden lake that fills a steep-sided glacial basin on B.C.'s east flank at 5,300 ft. This lake isn't easy to find, but it is 2WD accessible. Like other "secret" Cascade lakes it's warmish, it's fishable, it's secluded, and it's not listed in other guidebooks. Here are some tips for explorers: first take a look at it on Google Earth. Then get a Sisters Ranger District map and a rugged car. Locate FS 790 on the map. At the highpoint of this road there's a short spur road that heads towards the lake. Look carefully to find the ATV-wide trail off this spur and then scurry about a half-mile to this "secret" nugget.

D R I V E

From Sisters take Hwy 242 west for 11 miles. Pass Windy Pt. and at MP 81 turn left into the signed trailhead parking.

♦ **Drivetime from Bend: 33 mins**

Tired puppies

Mt. Washington

Whitebark Pine

WHATEVER WHATEVER WHATEVER WHATEVER WHATEVER WHATEVER WHATEVER WHATEVER WHATEVER WHATEVER

Meet the Beetles! (Getting to know our bark beetles): Rice-sized female beetles bore into the bark of stressed pine trees. The tree will try to repel the attack by oozing pitch in an attempt to drown and expel the invaders. A weakened tree in an overburdened forest will not be able to repel the attack. Eggs are then laid in a "gallery" between the bark and wood. As the larvae grow they tunnel through the wood and into the bark (leaving the rutted patterns you see on deadwood). Adult beetles eat an exit hole through the bark and fly off to attack another tree. Look for pitch tubes on the tree bark, sometimes with a dead beetle stuck to them. Also, look for beetle exit holes that look like BB holes.

WHATEVER WHATEVER WHATEVER WHATEVER WHATEVER WHATEVER WHATEVER WHATEVER WHATEVER WHATEVER

52 DEE WRIGHT OBSERVATORY
The McKenzie Pass lava castle

Hike: easy short interpretive trails

OBSCUROMETER

- elevation: 5,325 feet
- free
- vault toilets
- dogs: leash required

Observatory from Interpretive Trail

The Dee Wright Observatory is a fascinating stopping point amidst the other-worldly lava flows atop McKenzie Pass. First-timers driving over the uber-scenic Highway 242 simply can't believe the spectacle that awaits their eyes, and there's no place better along the highway to take it all in than Dee Wright's odd little castle. This observatory is a small castle-like room built circa 1934 by the CCC out of actual lava rock. Dee Wright himself was a Forest Service employee who had worked in the surrounding Cascades for 24 years. The observatory is named in his honor because he was the foreman for the construction, but sadly died before the observatory was completed.

The observatory has an open-air indoor room for when it's nasty out, and a roof-top viewpoint sporting a large bronze mountain-identifying compass. This observatory, as simple as it is, will definitely be able to answer all the oft-asked questions of "which peak is that and how far away do you think it is?" Below the observatory there's a mini-pavilion with some historic-info signboards which detail the peculiar histories of this lava landscape.

Here's what the *Bend Bulletin* had to say in July 1925 about the newly paved McKenzie Pass Hwy:

"The McKenzie Highway opens the way to an outdoor country whose natural beauties are unexcelled anywhere in America. Its charm is so great that none who have ever seen it can ever lose the desire to come back and see it again. The time will come when it will be a great popular playground, visited annually by thousands where now only hundreds come.

The lover of Oregon's outdoors says this with a trace of sadness. A part of the charm of the McKenzie country is its unspoiled and primitive wildness. This particular charm will disappear when there are tourist camps and dance halls and jazz bands and yesterday's newspapers and tin cans at all the beauty spots that are now remote and wild and lovely.

But all of that is a part of the price of progress. We cannot have our cake and eat it too. We cannot attract tourists to Oregon in vast and profitable numbers and still retain the solitude and the unspoiled grandeur of the present."

D R I V E

From Sisters take Hwy 242 west for 14 miles. The observatory is atop McKenzie Pass at MP 78.

➤ **Drivetime from Bend:** 40 mins

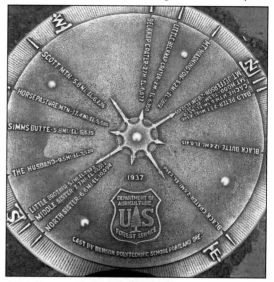

HIKE: Don't miss the half-mile paved pathway that begins near the observatory's front steps. This path is an easy stroll through some pretty cool lava terrain enlivened further by a scad of info signs.

Watching the 2003 B&B Fire begin near Mt. Washington

53 MᴄKENZIE PASS WAGON RD
Walk a remnant of the historic wagon road

Hike: 1.5-mile one-way rough lava-walk (or shorter)

OBSCUROMETER

- elevation: 5,200 feet
- free
- toilet at Dee Wright
- dogs discouraged (ouch, sharp lava)

To explore a little historical nugget that few know about and even fewer have explored, look no further than a few steps past McKenzie pass' Dee Wright Observatory. Surprisingly, a neat 1.5-mile section of the rugged pre-1920 McKenzie Pass wagon road still exists amidst the unforgiving Belknap lavas. Back in "the day" the McKenzie Pass road was the ONLY route over the Central Cascades from Eugene to Sisters/Bend. The only other route was the Mt Hood route thru Gov't Camp and into Madras. This McKenzie route began as a wagon road in the 1870s and gradually matured into a car-drivable route around

Circa 1900

Photo courtesy of Bowman Museum

1910. The 1910 "improvements" to this route lead to newspaper-reported speed records over McKenzie Pass—whereas a wagon once took <u>5 days</u> to cross, a car could then do it in <u>a day</u>. Today it takes just over two hours to drive from Bend to Eugene.

This wagon road route was superseded by the present-day Hwy 242 in 1920 when extensive dynamiting and back-filling cleared a direct and less

Hike

The wagon road's descent out of the lava

steep and twisty roadway. By 1925 this new highway had been paved and gone were the days of an agonizingly slow journey from Sisters to Eugene.

Nowadays a walk on this forgotten route lends a great

D R I V E From Sisters take Hwy 242 up McKenzie Pass. Keep going past Dee Wright Observatory (MP 78) for only .4 miles more and turn right into the easy-to-miss PCT parking area.

→ **Drivetime from Bend: 40 mins**

perspective on how slow things change in the Belknap lava fields and how little has been "spoiled" by 100 years of increased tourism (see newspaper in Dee Wright entry). Take a slow walk on the old road and ponder how travel has changed in 100 years. Imagine trying to drive a Model-T

Black Crater

Dee Wright ➤

Road

over this torturous lava surface. Notice how 100 years later only small trees grow in the bed of the old road. Telephone poles still line the route or lay where they fell. Notice the rounded lava rocks on portions of the road bed, smoothed down by 50 years of wagon wheels! Maybe you'll find a fun artifact like a 1910 penny! (I found the penny and then left it as it lay…if you spot it, please leave it also…and send me a photo that I'll post on the blog!)

For history nuts it's fascinating that this route is visible on Google Earth—look for the two tree islands west of McKenzie Pass and zoom in on the faint line heading west.

HIKE: From the PCT trail-head head overland NW along the left (eastern) margin of the lavas. In a few hundred yards (5-8 minutes) look for the obvious wide defunct road grade descending from the lava onto the sands. If you get to a heavily-treed area, you've gone too far. Walk the road until your curiosity abates. It's 1.5 miles to where the remnant merges with Hwy 126 near Craig Lake. At the minimum at least walk 10-15 minutes to where the trees have re-colonized the roadbed.

54 MATTHIEU LAKES LOOP TRAIL
A quintessential High Cascades loop

Hike: moderate 7-mi. semi-loop with optional 2-mi. one-way extra

OBSCURE POPULAR
OBSCUROMETER

- elevation parking: 5,350 feet
- elevation S. Matthieu Lake: 6,000 feet
- free
- vault toilets
- dogs: no rules

Map page 219

The "normal" trail looping around the Matthieu Lakes is good, but if you add in a start/finish at Dee Wright Observatory instead of the boring horse trailhead…then you've got a Quintessential Cascades experience! Here's why: starting at the "normal" Lava Camp horse trailhead you park in a dusty viewless road-end with an hour's hike before the first views. But, if you start at Dee Wright instead, you add a little over a mile to the entire route by traversing the intriguing lava-flow PCT section at both the start/finish of the hike. This lava traverse features smashing views all around and is simply WAY more interesting than the shorter route. And, finishing up the hike, you'll be at Dee Wright where you can pop open a bevvie to toast the mountain views rather than simply ending up at a dusty viewless trailhead.

North Sister

Middle Sister

South Matthieu Lake

This trail is unquestionably the showpiece trail of the McKenzie Pass. Here's the run-down of this hike's exclamation points: an easy mile of stunning lava field, jaw-drop volcano views from Middle Sister to Mt Hood, and two chilly yet swimmable lakes…all for a measly 700-foot elevation gain. Want more? Then for an extra bonus jaunt you can make a 4-mile out 'n' back from South Matthieu Lake to see, sun, and swim at rarely-seen Yapoah Lake.

It's hard to beat this hike…rarely do you get such stunning scenery for such a minimum of heavy breathing!

HIKE: Park at Dee Wright's westernmost spots and begin by walking down the Hwy shoulder for 200 yards to pick up the easy-to-miss PCT on the left side. Zigzag a mile through the PCT lava field, and then descend to the forest and the junction with the trail from the Lava Camp. Go right for .5 miles to the junction—the beginning/end point of the loop. Go left for the easy 2.5-mile climb to South Matthieu. After 2 miles the view will open up to see North and Middle Sisters looming large, while to the north the Cascades peaks march like sentinels over Belknap's lavas and

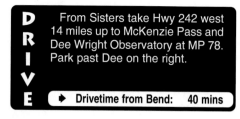

D R I V E From Sisters take Hwy 242 west 14 miles up to McKenzie Pass and Dee Wright Observatory at MP 78. Park past Dee on the right.

➤ Drivetime from Bend: 40 mins

the 2003 B&B burn. Down below is a glimpse North Matthieu Lake as well as the entire Yapoah Crater lava field. Quite the view!

Soon you'll arrive at the loop junction where a right will take you down to North Matthieu and then back to the car...but first head straight to see South Matthieu Lake. This lake is a PCT camper's favorite and you'll often see tents around it, but at 6,000 feet, it stays a tad chilly for much swimming. Circling the lake, at the eastern side you'll see the Scott Pass trail junction—this is the way to Yapoah Lake if you're up to an extra 4 miles and 500-foot descent/ascent. If not, then head back north, descend .5 miles to North Matthieu, explore its shoreline, then 1.5 miles down to the loop junction and left back through the lava a mile to the finish.

For a side trip to unsigned Yapoah

Washington 3-Fingered Jefferson Hood

North Matthieu Lake

Lake, take the Scott Pass trail for 1.2 miles downhill (500-feet elev loss). About a mile into the descent there are two long switchbacks which signal the upcoming unsigned path you'll need to find. A couple of minutes past these switchbacks look carefully for a path heading to the right, some-

times marked with sticks. If the main trail flattens out then you've gone 200-300 yards too far. This well-trodden side path heads up/down .3 miles to Yapoah's sandy lake shore.

Yapoah Lake beach

55 OBSIDIAN TRAIL
North Sister splendor on the PCT

Hike: difficult 11-mile semi-loop

OBSCUROMETER

- elevation parking: 4,800 feet
- elevation top: 6,600 feet
- fees: Forest Service permit req'd
- vault toilets
- dogs: no rules

The Obsidian Trail features sweeping views of North and Middle Sisters, alpine meadows dotted with springs and tarns, a 20-foot waterfall, and amazingly marbled obsidian—all in a long 11-mile day hike. The colorfully banded obsidian glass is everywhere at the top elevations of this loop—walls, gullies, boulders, hunks, and flakes—all colored with Mother Nature's fingerprints.

Obsidian swirl

Alas though, the moderate elevation gain (for such a long length) combined with the great visuals and rare obsidian has lead to overuse of this trail and the obsidian area. Backpackers and PCT hikers all want to camp around the hyper-scenic, yet sensitive alpine meadow. Thus, years ago the Forest Service implemented a permit system in order to try to regulate the overuse of this Wilderness Area. (The Forest Service is charged by the 1964 Wilderness Act to attempt to preserve the "wilderness" character

North Sister

Tents

Tarns   Obsidian Meadows

of the designated areas. Places like the Obsidian Trail were failing as a wilderness, as are the current usage numbers at Proxy Falls, South Sister and Green Lakes. Don't be surprised in the future to see permitting also for these too-popular areas.) Thus, a free permit is required to either day-hike or backpack on the Obsidian Trail. Call ahead to reserve one from the McKenzie Ranger Station— 541-822-3381. They can fax the permit to either the Bend or Sisters office for pick-up.

Despite the Obsidian Trail's popularity, this trail is

hardly the best one around. Half the length of the trail is rather boring, and then the good half is often crowded with hikers. In essence, for the 11-mile total you get 6 boring miles through view-less forest and over a lava

D R I V E

From Sisters take Hwy 242 west. Pass Dee Wright at MP 78 and head down to MP 71. Just past Scott Lake turn left at the signed trailhead.

◆ **Drivetime from Bend: 51 mins**

field, then a 5-mile loop of interesting sights and terrain (but crowded). Why this not-that-remarkable area gets so much use is that it is a good base for North Sister climbers and also for backpackers doing longer routes around the Sisters. As a day hike the Obsidian Trail isn't too much more remarkable than other hikes in the area. Extending a Matthieu Lakes hike (54) or doing Scott Mtn (57), or Thayer Lake (49) may be better options with much less planning hassle for the day-hiker.

Obsidian Falls

HIKE: The trail begins with an easy 3 miles through a Hemlock forest. Then you'll contour up and through Collier Cone's lava flow (the same flow that dams-up Linton Lake farther down the valley). After hopping across White Branch Creek the trail forks and begins the loop section. Head right towards Linton Meadows. The next 1.5 miles showcase the first obsidian hunks and the first of three trailside Mazamas plaques. At the junction with the PCT go left, arriving shortly at Obsidian Falls. Above the falls are the meadows where it's easy to spend an hour at the springs, ponds (tarns), and investigating the red-yellow-black whirly-swirly obsidian

outcroppings. The next mile of the trail sports lots of mountain visuals as it drops to a flowing creek and junction. To finish the loop take a left onto "Glacier Way Trail 4336" and descend .75 miles back to the loop junction. Go right, through lava again, then 3 miles back to the parking.

NOTE: The map shows Spring Lake at the end of a .5-mile spur near the trailhead. It looks inviting for a dip after a long hike, but No—it's spring-fed cold with muddy shores after a wicked-steep descent. Skip it.

WHATEVER WHATEVER WHATEVER WHATEVER WHATEVER WHATEVER WHATEVER WHATEVER WHATEVER WHATEVER

Plaques for Bronaugh, Montague, and Prouty were placed early in the 1900's by the Mazamas Mountaineering Club to honor esteemed members.

RICHARD
1852 WARD 1936
MONTAGUE

WHATEVER WHATEVER WHATEVER WHATEVER WHATEVER WHATEVER WHATEVER WHATEVER WHATEVER WHATEVER

Hike: easy/moderate 1.3 miles one-way

OBSCUROMETER

- elevation trailhead: 4,800 feet
- elevation lake: 5,200 feet
- fees: $5 NW Pass
- vault toilets
- dogs: no rules

Benson Lake is the first stop on the Scott Mtn hiking loop (57) if you hike the loop clockwise, and it may be the Central Cascades' most overlooked lake. "Overlooked" in that most people have no idea of its hidden beauty, rather than "overlooked" like people know to scramble up the lake's north ridge for the surprisingly dramatic view! If you're a keen photographer, then bushwhack around to the rocky NW ridge and Benson Lake will pop to the top of your Favorites list faster than you can twirl your polarizing filter. The lake is fairly popular in the summertime, as it makes for an easy backpack destination…but few hikers know that a venture to its far side is way worth it.

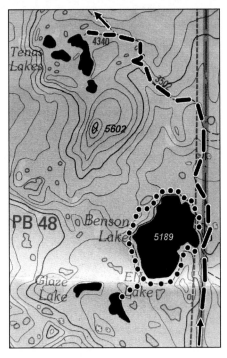

Benson is not your typical shallow basin-type lake (like Scott Lake). Benson is a deep rock-bound bowl of yummy indigo blue with plenty of ridgetop viewpoints to help you see deep down into the blue—a little like Crater Lake's rim. But Benson isn't just a look-at-me beauty—it's also come-jump-into-me fun! As the trail approaches the lake, turn left on the "near" shoreline path and in a couple of minutes you'll find a downed-log diving board and a perfect jumping rock. Yes, perfect—it may be one of the Cascades' best hucking rocks…perched above 20-30 feet of crystal clear azure…Geronimo!!!

If Benson on a summer weekend is too busy for your tastes, or you're just the bushwhack-to-find-Cascades-secrets type, then there are two small swimmable lakes just west of Benson's western ridge—Elf and Glaze Lakes. The two lakes are connected by a dry 100-yard streambed. For sunning privacy Elf has the nicest flat rocks on its far shore, but both lakes are worth a scouting. To find them from Benson's jump-off rock, look across to the small rockslide on the west shore. You'll need to find the faint paths that head over to this rockslide, ascend the ridge behind it, log-hop over the blow-down, and then descend a minute down to Elf Lake. It only takes about 5 minutes from Benson's western ridge.

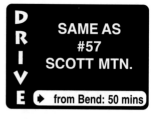
DRIVE

SAME AS
#57
SCOTT MTN.

▶ from Bend: 50 mins

Now, here's the part about Benson's sweetest view. Above the jump-off rock there's a ridge that sports a fair view of the Three Sisters, and this is good enough for most folks. But, if you navigate the far (north) shore's faint path over to the prominent ridge, then ahhhh, you'll witness one of the Cascades' finest compositions—the Three snowy Sisters rising dramatically over the bowl of deep indigo!! SO many people hike by Benson without a

Scott Lake Trailhead Camp

clue as to this view because the "trail" side of the lake gives you no indication of this unexpected wonder. Now you know—GO SEE!!

HIKE: (See also Scott Mtn loop entry 57) From the Scott Lake trailhead take the Benson Lake trail from the signboard. The lake is in 1.3 miles. A footpath of sorts circles the lake.

Benson's far-side view

Jumping rock

Hike: moderate 9-mile loop

- elev. parking: 4,840 feet
- elev. Tenas Lakes: 5,475 feet
- elev. Scott Mtn: 6,100 feet

- fees: NW Pass ($5 at T'head)
- vault toilets
- dogs: no rules

Map page 220

It's hard to make a better loop hike than this! This loop has it all, and then some. It starts with a postcard-perfect view of the Three Sisters reflecting in tranquil Scott Lake, then it traipses past Li'l Scott Lake on the

way to Hand Lake. Hand lake is notable in that it is blocked up by a wall of chunky black lava which oozed down here from Belknap Crater atop McKenzie Pass— pretty cool! As you pass the lake on the trail, to add interest to the already-interesting area, you can look for a pioneer wagon road, built by John Craig

Scott Lake

circa 1862, that made a short traverse through the lava on its way over the McKenzie Pass. Finding the little-known wagon trail makes for a short and interesting out 'n' back side-diversion. The trail then leaves the lava to climb up to Scott Mtn where a stunning west-side-of-the-Cascades awaits. Wow is an understatement!

One of the Tenas Lakes   **Scott Mtn.**

Then, after all this good stuff comes more good stuff. Heading down and back towards the parking a short side-track leads to the Tenas Lakes. "Tenas" means 'little' in Chinookan... and what you'll find here is

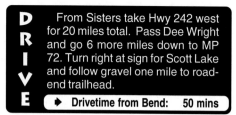

D R I V E

From Sisters take Hwy 242 west for 20 miles total. Pass Dee Wright and go 6 more miles down to MP 72. Turn right at sign for Scott Lake and follow gravel one mile to road-end trailhead.

➡ **Drivetime from Bend: 50 mins**

a group of small lakes primed for a wash-the-sweat-off dip. These lakes are all warm by August, and if you scout around you'll surely find one to your liking. Or, maybe you'll continue on the loop another mile to bigger, bluer, and more scenic Benson Lake (56). Oh my, talk about an embarrassment of riches!! From Benson it's 1.3 miles back to the car where you can lug the cooler over to a lakeside spot on Scott Lake and toast to one of the best loops in the Cascades...a diem well carpe'd!

Mt. Jefferson

Three-Fingered Jack

Mt. Hood

Hoodoo Butte

Hayrick Butte

The view north from Scott Mtn.

HIKE: Going counter-clock is wise—start past Scott Lake, skirt Hand Lake, summit Scott, then return past Tenas and Benson Lakes. From parking start on the Hand Lake road/trail that skirts Scott Lake and then soon Li'l Scott Lake also. The trail narrows and then goes about 1.5 miles to Hand Lake and its Belknap lavas—this lava flowed down from Belknap Crater, not the two small craters on the northern horizon (check Google Earth.) The next 1.5 miles contour the lava flow—look closely just after the lava begins to find the lava-crossing wagon road. A mile after the wagon road you'll reach a junction sign "Bunchgrass Ridge/Hand Lake". TURN LEFT here onto the unsigned trail that climbs into the forest for 1.8 miles to the Scott Mtn junction. Go right to climb .7 miles to Scott's summit, then descend, stay right, and complete the loop. From the Scott Mtn junction it's 1 mile to Tenas, then another mile to Benson, then 1.3 miles from Benson to the car.

58 LINTON LAKE/FALLS TRAIL

A lake with *secret* waterfalls pouring into it

OBSCUROMETER (OBSCURE—POPULAR)

Hike: moderate 1.7 miles one-way w/optional steep scramble

- elevation parking: 3,600 feet
- elevation lake: 3,600 feet
- free
- vault toilets
- dogs: no rules

Lava dam

Obsidian Creek beach

Majestic old-growth, towering secret waterfalls and a unique lava dam highlight a trip to pristine Linton Lake. Sounds pretty good, huh? Too bad most guidebooks bore you into skipping this hike with tripe like, "hike moderately two miles past old-growth to chilly Linton Lake with its attendant falls." Gah, that's hardly inspiring.

Who wants a dull hike to see "attendant falls" when you've got the glories of the McKenzie all around you? Nobody. But, Linton's Falls aren't "attendant"...they're AWESOME! The other writers just haven't seen them up close.

Here's what a trip to Linton Lake really offers. First off the easy/mod trail contours 1.7 miles through the lava bed that at one time poured down the Hwy 242's glacial valley and hooked a left to pour into and dam up this stream canyon. The trail then descends to the lake and ends at the Obsidian Creek lakeside campspots and beach. Sure, the lake is always a bit chilly, but the spacious sunny beach is a pleaser for picnicking, fishing, or wading/sunning. This is enough to satisfy most folks, but the wonders of Linton don't stop here...no way.

Hiking in, as you near the lake, you'll begin to hear a soft roar, and if you peer through the trees you'll see, across the lake, Linton Creek pouring down an 800-1,000-foot wall of forest.

110-foot Linton Falls

You'll only see one of the top tiers of this juggernaut series of waterfalls though. To see the rest you've got to be a gung-ho scrambler. These waterfalls are one of Central Oregon's best-kept secrets, a secret that WaterfallsNorthwest.com

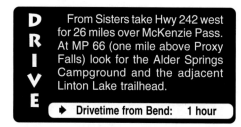

D R I V E From Sisters take Hwy 242 west for 26 miles over McKenzie Pass. At MP 66 (one mile above Proxy Falls) look for the Alder Springs Campground and the adjacent Linton Lake trailhead.

◆ **Drivetime from Bend: 1 hour**

says, *"makes a strong claim on the title of Best Waterfall in Oregon."* These waterfalls are hardly "attendant"…these waterfalls make Sahalie and Koosah look like babies…go and gawk!!

Whether you come for an easy day hike, come for an overnight back-pack at one of 4 lakeside campspots, or come to charge up a steep hillside to plunder rarely-seen cataracts…Linton Lake is sure to please!

To see the waterfalls: From Obsidian Creek find the .3-mile shoreline path that log-hops over to the mouth of Linton Creek. Arriving at the creek's campspots, look for a scramble path leading upwards over and under logs. This steep scramble is for adventurers only. The first 110-foot double falls is only an 8 to 12-minute scramble on an obvious path….leading to an excellent photo-perch. Most folks are satisfied with this and head back… but not you. Up you go to have a look at the lip of these falls and then another 7 minutes of rougher path until WOW, tier #2 thunders through the forest up ahead! Want more?? You've only seen half of these secrets, but seeing the rest demands clawing your way higher as the path disinte-grates into a steep loose grapple for the next 20 minutes. Very few people have ventured any higher. Are you up for it?

Waterfall #2 of ???

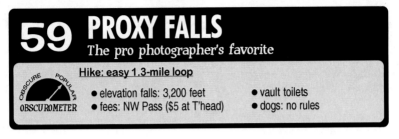

59 PROXY FALLS
The pro photographer's favorite

Hike: easy 1.3-mile loop

OBSCURE — POPULAR
OBSCUROMETER

- elevation falls: 3,200 feet
- fees: NW Pass ($5 at T'head)
- vault toilets
- dogs: no rules

A super-popular loop trail visits both Upper and Lower Proxy waterfalls after touring a bit of lava jumble and some massive old-growth forest. This trail has such a well-deserved reputation for ease and beauty that almost everyone driving over McKenzie Pass stops for a 30-60 minute jaunt. Avoid weekends if you can because it's often hard to find a place to park.

Crowded or not, both waterfalls are beauties. Lower Falls, surprisingly, is one of the most pro-photographed waterfalls in the NW. The Lower

Falls cascade about 200 feet down a glacially-carved wall…but it's not the viewpoint view that enraptures the pros. Everyone with a huge lens and a tripod over their shoulder is headed down the slippery scramble path to the base of the falls. Down there they set up close to the bottom of the falls, close enough that the mist can tickle their pixels! Proxy Falls made the recent cover of the guidebook *Photographing Oregon*, as well as the header of the WaterfallsNorthwest.com website (see the blog for pix and linx).

A second spur trail leaves the loop to see Upper Proxy Falls. It's shaped like a mossy stairway to heaven and it pours into a mysterious pool that has no outflow—it all soaks into the lava.

The Proxy waterfalls are good to visit any time the McKenzie Hwy is open (late-June to Nov.)…but for locals the best time to have a look is in late October. The drive on Hwy 242 down from the pass will treat you to an explosion of vibrant Fall colors as the Vine maples change with the season….and the tourist crowds will be back home and the kids in school. The entire McKenzie/Santiam driving loop is fantastic in late October!

HIKE: Signboard at the parking area details the 1.3-mile route. The lava flow that the trail traverses is Collier Cone's flow that oozed down from North Sister to fill the glacially-carved valley and damming-up Linton Lake (58). If you look on Google Earth you can vividly see the lava flow and how it stopped just past Proxy Falls.

D
R
I
V
E

From Sisters take Hwy 242 west for a total of 27 miles. Just past the signed Alder Springs/ Linton Lake trailhead, at MP 65, slow down for Proxy's roadside parking. If you're coming from the west up Hwy 242, just watch the MilePosts for #65.

◆ **Drivetime from Bend: 1 hour**

A forest pixie

Author's note: *Regrettably, the sylvan forest pixie that was frolicking nakedly at Upper Proxy Falls now is ashamed of her exposure. Certain members of the Bend retailer community have shamed the author into adding a smiley to hide the "offensive" nipple that peeked out. As harmless as the sight of a female breast is, especially when the female is an actual creature of the wilderness...the author now bows to the realities of retailing... the conservatives have won this minor skirmish. Check the blog to see the original photo in color, and maybe even more...but beware, cuz you may see a boob—yikes!*

Lower Proxy Falls

133

60 COUGAR HOT SPRING
Shangri-La

OBSCUROMETER
OBSCURE — POPULAR

Hike: moderate 7-minute walk
- elevation: 1,800 feet
- fees: $5 daily or $50 yearly pass
- No alcohol at pools, nor glass bottles of any sort
- vault toilets
- dogs: there is a designated dog area next to spring— no dogs near the pools!

Cougar Hot Spring is my favorite hot spring in America! It's also one of the busier natural hot springs in the west— hundreds of people a day LOVE Cougar! There's much to love: the setting is a jungly old-growth forest where the spring gushes forth from a tiny rock cave. After the spring's first one-foot waterfall it collects into the first of five successive pools, each big enough to

hold 6-12 people. The first crystal-clear pool can be a hot-hot 107°-ish, but each successive pool gets a couple of degrees cooler, so just like Goldilocks and the three bares, everyone can find one that's "just right."

The five soaking pools have been altered and "improved" by Friends of Cougar for eons, and the latest improvements—in spring '09—have yielded wonderful natural rock-bottomed pools that waterfall into each other. One of the best aspects of Cougar is that you can move pools if you don't like the immediate company. There are helpful stone steps and handrails, as well as a small changing area to hang your clothes.

And…about the clothing: Cougar is definitely CLOTHING OPTIONAL, leaning way nearer to No-Clothing-At-All. Think Eugene, think naked hippies mixed with Burning Man mixed with authors mixed with all other sorts. Don't come expecting bathing suits. Come expecting a wonderful natural experience where you can comfortably shed some of society's trappings and hang-ups about body image. At Cougar you'll find all kinds of bodies on display…super fat and bone-skinny…wrinkles of age and smoothness

New shelter ➡

The top 3 pools

Note: the forest service calls the springs "Terwilliger," but locals don't.

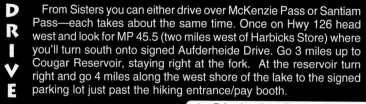

D
R
I
V
E

From Sisters you can either drive over McKenzie Pass or Santiam Pass—each takes about the same time. Once on Hwy 126 head west and look for MP 45.5 (two miles west of Harbicks Store) where you'll turn south onto signed Aufderheide Drive. Go 3 miles up to Cougar Reservoir, staying right at the fork. At the reservoir turn right and go 4 miles along the west shore of the lake to the signed parking lot just past the hiking entrance/pay booth.

➤ **Drivetime from Bend:** **90 mins**

of youth…penises both short and long…boobs hither and yon…hairy backs and hairy muffs…kids of all ages…tatts, piercings, scars, dreads… everything goes and everything's OK!

What you won't find at Cougar is a mess. The Forest Service instituted a fee a bunch of years ago and now Hoodoo Services operates the concession. There is a booth at the trail entrance where an actual person will collect the $5 per-person day fee. These fees go to good use, though there are those who'd still protest. But, if you had visited in the last years

Rider Creek Falls

before the fee, what you saw was a mini Rainbow Gathering all-day hangout at the pools… there were kids hustling you for change or rides back to the Hippie Hollow camp… there were car break-in issues in the parking area…Cougar seemed dirty. Many people didn't like their favorite hot spring anymore. But not anymore, as the fee keeps the place from being over-run and pays for daily clean-up of the beer cans, cig butts and other inconsiderate rubbish. The fee also supports outhouses at both parking and springs, and it pays for a weekly scrub-down of the rock pools by the diligent and always-smiling Maria (Thursday mornings).

Cougar is a paradise! Come in the early morning and watch the sunbeams streak and swirl through the steam in front of the moss-draped nurse log. Come mid-day to lay-out and diminish your tan lines. Come in the evening shade and watch the light play on the far canyon wall, reveling in another incomparable McKenzie day.

One thing that few visitors know about is the 30-foot waterfall that graces Rider Creek just a 10-minute scramble from the springs. Just below the bottom hot spring pool Rider Creek gurgles by, unnoticed by most everyone. If you feel like a little mossy Oregon-y stream adventure to take a break from all the relaxing, then follow the path that heads right from the lowest pool. The first 100 yards is difficult, but then it's a fairly simple rocks 'n' logs scamper up to the photogenic waterfall. Bare feet won't work, sandals are only OK, and shoes are best.

Hike: short hike to lake

OBSCUROMETER

- elevation lake: 3,300 feet
- free
- no toilets
- dogs: no rules

Hidden Lake is a skinny-dipper's pond. It's no different or more attractive than the thousand other Cascade lakes scattered throughout the nearby forests...there's neither nice beach nor shoreline, nor is it warmer than any other Cascade lake. Thus, the only reason or purpose for going should be

to join in and continue the 30-year tradition of skinny-dipping at this little pond.

Please let me get personal for a moment here. It's probably obvious by this time in this book that I like being naked in the woods...I and lots of others too. So, the only reason I'm putting Hidden Lake in my guidebook is to alert other skinny-dippers to a spot where nakedness is the norm rather than secretive solitary pursuit. The way our society has devolved, people "caught" naked out in the wilderness by clothed folks still feel ashamed and most often will move to cover up at least somewhat in order not to "offend." Personally. I think this "norm" sucks! A better norm would be that nudity at a wilderness lake would be **expected**, just like as female toplessness is on a European beach. I'm not talking about getting naked at Suttle Lake or Elk Lake...I'm talking about off-the-path lakes and rivers. That's the agenda I promote. To that end, the more people I can encourage to try the feel the fun of skinny-dipping, the

more I hope they'll enjoy it...and the more the stigmatization of being naked in nature will gradually wane. Just my hope.

So, if you'll skinny-dip, make a fun outing on a sunny day to Hidden Lake. If you don't skinny-dip, then don't go and bother the naked folk there, because you'll pass hundreds of other lakes on the way that'd be much friendlier for bathing suits.☺ If you don't like to see naked hippies, then consider this entry helpful by steering you away from a known spot.

Here's the main fun attraction of Hidden Lake—there's big log rafts covered with plywood tops that nekkid folks can paddle around the pond on. The biggest one was once a party barge with an upper deck for lounging and jumping! Back in the body-freedom heyday of the 70's the lake was reputed to be a naked-hippie Shangri-La.

DRIVE

?

➤ from Bend: 2 hours

Nowadays it's just a lake where camping has been prohibited, some ramshackle rafts are still floating, and naked people are still swimming and paddling and laughing. Don't miss paddling over to the "far" shore to disembark and check out the short and peculiar in-flowing stream.

Come join in…get naked and you'll feel welcomed, come to gawk and I, for one, will curse you. To that end, I won't even give directions as to how to get to the Hidden Lake. If you're a skinny-dipper I know you'll make the effort to find it on a map, but if you have an unyielding attachment to your bathing suit, then please use this book to find Robinson Lake (64), Benson Lake (56), or Matthieu Lakes (54).

What I will tell you is that the lake is 2WD-able, about 8 miles from Cougar Res off spur road 260. See ya there!

Plywood raft

Hike: 100-yard walk to riverside pool

OBSCUROMETER

- elevation: 1,900 feet
- free
- dogs: discouraged

- no toilets
(at Olallie Camp 1 mile south,
or Sahalie Falls 8 miles north)

Deer Creek (or Bigelow) hot spring is a small natural hot spring seeping from a cave overhang within arm's length of the swift-flowing McKenzie River. This is a small intimate pool is good for only a handful of people. Expect nudity.

Most of the pool is just-more-than-lukewarm, but if you shimmy into the back "cave" area, you'll then feel the HOT water seeping out from the far corners. This hot spring can get super-popular on summer weekends, and when it's full, it's full (no room for you)...but it's unpredictably hit-or-miss. There are some nearby undeveloped campsites that are popular with hot-springers (and also with Mtn Bikers riding the McKenzie Trail). Hikers and bikers will pass above you on the McKenzie River trail...and occasionally fishermen will float by on rafts. In winter and early spring the hot spring pool is flooded by the ice-cold McKenzie.

There's a great serenity to this pool. The sapphire McKenzie River rushes by just an arm's-length away and in the springtime (or rainy times) a delightful symphony of drips sprinkle from the mossy cave overhang. In the autumn the yellow-red maple leaves float down to land in the pool all around you. Quite nice...don't tell anyone.

Looking out of the misty cave

D
R
I
V
E

The Springs are on Hwy 126 near to Belknap Hot Springs Resort and the junction of Hwy 126/242. On Hwy 126 at MP 14.5 turn onto signed Deer Creek Rd and go .25 miles, cross the bridge and park on the right. The spring is on the downstream west side of the bridge, about 75 yards from the bridge.

➧ **Drivetime from Bend: 70 mins**

An autumn soak

63 TAMOLITCH FALLS/ BLUE POOL TRAIL
A 100% wonderful trail

Hike: easy 2-miles one-way to pool

OBSCUROMETER

- elevation parking: 2,200 feet
- free
- toilets at campground
- dogs: no rules

Along the McKenzie River are some of the finest Oh's in Oregon. This 2-mile section of the much-longer McKenzie River trail is simply gorgeous, simply eye-popping! Tamolitch Falls ("bucket" in Chinookan...the "Blue Pool" in local lexicon), is the destination of this pleasure hike. The pool is bizarre...So Blue, So quizzical, So Oregon...So magnificent! In essence

McKenzie River

the Blue Pool is the spot where the McKenzie River re-appears on the surface after making an underground detour through the lava flow that filled-up the McKenzie's ancient canyon (see blog for vibrant Google Earth views of the flows). With a silent and mysterious whisper the McKenzie "springs" back to life in a giant translucent mini-lake...then begins its flow anew, heading downstream along the route of this trail. You need to see it to believe it!

The Tamolitch Falls trailhead is on Hwy 126 5 miles south of Sahalie Falls or 8 miles north of Hwy 242 junction. Just north of MP 11 on Hwy 126, turn down at signs for Trailbridge Camp/ Smith Reservoir. Go across bridge then immediately right onto FS 655 for .3 miles to parking spaces. The trail is up the hill a few yards heading upstream.

➤ **Drivetime from Bend: 1 hour**

Since regular hiking verbiage fails to capture this wonder, here's a likely metaphor: Take a bottle of Bombay Sapphire Gin and pour it over a collection of green leaves, rocks and moss. It'll be blue in the bottle yet clear as it flows. Imagine an icy sapphire martini that never diminishes as it pours out of the glass—that's the Blue Pool. Let's have a toast!

The entire 2-mile hike to Tamolitch is a non-stop pleasure of rushing riversong, old-growth grandeur,

Tamolitch Falls
June 2008

Blue Pool

and quaint stream bridges. An easy hike doesn't get any better than this one. Don't miss this gem—it'll be one you'll remember!

HIKE: The easy-ish trail is never steep, but it does have some bumpy lava sections. It's a straightforward 2 miles to the Pool then back. The first 1.25 miles you'll be along the gorgeous river, then the final .75 miles you'll climb away from the river and through the lava field before popping out on the pool's rim. This lava flowed about 1,600 years ago, first damming up what's now Clear Lake, then creating the falls at Sahalie, Koosah...and Tamolitch. At Tamolitch take an extra jaunt a little above the pool to hear the quiet of the forest and see the now-dry channel before heading back. Before the Smith Diversion Reservoir was built in 1966 this channel flowed more often, but now the channel only flows during the rainiest of spring times (the McKenzie's flow is diverted upstream at Carmen Reservoir—near Koosah Falls—to make power at the powerhouse at Trailbridge Res—at the bridge before the trailhead.) Returning on the trail, notice how the sharp lava gives way to smoothed river stones as you abruptly leave the lava field.

64 ROBINSON/KUITAN LAKES TRAIL
Two small swimmable lakes

Hike: easy 0.3-mile or 1.2-mile one-way

OBSCUROMETER

- elevation: 3,900 feet
- free
- bring floaty, bug repellent, PBR

- no toilets
- dogs: no rules

Robinson and Kuitan Lakes are two small lakes nestled in the thick forest just inside the Mt Washington Wilderness boundary. Both are shallow enough that by mid-summer they're warm and skinny-dippable, and this is the main attraction of this duo—intimate privacy! Neither lake sees many visitors. These aren't lakes that'll Wow you with Cascades grandeur, but rather they're lakes that'll sooth you with their off-the-beaten-track silence. Robinson Lake, just a 7-minute walk from the car, isn't a lake that'll host many people. Basically there's one lakeside campsite with brush-free water access. Whoever gets there first "gets" the lake—if you arrive hoping for a private lake, then don't temper someone else's experience who got there first...move on to Kuitan Lake.

Kuitan Lake is just another mile up the Hand/Benson trail from Robinson, but way less known. Same deal at this lake...no views or attractions other than a private woodsy lake and campsite hidden in the forest. Nobody watching you strip 'n' dip except your boyfriend ☺. Super fun is the 100-foot fir that fell into the lake and now acts as both balance beam and diving board!

Since all the water near in this region—in Clear Lake or the McKenzie—is near freezing, Robinson or Kuitan Lake is a good place for a rinse after a long day of hike or bike...and the 7-minute walk makes Robinson full-cooler friendly ☺!

Robinson Lake

HIKE: From the parking area a 4-minute 1,000-foot walk brings you to a Hand Lake/Benson junction. Go left for 3 more minutes to Robinson.

For Kuitan head right, but since Kuitan is not signed off

D R I V E On Hwy 126 at MP 8 (2 miles south of Sahalie Falls), turn onto signed Robinson Lake Rd and drive 4.3 fast gravel miles to the road-end parking (just an 8-minute drive from Hwy 126).

➤ **Drivetime from Bend:** **75 mins**

the trail, you'll have to keep a sharp eye out for its faint and unmarked access path. So, at the trail junction check your watch. Begin the easy 20-minute (1 mile) walk and in 17 minutes take note when you cross a

Kuitan Lake

deep gully. Check your watch here and in 3 more minutes look sharp for the faint path heading left to the lake, possibly marked by a cairn (just before the trail makes a 90° right bend.) The lake is just a couple minutes through the woods— you'll see the clearing ahead. Kuitan Lake is only a couple of minutes

off the trail, so don't just amble too far if you don't think you took the proper turn—backtrack to the trail again, then back to the gully to re-orient.

From Kuitan Lake the trail continues towards Scott Mtn and Hand Lake —bring a map if you want to venture farther.

Kuitan campsite

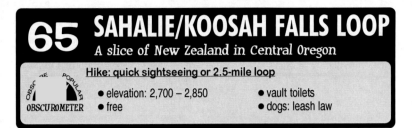

65 SAHALIE/KOOSAH FALLS LOOP
A slice of New Zealand in Central Oregon

Hike: quick sightseeing or 2.5-mile loop

OBSCUROMETER

- elevation: 2,700 – 2,850
- free
- vault toilets
- dogs: leash law

The trail between Sahalie Falls and Koosah Falls is the prettiest short riverside trail anywhere in Oregon! That's saying a lot in our state of wonder-landscapes, but this li'l slice of rushing, churning, bubbling nirvana **Delivers**! Imagine… two surging 80-foot waterfalls, crystalline turquoise waters, old-growth firs, cedars, and hemlocks, and thick pillows of spongy moss covering the exposed chunks of this young lava flow…WOW, it's like a slice of distilled New Zealand in our own back yard! (count 'em, that's 3 exclamation points thus far ☺.)

There are two ways to experience the wonders on this stretch of the McKenzie River. You can park at either waterfall and simply walk the easy half-mile trail between them, or, better yet, hike a loop by going up one

side of the river then down the other, passing the two waterfall in both directions. In summer both waterfalls can be very busy because they're on every tourist map, well-signed, and just steps off the highway. For a little more sense of seclusion hike the loop. The far bank feels remote—you probably won't even notice the people at the viewpoints, and the roar of the falls drowns out the annoying tourist chatter. Chances are you won't hear a tourist comment, "hey wasn't this the slice of river used in the movie *Seraphin Falls* where Pierce Brosnan hucked over Sahalie Falls and also in *Homeward Bound* where the cat took the

Sahalie Falls in an actual 1971 Playboy *ad*

D
R
I
V
E

From Sisters take Hwy 20 west for 26 miles. Once over Santiam Pass then stay left at the Hwy 20/22 junction. Go 3 more miles then turn left onto Hwy 126 towards Eugene. Pass Clear Lake and at MP 6 turn into the signed Sahalie Falls parking, or head .5 miles farther to turn into and park at the less-busy Koosah Falls parking.

➤ **Drivetime from Bend: 1 hour**

plunge?"…but if a local was there, she might reply, "Yup, it is…and did ya know that Sahalie Falls was also used in national ciga-rette ad in the early 70's?" This is what tour-ists talk about around these spectacular waterfalls…not whether their poodle has pooped yet or whether grandma is carsick.

Ok, back to reality. Really venturesome hikers, once across the canyon on the loop, can

Koosah Falls

look for the slippery path leading down to the ever-misty alcove <u>behind</u> Sahalie Falls where mists, mosses, rainbows, and thunder await the brave!

Overall, the beauty of the upper McKenzie River is eye-boggling! This short section of aquamarine crystal-clarity, bookended between two thun-derous waterfalls, is undoubtedly one of Oregon's finest exclamations!! (count 'em!!)

HIKE: Start at either waterfall. The loop is best hiked clockwise—downriver first. It's about 1.25 miles on each side of the canyon with bridges at either end. Heading downstream, a few minutes past Koosah turn right, cross the bridge, and then turn right onto the trail again by the toilet. Now head upstream, pass both waterfalls and Sahalie's wet scramble path, until you get to the upper footbridge over the river. Cross the bridge and go right back to the parking lot.

WHATEVER WHATEVER WHATEVER WHATEVER WHATEVER WHATEVER WHATEVER WHATEVER WHATEVER WHATEVER

Holy !!! In July 1998 Shannon Carroll, a 20-year-old female kayaker, kayaked over 78-foot Sahalie Falls to set a world record (since surpassed).

WHATEVER WHATEVER WHATEVER WHATEVER WHATEVER WHATEVER WHATEVER WHATEVER WHATEVER WHATEVER

66 CLEAR LAKE
An ice-cold hyper-clear lake

Hike: easy 4.5-mile lakeshore loop

OBSCURE POPULAR
OBSCUROMETER

- elevation: 3,016 feet
- free

- vault toilets
- dogs: no rules

Clear Lake is one of the numerous spring-fed lakes dotting the Cascades that feature amazingly clear aquamarine water. Surprising though is Clear Lake's unique origin. Only about 3,000 years ago local lava flows from Sand Mtn oozed down the slope to the east to dam both the inflow and outflow of a section of the McKenzie River. The waters still course through the lava, but now underground, to emerge as springs to fill the newly-created lava-dammed Clear Lake. As the new lake filled it drowned the surrounding forest then over-spilled its lava dam, creating a new "headwaters"

for the McKenzie River. The lake's waters are so cold and algae-free that the 3,000-year-old drowned trees don't decay much, and today you can still see the famed submerged stumps near the north end of the lake (either via trail or boat). The ice-cold spring water that fills the lake is SO clear that if you rent a rowboat to paddle around, most of the time you'll be looking down into the water at the scenery rather than up at the surrounding mountains and forest—how unique!

Clear Lake is popular and packed on summer weekends. Most people come to camp, boat, fish, and picnic. This leaves the lakeshore trail relatively uncrowded. The trail is super-neat with plenty of eye-candy. It weaves

Rental rowboats

on a paved portion through the lava flow, it crosses a bridge at the outflow "headwaters", it skirts the Great Springs that literally gush the lake-filling flow, it views the submerged stumps and the distant Three Sisters, and it rubs elbows with old-growth the entire way.

Too much good stuff! (Be aware that the trail is open to Mtn-bikes.)

FYI: If you're a Google Earth enabled person, you gotta check out this lake and its lava flows. If you're not yet a Google-Earther, then

**D
R
I
V
E**

From Sisters take Hwy 20 west for 25 miles over Santiam Pass. Stay left at the Hwy 20/22 junction, then in 3 miles turn left onto Hwy 126 towards Eugene. In 4 miles turn left at signed entrance to the Resort.

➜ **Drivetime from Bend: 1 hour**

this lake is reason to be. Now you can just click "earth" on Google Maps to get the 3-D aerial view of the lake. What you'll see is how the lavas poured down the hillside from the Sand Mtn cones (69) to dam-up the lake, as well as to fill the McKenzie's canyon…creating the both Sahalie and Koosah Falls. A must-see!

Clear Lake Resort: The Resort has cabins for rent, an old-timey café/ restaurant, some groceries (no beer), and rowboat rentals.

There's no phone when you step back in time into this Resort, and if they catch you trying to check your iPhone, they grab it and chuck it in the lake!

HIKE: The easy 4.5-mile trail circles the lake. Start and finish the loop at either the Resort or Coldwater campground. The SW part of the loop is busier with the Resort and campground, while the NE portion has the best views, springs, and submerged stumps.

North trail view over lake, resort, and Sisters

WHATEVER WHATEVER WHATEVER WHATEVER WHATEVER WHATEVER WHATEVER WHATEVER WHATEVER WHATEVER WHATEVER

Springs fill the lake year-round with 38-degree water. The lake never freezes, but it doesn't warm up either. Only polar bares dare to swim.

WHATEVER WHATEVER WHATEVER WHATEVER WHATEVER WHATEVER WHATEVER WHATEVER WHATEVER WHATEVER WHATEVER

67 IRON MOUNTAIN TRAIL
An excellent July wildflower-view peak

OBSCUROMETER

OBSCURE   POPULAR

Hike: moderate 1-mile one-way or mod/diff 2-mile one-way
- elevation trailhead: 4,000 or 4,800 feet
- elevation peak: 5,455 feet
- fees: NW Pass
- vault toilets
- dogs: no rules

Iron Mtn from upper trailhead

In the first week of July, every year, Iron Mtn's 5,455-foot former lookout site tops every "in-the-know-hiker's" must-see list. This peak <u>always</u> features neck-spinning views that range from Coast Range to WA State to southern Cascades... but it's only in the first couple weeks of July that the trailside slopes literally explode into a technicolor wildflowery flourish!! **Yup, Iron Mtn sports THE BEST wildflower show in the Central Cascades, while also delivering a jaw-drop viewpoint. A must-see!**

Of course the wildflower bloom can vary, but ask any Ranger and they'll all say, "first week of July." Just try to be within 7-10 days and surely you'll catch most of the bloomarama.

New for 2009 is a 24-by-24 view platform that replaces the old lookout (removed in 2008). Here are some "look-fors" from the new platform: a western gaze will reveal a Willamette Valley haze band topped by Corvallis' 4,097-foot Mary's Peak (it angles down and right), with a glimpse of Sweet Home's Foster Reservoir a bit closer in. To the north you'll see Mt Adams showing left of Hood with Coffin Mtn (70) on Hood's right shoulder. Look east for every Central Cascade peak and note Scott Mtn below Middle Sis

and Mt Bachelor peeking around South Sis. To the south the big sprawling mountain is Diamond Peak. Binocular'd folk can attempt to spot 4 nearby fire lookouts—Coffin to the north, Black Butte and Sand Mtn due east, and Carpenter Mtn on the little rock nipple just left and foreground from Diamond Peak.

HIKE: Here are the two easiest routes:

1st) From the Hwy 20 parking area the trail crosses the highway then ascends steeply for two miles to the peak (1,400 vertical feet). In a mile you'll junction with the 2nd trailhead trail for the final mile to the top.

D R I V E

There are 3 different trailheads for an Iron Mtn hike. Here are directions for the two shortest routes. Check the blog for the longer route.

Coming from Sisters over Santiam Pass you'll need to keep left at the Hwy 22/20 junction (to Albany) and then stay straight on Hwy 20 at the Hwy 126 fork. The first Iron Mtn trailhead is on Hwy 20 at MP 63, 8.6 miles past the intersection of Hwy 126.

For the shorter route, pass the first signed roadside trailhead and in .8 miles slow down and prepare to turn right on the sud-denly-appearing FS 035, signed to Iron Mtn (MP 62.2). Follow this uphill, staying right always, for 2.5 fast gravel miles to the road-end trailhead.

➡ **Drivetime from Bend: 70 mins**

2nd) From the upper trailhead go one minute then left and then quickly right following the Iron Mtn pointer for just a mile to the peak (650 vertical feet).

There is another route—a loop from Tombstone Pass that heads over near Cone Peak first before climbing Iron, then descending to the highway and working back to the car. This is the complex loop William Sullivan describes in his book. Check my blog for a Google map of the route and some extra directions—the route is somewhat complicated and tricky.

Mt Adams   Mt Hood   Mt Jefferson

Iron Mountain Lookout

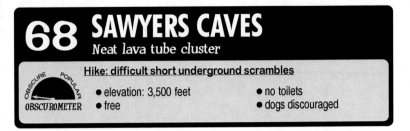

68 SAWYERS CAVES
Neat lava tube cluster

Hike: difficult short underground scrambles

OBSCUROMETER

- elevation: 3,500 feet
- free
- no toilets
- dogs discouraged

Sawyers Caves are a group of short lava tubes sporting an interesting variety of features. Thousands of cars pass by these caves daily, but since the Forest Service "unsigned" them a decade ago, few people know to stop. The two main caves are up and left from the former parking area. In about 100 yards you'll find a big opening with a large skylight. This cave goes in about 300 feet over a rugged bottom surface. Bring a lantern or multiple flashlights and a hat to protect your noggin from bumps. There's a breakdown section that you'll need to negotiate—if you've got enough light you'll see some reddish ropey "pahoehoe" lava, resembling redwood bark, and also a neat little side passage. Further, the cave opens again for easy walking over a floor featuring great swirls of ropey lava—maybe the best display of "pa-hoe-hoe" in any of Oregon's easily-accessed caves!

D R I V E

From Sisters take Hwy 20 west 28 miles. After Santiam Pass stay <u>left</u> at the Hwy 20/22 split and check your odometer. Go 2.2 miles from the split. Slow down when you see the big yellow sign "Trucks: Length Restricted". The former parking area is on the left side across from this sign, but since ODOT blocked the parking area with boulders, you'll need to park on either side's Hwy shoulder (I guess that's how they made it "safe".) If you get to Hwy 126, then you've gone one mile too far. Or, if you're coming up from Hwy 126, after the junction with Hwy 22 the caves are exactly 1.0 miles on the right side.

➨ **Drivetime from Bend: 51 mins**

Cave-end Pahoehoe lava ➜

Past this first cave entrance a faint path continues into the forest. A big tube awaits in a few hundred yards with a land-bridge spanning the openings. The caves here are jumbled, super-rough going, and not that interesting… but the land-bridge is cool.

Octopus hunting

Finally, back at the parking area, down and right about 100 feet are two short crawl-tubes. The farther one is eerie. You have to lower yourself into it then duckwalk and crawl. Thirty feet into it there appears to be a sleeping octopus—yikes! Be brave, go look.

WHATEVER WHATEVER WHATEVER WHATEVER WHATEVER WHATEVER WHATEVER WHATEVER WHATEVER WHATEVER

The eye has two types of cells for vision. Cones are for color and detail in daylight and rods are for black and white vision in low light. It takes the eye a gradual 10–30 minutes to adjust from cone vision to rod vision. Thus, when entering a dark cave with just a flashlight, your cones won't work in the dim light, but ever-so-slowly your rods will activate and begin to "see"—though only in black and white with little detail. On the other hand, if you bring a bright lantern into the cave, your cones will still function and you'll be able to "see" the colors and details of the cave features. When entering a dark cave it's best to sit in the dark entrance for a few minutes to let your eyes begin to adjust and "see".

WHATEVER WHATEVER WHATEVER WHATEVER WHATEVER WHATEVER WHATEVER WHATEVER WHATEVER WHATEVER

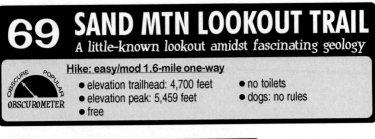

69 SAND MTN LOOKOUT TRAIL
A little-known lookout amidst fascinating geology

OBSCUROMETER (OBSCURE / POPULAR)

Hike: easy/mod 1.6-mile one-way

- elevation trailhead: 4,700 feet
- elevation peak: 5,459 feet
- free
- no toilets
- dogs: no rules

The Sand Mountain lookout is one of the Deschutes Nat'l Forest's hidden and almost-forgotten gems. A hike up to the lookout is WAY WORTH IT!

Sand Mountain is an 800-foot cinder cone that's a lot like Lava Butte south of Bend. It's got a staffed lookout atop it, a gradual road/trail up it, ancient lavas spewing from its flank, a deep crater bowl…and simply smashing views!! This viewpoint is in the "almost-forgotten" category because it gets little or no publicity. Forest Service maps quizzically don't show the lookout. Sullivan wrote about it in the mid-90s, but in his current editions Sand Mtn is just a wee back-pages footnote. Mostly the only people who know of Sand Mtn are the ATV'ers who roam the OHV tracks between Sand Mtn and Big Lake. Fortunately the ATVs are not allowed up Sand Mtn—the surprisingly excellent view is kept for hikers, bikers, and horses.

In summer the lookout is staffed by volunteers—part of the group that re-habbed the lookout back in 1989. These dedicated volunteers are glad to see visitors and help explain all things Central Cascades.

Sand Mtn. Lookout

D
R
I
V
E

You need a decent-clearance vehicle for this route—2WD is OK, but clearance is a factor.

On Hwy 20/126 heading west out of Sisters ascend Santiam Pass and at the top (MP 80) turn south onto Hoodoo/Big Lake Rd. Go 3 miles towards Big Lake. Just past a Big Lake Camp fork, in an area of wooden rails, angle right onto the signed dirt road FS 810. It's a slow, bumpy 3 miles from here to the trailhead because the road is so roller-coastery from all the ATV use. From the road you'll see Sand Mtn and the lookout ahead. Park at the Sand Mtn sign/gated road. FYI...if you have a Ranger Map and wonder if you can get out of here by continuing west—you can't, the road 866 is gated shortly ahead.

→ Drivetime from Bend: 1 hour

The 360° view from the lookout is so neck-swivelingly superb that pix just won't do it justice. Here's a rundown of fun stuff to look for. (If you fail to bring a Sisters Ranger District map and binoculars, then it'll be only you who misses out on some of the best west-side peak-spotting around). First off you've got 130 miles of Cascades peaks from the tip of Mt Hood south to Diamond Peak. Clear and Fish Lakes are below to the west and Big Lake to the east. Due west is the distinctive thumb of Iron Mtn slotted in a gap (67). The north skyline is dominated by Coffin and Bachelor Mtns (70). Around Santiam Pass' Hogg Rock you'll see extensive 2003 B&B burn. To the east you'll see distant Haystack

Mt. Jefferson — Three-Fingered Jack

The view northeast

Butte (Madras) to the left of lookout-topped Black Butte, with the Ochocos' distant pointy Pilot Butte right of Cache Mtn. To the south Diamond Peak is the large snow-cap peak with Waldo Lake's The Twins (30) and Maiden Peak (with the knob) to its left. Below Sand Mtn's crater look for the sub-cone which spewed the lavas that flowed down just 1,500 years ago to dam up Clear Lake and create the drops of Sahalie and Koosah Falls. Wow...bring a map!

About Big Lake: Big Lake is like a fun summertime outdoors carnival. There are huge campgrounds all along the lakeshore, with a number a kids' summer camps too. The lake is busy-busy with all sorts of wave-runners, motor boats, and basically anything else that can float. ATVs roar around from the nearby OHV areas. In a nutshell, it's summertime family-time mayhem...which hordes of people LOVE. Go see Big Lake with this in mind and you'll have fun! FYI: Patjens Lake loop is a bore.

HIKE: Head up the cinder cone road 1.3 miles to the road-end "corral" then continue up past the sign to find the signed trail .3 miles to the top.

Hite: two different moderate trails

OBSCUROMETER

- elevations: 4,800 to 5,900 feet
- free
- no toilets
- dogs: no rules

Coffin and Bachelor Mtns are two adjacent peaks situated between Mt Jefferson and Detroit Lake. Coffin Mtn, at 5,771 ft, is the better-known peak because of its recognizable flat-topped silhouette, its dazzling July wildflower show, and the staffed lookout on its peak. Bachelor Mtn (Coffin's neighbor) is lesser-known but no less attractive. Bachelor Mtn is actually higher, at 5,950 ft and features both a more enjoyable trail and a much better view of Mt Jefferson. Fortunately, both these peaks are accessed by the same FS road and the trailheads are only a mile apart.

Here's how to choose which mountain to hike: Coffin has the better wildflower show of the two, but Bachelor has better views and a nicer trail. The wildflowers go crazy the first two weeks of July. Thus, if you're hiking then, go up Coffin for its non-stop flowers 'n' views extravaganza. But, if you're visiting any time after mid-July, then go up Bachelor instead. Bachelor's 2-mile trail is better, there'll still be some flowers, and the view at the top is 360° of excellence (Bachelor somewhat blocks Coffin's view of Jefferson).

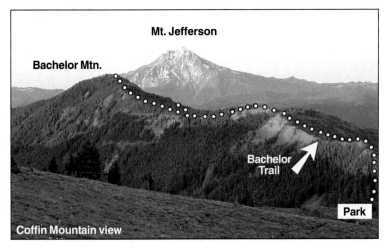

Mt. Jefferson

Bachelor Mtn.

Bachelor Trail

Park

Coffin Mountain view

Coffin Mtn: *Trailhead 4,750 ft – Peak 5,750 ft. Trail: Mod/Diff 1.5 miles one-way.*

From the signed trailhead the trail ascends relentlessly for 1.3 miles and then levels a bit as it contours to the right (east) side of the craggy flat-topped peak. The lookout, perched above the east-facing cliffs, is staffed from July-Sept (bring a little candy or chips and you may "sweet"-talk your

D
R
I
V
E

FYI—even if you're not a hiker, the drive to Buck Mtn's slope is WORTH IT!

From Sisters take Hwy 22 over Santiam Pass towards Salem. Turn right at the Hwy 20/22 fork and go 12 more miles to signed Straight Creek Rd at MP 69 (3 miles north of Marion Forks.) Turn west onto Straight Creek (FS 11) and ascend 4.1 miles then angle right onto gravel FS 1168. You'll continue ascending for 4 more miles and after contouring around Buck Mtn's excellent view-slope you'll see spur 450 leading left 100 yards to Coffin's trailhead. To find Bachelor continue straight for .6 miles then turn left at the fork for .6 more to the road-end unsigned trailhead.

➡ **Drivetime from Bend: 90 mins**

way into a tour. Ignore the buildings on the west side of the peak—there's nothing to see to the west except clearcuts.

Bachelor Mtn: *Trailhead 4,800 ft – Peak 5,950 ft. Trail: Moderate 2 miles one-way.*

The trailhead is unsigned, but the obvious trail begins where the road ends. The trail as-

Coffin Lookout and heli-pad

cends through nice forest before breaking out onto the view-laden ridge that leads 1.0 miles onto the mid-hike plateau. This plateau, besides offering a nice breather, has great visuals because of the stark forest of standing snags left over from the mid-70s Buck Mtn burn. After a .25-mile jaunt over the plateau you'll re-enter the forest and take a left at the signed Bruno junction for the last steep .7 mile climb to the former lookout site. Jefferson is the obvious highlight, but look to its right to try to spot Marion Creek's double falls (71).

Bachelor Mtn. Trail Plateau

71 MARION LAKE TRAIL
Big pristine lake with hidden waterfalls

Hike: easy/moderate 5.2-mile semi-loop

OBSCURE — POPULAR

OBSCUROMETER

- elevation parking: 3,400 feet
- elevation lake: 4,100 feet
- fees: NW Pass (at trailhead)
- vault toilets
- dogs: no rules

Ever hear of Marion Lake's huge twin waterfalls— Marion and Gatch Falls—which combine for a 160-foot drop? Few people have. They're Marion Lake's best-kept secret...just a quick 7 minutes off the well-used trail. Combining them with a visit to the big lake will make for a rousing outing!

B&B Burn

View from the ridge

Marion Lake is a biggie, and even though it's a bit busy on summer weekends, at least everyone has to actually WALK a trail to get there, as opposed to drive-up lakes like Big Lake or Suttle. The trail to the lake is an easy-going joy. It's wide, never too steep, and only about two miles to the lakeshore. Along the way you'll pass marshy Lake Ann and its peculiar rumbling outflow.

Arriving at the Marion Lake, a day-use area spans the north shore with plenty of access points and views to far-off Three-Fingered Jack and the 2003 B&B burn. Marion is swimmable, but it does stay on the chillier side. Bring a blow-up floaty or find a place on the Peninsula's lava rocks to warm your buns after a quick dip! The "Peninsula" is a lava hillside poking

Three-Fingered Jack

Peninsula shoreline

into the lake midway along the day-use shoreline. If you climb it you'll get a peek at Jefferson's peak, but if you want a really good view you'll have to scramble up the lava pile in back of the Peninsula (begin up the forested slope opposite the Peninsula then continue up the blocky lava 200 feet (5 minutes) to the knob— the view here is WOW—big Jefferson one way and the entire lake the other!)

What makes this easy jaunt to a big Cascade lake even better is the side-trail that leads to a "hidden" pair of waterfalls. Sullivan mentions them, but does a lousy

D
R
I
V
E

On Hwy 22, 15 miles south (towards Detroit) of the Hwy 22/20 split, look for Marion Creek Rd at MP 66.5. Turn and set your odometer. At the 3.3-mile mark, note FS 850 on the right—with the closed green gate. This is the access point for Gooch Falls. Continue another mile to the trailhead.

▶ **Drivetime from Bend:** **90 mins**

motivating a look-see. Here's what you'll find at this double-tiered water-fall: **WHOA!** No mere trickles here…these twins are 160 feet of WOW, with some sunny and misty spots to sit and enjoy the spectacle. The path to the falls is faint and requires some steep scrambling, so don't go if you're a wuss. Between the two drops is a little churning pool that's just divine on a hot sunny afternoon. The pool is wade-able and the rocks sit-able…and surprisingly, the falls' mist blows sideways, leaving the little area pleasantly warm. Courageous folks will love the "Cedar island" and it's views of distant Coffin/Bachelor Mtns (entry 70.)

HIKE: This is a semi-loop trail—1.6 miles to a junction where a 2-mile loop begins which tours both lake and waterfalls.

When you get to the junction, in order to find the faint path leading to the falls, go right onto the "Outlet Trail" and begin counting your steps. In 213 steps, just as the trail levels a bit and bends right, look for the unmarked faint path on the right. Take this path 5 minutes towards the sound of the stream then trend right as path becomes fainter towards the lip of the falls. Once you find the lip head right to find the steep 3-minute scramble down.

Once back on the main trail to the lake, head .5 miles to the outlet then left along the shore .75 miles to the "far" shore clearings where you'll go left and pick up the unsigned, yet obvi-ous when you've found it, trail back to the junction.

Gooch Falls. If one hid-den waterfall isn't enough, head back down the road 1.0 miles from the trailhead and park at the FS 850 gate. Walk 250 yards be-yond the gate and when you arrive at the former parking area, listen for the falls and find the faint trail which leads a couple of minutes past Mr. Gooch's corral to a cliff-edge viewpoint. Check blog for overview map.

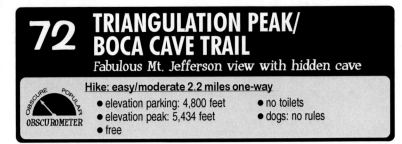

72 TRIANGULATION PEAK/ BOCA CAVE TRAIL

Fabulous Mt. Jefferson view with hidden cave

Hike: easy/moderate 2.2 miles one-way

OBSCUROMETER

- elevation parking: 4,800 feet
- elevation peak: 5,434 feet
- free
- no toilets
- dogs: no rules

Triangulation Peak's 5,434-foot former lookout site provides about the easiest up-close-and-personal look at Mt Jefferson you'll ever get – just 7 miles away (as the Google Earth ruler flies). Surprisingly, this face-to-face with Jefferson is relatively painless to achieve since you drive up 3,000 feet on a good forest road and then only have to hike 2.2 miles and ascend 650 feet. Thus, good bang-for-the-buck! (Pamelia Lake's Grizzly Peak is nearer to Jeff, but requires a tough 5-mile 3,000-foot gain).

To sweeten the allure of an excursion to Triangulation Peak is the semi-secret Boca Cave hiding on the east side of the peak that enables one of the most unique photographic framings of a Cascade peak anywhere in the Cascade Range. The cave is a neat spot—make the extra effort to see it!

At the former lookout site there's little evidence of the 1950s tower, but the 360° view is a stunner! You can see at least two other nearby lookouts: to the SW binoculars will show the cabin atop craggy Coffin

Mt. Jefferson

Mtn (70) and directly north to the right of Hood you'll easily see the 50-foot tower atop 5,617-foot Sisi Butte. Past Sisi Butte you'll get a clear view of Mt Hood with its postage-stamp Palmer Glacier ski-slope (with Timberline Lodge hiding in the trees directly below it). Past Hood you may see the tip of a mountain that would appear to be Mt Adams, but no, Adams hides just behind Hood's left shoulder—remarkably, the distant peak is Mt Rainier!

HIKE: Head east on the almost-level trail for 1.5 miles and look for the unsigned lookout trail which forks off to the right and upwards (it's the only fork you'll come to.) Climb this steeper trail .7 miles to the summit.

To find the Boca Cave you'll need to head 200 yards NE from the lookout site along the ridge towards Olallie Butte. You'll pass some campspots and at the last one look for a footpath heading down and right. As you descend there'll be a huge rock ridge to your left as you scramble down the steep path for about 150 vertical feet (5 minutes) until it contours back left around the face and into the large cave mouth.

D R I V E

From Bend head past Sisters and over Santiam Pass staying right onto Hwy 22 towards Detroit. Go 26 miles down Hwy 22 and look for McCoy Creek Rd at MP 56.2 (this is one mile before Idanha and 6 miles south of Detroit.) The trailhead is 9 miles up McCoy Creek Rd, the first 4 miles are paved and the next 5 miles fast 2WD gravel. At 7.7 miles is a big intersection with the McCoy Cabin – head right and continue 1.3 more miles. Just past a view of Mt Jefferson, take the next right onto oft-signed FS 635 and you'll see the trailhead sign immediately on the right.

◆ **Drivetime from Bend: 95 mins**

FYI: A neat stop on the way up/ back is the McCoy-Santiam Snow cabin 7.7 miles up the access road. It's a rustic log cabin, open to the public, with a wooden plaque inside spelling out the details of its existence.

Mt. Hood

Sisi Butte

Timberline Lodge

The view north

Boca Cave

Hike: difficult 1.8 miles one-way down to lake

OBSCUROMETER

- elevation parking: 4,400 feet
- elevation lake: 3,700 feet
- elevation phantom: 4,500 feet
- free
- no toilets
- dogs: no rules

Tumble Lake is a fair-sized "cirque" lake nestled in a bowl of charismatic rocky escarpments. At the lake's far end there's a shoreline studded with flat sunning/picnic rocks and also an extensive log jam that's fun to log-hop.

Tumble Lake gets swimmably warm in August, and given its remoteness, it'll probably be just you and the friendly salamanders frolicking in this oh-so-scenic cirque. For whatever reason, Tumble Lake seems to spawn a gaggle of sala- manders and it's quite a unique experience to actually swim with the sallies!

Tumble Lake

What sets Tumble Lake apart from most of its Cascade lake neighbors is that just 100 yards downstream of the lake's outflow the stream "tumbles" over a 120-foot cliff to begin its rush down to Detroit Lake. If you pick your way along the far side of the stream you'll soon find a sun-drenched water- fall ledge with a great view of Detroit Lake and its nearby peaks—quite a nice hidden addition to the obvious charms of this lake.

Plentiful Salamanders

NOTE: There is a trail up from Detroit Lake, but it climbs too high before then descending to the lake—ouch. Skip it.

HIKE: From the roadside parking the trail begins up over a steep hump then trends up and left for .5 miles to a sign- post junction (look for the lake below through the trees). Straight ahead is the long trail down to Detroit Lake, so instead go right and begin the steep 1.3 mile de- scent to Tumble Lake. At the lake head left on the user path and pass a couple of campsites before getting to the logjam outflow area.

D
R
I
V
E

(It's 20 min from Detroit to Tumble Lake.) A map is a good idea here…or at least a photo of one.

At Detroit Lake town (MP 50 on Hwy 22), go west over the Hwy bridge and turn immediately onto FS 2223 up French Creek. Set your odometer here. Go 4 paved miles then fork left onto the gravel FS 2223 and go 3.8 uphill miles more to the semi-unsigned left-hand shoulder trailhead parking for Tumble Lake (if you come to a ridge-top road fork, you're a bit too far). The trail begins up a steep dirt bank.

To continue to Phantom Bridge, pass the Tumble Lake trail and in just 500 yards fork to the right. In another .5 miles you'll pass under the powerlines again where a bunch of spur roads cluster…but you want to go right on an obvious (yet unsigned) fork that stays high on the ridge. In 2 more miles, as this road begins steeply down, you'll take a right fork upwards on the narrower double track that quickly dead-ends at the unsigned Phantom trailhead.

➡ **Drivetime from Bend: 2 hours**

PHANTOM BRIDGE is a natural rock arch span perched on a ridge a couple miles past Tumble Lake. For sure it's an interesting natural phenomenon, but it's a long drive to see just by itself. Thus, it's best plan an excursion to see both Tumble Lake and the arch together.

(**HIKE:**) From Phantom's road-end trailhead begin up the wide path (which soon narrows) for about 6 minutes, and as you enter the trees, look for an unsigned righthand path that heads upwards next to a big downed tree…the arch is just 50 feet up this path. Go ahead, be a daredevil…dare to walk the arch??!! For arch lovers, also see next entry.

View from Tumble Falls

Hike: various
- elevation river: 1,000 feet
- elevation arch: 3,300 feet
- elevation peak: 5,000 feet
- free
- vault toilets
- dogs: no rules

OBSCUROMETER

The Santiam River canyon near the long-gone town of Niagara hosts a cluster of neat excursions. The area gets little attention because it's run by both County Parks and the Santiam State Forest—neither as well-publicized or mapped as the bordering Nat'l Forest. Thus, you won't find these interesting "points of interest" on the Nat'l Forest maps.

Along the Santiam River you'll find the ruins of Niagara's late-1800s town site with some explorable ruins along the river. Driving up the gravel road adjacent to the riverside park you'll find an obscure trailhead to a largish rock arch, and then 2 miles beyond another trail to Rocky Top's, 5,000-foot former lookout site. It may not be worth a two-hour drive just to see this stuff, but if you're in the area or passing through, then these seldom-seen features are worth a look.

Niagara County Park. This small park is the site of a failed town/dam/mill site on the Santiam River at the Niagara narrows. The parking area has a sign detailing the fruitless efforts of the pioneers. A staircase leads down from the parking lot to the ruins of the dam and mill works, as well as the spot where the entire surging river squeezes through a narrow 5-foot channel—quite impressive! There's a big sunny swimming hole with SevenMile Falls cascading just across the Santiam. A better swimming hole is .3 miles upriver on the park's gravel road where an angled expanse of sun-warmed rock tilts into the chilly emerald waters.

Santiam Rock Arch.
The Santiam Rock Arch is an impressive span! A fin of rock juts out over steep Sardine Creek canyon and rock has fallen away on the underside to leave a fairly large archway. Scramblers can bushwhack to get on top of the arch where you'll find a nice sunny perch overlooking a wink of

Santiam Arch

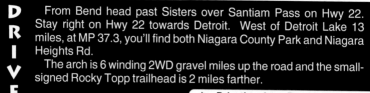

D
R
I
V
E

From Bend head past Sisters over Santiam Pass on Hwy 22. Stay right on Hwy 22 towards Detroit. West of Detroit Lake 13 miles, at MP 37.3, you'll find both Niagara County Park and Niagara Heights Rd.

The arch is 6 winding 2WD gravel miles up the road and the small-signed Rocky Topp trailhead is 2 miles farther.

→ **Drivetime from Bend: 2 hours**

Big Cliff reservoir as well as the gurgling sound of Sardine Falls down in the canyon. This arch is more impressive than Phantom Bridge (entry 73) but don't expect Delicate Arch or anything jaw-dropping. The arch is appealing to those who love geologic oddity.

To find the scramble up to arch's top, head back up the trail about 100 feet until you can't see the rocky wall any more and then just scramble up. Rock-climbing isn't necessary—head further uphill to find a safe walking route.

To get to the trailhead drive 6 miles up the gravel Niagara Heights Rd following signs at every intersection and park at the large Santiam Forest "Arch" sign. Walk downhill on the steep switch-backed path for .4 miles to the arch.

Rocky Top Lookout. A steep 0.8-mile trail heads 700 vertical feet up to Rocky Top's 5,014 foot knob. This former lookout site still has some lookout remnants—scout around to find a 1945 inscription. Rocky Top also boasts a view from Mt Adams to the Three Sisters with a neat view of Jefferson's NW side...as well as a west view over the hazy Willamette Valley and Coast Range. Look for Coffin Mtn (70) directly in front of 3-F Jack and Iron Mtn (67) down and right of South Sister.

The signed trailhead is another 2 miles up the road from the arch.

View from Rocky Top

Mt. Jefferson

Triangulation Peak

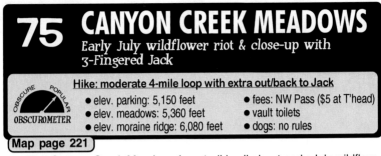

75 CANYON CREEK MEADOWS
Early July wildflower riot & close-up with 3-Fingered Jack

Hike: moderate 4-mile loop with extra out/back to Jack

OBSCUROMETER

- elev. parking: 5,150 feet
- elev. meadows: 5,360 feet
- elev. moraine ridge: 6,080 feet
- fees: NW Pass ($5 at T'head)
- vault toilets
- dogs: no rules

Map page 221

The Canyon Creek Meadows loop trail is all about early-July wildflowers and a superb up-close look at Three-Fingered Jack's glaciated maw. From Jack Lake a fairly easy trail winds through the remnant forest of 2003's horrendous B&B Burn before delivering you into Canyon Creek's sing-song meadows. These meadows, around July 4th, are arguably Central Oregon's finest wildflower showcase (Iron Mtn would argue loudest [67]). But it's not only flowers that color this trail. Their rainbowed array conspires with Three-Fingered Jack's spires to inspire some Wows (sorry about that). Approaching ole' 3-Fingered you'll see his magnificently striped innards highlighted by some glistening glaciers. The stratification of this Strato-volcano is plain to see when you venture off the main loop and head towards Jack's moraine meadows. FYI, for photographers pre-noon light is best on east-facing Jack.

For an easy outing, just hike the official Forest Service signed loop, but if you're up for some serious jaw-drop beauty, then you've got to follow the user-path a mile to Jack's moraine hill, then scramble up the rocky slope to the moraine rim where either a puddle of snow will await your eyes below, or in Aug/Sept probably an iceberg-pocked glacial lake. This moraine lake

Jack's craggy face

Meadows

D
R
I
V
E

Note: the last 6 miles to the trailhead are rough washboard, but 2WD OK.

From Sisters take Hwy 20 west for 11 miles. Near MP 89 turn right onto Jack Lake Rd (FS 12). Go 4.2 miles then left onto FS 1230. Go 1.6 miles, passing Jack Creek, then stay left onto gravel. In 1.0 miles stay left again onto FS 1234. Now bump-bump your way 5 miles to the lakeside trailhead.

➡ **Drivetime from Bend: 1 hour**

View south from Three-Fingered 's ridge

spills-over to form Canyon Creek. The gung-ho-ist of hikers will then continue to the top of the south ridge for views back down on the entire panorama—Jefferson to the north and a Sisters line-up to the south. Whew...it's way worth it!

Once you retreat back to the main loop you'll pass a small waterfall and a junction trail over to Wasco Lake (.7 miles) and beyond. At wildflower time Wasco will be too chilly to swim, but if you're hiking in August, then Wasco is nice for a dip.

Overall, the scenery on this loop is unforgettable no matter when you visit. It's places like this that makes an author try to dissuade you from hiking trails like Black Crater (51).

HIKE: The trail begins by skirting Jack Lake on the right. In .3 miles comes the loop junction. Head left 1.75 miles to the first meadow. The loop continues to the right, but the optional trail heads faintly left here, for a steep mile, to Jack's moraine lake. Retracing your steps back to the loop, go left one mile to the waterfall/ Wasco Lake junction. Make an optional .7-mile out 'n' back jaunt to the lake or head straight 1.5 miles back to the car.

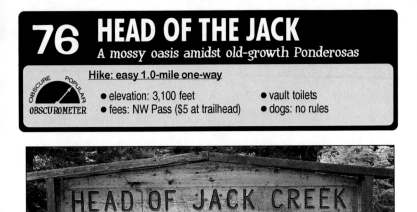

Hike: easy 1.0-mile one-way

OBSCURE POPULAR

OBSCUROMETER

- elevation: 3,100 feet
- fees: NW Pass ($5 at trailhead)
- vault toilets
- dogs: no rules

HEAD OF JACK CREEK

NORTHWEST FOREST PASS   PASSES   NO VEHICLES   YOUR PASS AT WORK

The Head of the Jack is the fun-sounding name of an area where a myriad of springs gurgle from a wooded hillside and accumulate into Jack Creek. Jack's Head is a long-time favorite amongst local campers because the campground is like a spacious Ponderosa park run-thru by an ice-cold creek. Campers often bring a milk crate to plop into the creek to chill all their camping "necessities"—Bud, Miller, Corona, Black Butte Porter etc etc. The creek is a mossy oasis rife with delicate wildflowers, somehow misplaced amidst the dry pine-needled park. Besides being just a nice forest creek, Jack Creek is super interesting to explore because, being a 100% spring-fed creek, it doesn't flood its channel every season to sweep away the fallen trees and limbs. Along Jack Creek the trees lay as they fall, apparently for a long, long time. The creekbed is laced with a lattice of downed trees and the trees have accumulated enough forest duff to create flowery/mossy

Jack Creek

From Sisters take Hwy 20 west for 12 miles. Near MP 89 turn right onto Jack Lake Rd (FS 12)(this is just east of Suttle Lake). Go 4 miles then left onto paved FS 1230. In .7 miles cross Jack Creek and turn left onto FS 1232. The campground is an immediate left or follow signage .5 miles to the far trailhead.

> ▶ **Drivetime from Bend:** 40 mins

islands of "land" in the middle of the creek—each with its own walk-the-plank tree-trunk bridge. Kids love playing hide 'n' seek chasing each other over the log bridges…and even if they fall off the creek's only 6-inches deep, so the adults don't have to supervise…they can sit around the fire and concentrate on the "necessities"!

Basically, you've gotta see Jack Creek to appreciate how unique it is. Some locals call it their favorite spot in all of Central Oregon! Bring the bikes, bring a Frisbee, bring a milk crate, and head to the historic Camp Sherman Store for necessities…then you'll be set for a great time at the Head of the Jack.

HIKE: There are two trailheads. You can drive a half-mile past the campground to park at the NW Pass ($5) trailhead for a shorter half-mile hike to the springs, but it's way better to park at the upriver end of the campground for free and hike a nice mile along the creek to the springs. That way, when you get back you'll be creekside in the campground, ready for a relax, rather than in the dull dusty trailhead parking lot.

From the campground the trail rambles an easy-as-pie 1.0 miles to the spring source where there's also a mini nature loop heading across a bridge.

A bridge over gurgled waters

The B & B Complex wildfire began on 8/19/03 and burned 91,915 acres—the largest fire in Deschutes Nat'l Forest history. It was attributed to lightning strikes that smoldered for ten days before weather conditions ripened for an inferno.

Hike: easy .25-mile stroll

OBSCURE — POPULAR
OBSCUROMETER

- elevation: 3,000 feet
- free
- vault toilets
- dogs: leash law

The famous Head of the Metolius is picture-perfect Central Oregon. A super-easy everyone-friendly paved path leads to a fenced view platform directly over the silently gushing stream. Tourist literature often touts an "instant river" or "springs gushing from the hillside"…but this isn't really the case. The springs do gush, but in a silent and low-key fashion…which sort of adds to their peculiarity. The flow is close to 50,000 gallons per minute, but you'd never guess from the tranquility. What makes the scene so arresting and fabled is the old-growth Ponderosas that line both the trail and the springs area…and then the perfectly framed view of Mt Jefferson rising over the meadows surrounding the springs.

Some people look around and puzzle, "where's all the water come from in such a dry place." Geologically the answer is fairly straightforward…but it's still hard to get your head around it. On the other side of Black Butte lies the Black Butte Ranch swamp, at 300 feet higher elevation. It seems that about a million years ago Black Butte sprouted up in the normal flow channel of the pre-Ice-Age Metolius. The stream backed-up into a lagoon and found it more expeditious to simply flow under Black Butte than around it. Voilà, instant river!

A family-friendly outing

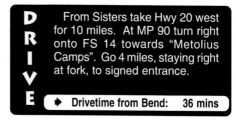

**D
R
I
V
E**

From Sisters take Hwy 20 west for 10 miles. At MP 90 turn right onto FS 14 towards "Metolius Camps". Go 4 miles, staying right at fork, to signed entrance.

➡ **Drivetime from Bend: 36 mins**

Mt. Jefferson

As seen in The Indian Fighter *movie (See Appendix 5)*

Stop by the Camp Sherman Store

CAMP SHERMAN

FLY FISHING ONLY

REPOR
FIRES H

Metolius charm, hatchery fun

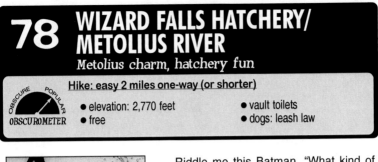

Hike: easy 2 miles one-way (or shorter)

OBSCURE · POPULAR

OBSCUROMETER

- elevation: 2,770 feet
- free

- vault toilets
- dogs: leash law

Riddle me this Batman, "What kind of wizard died to create a hatchery?" You'll find out the curious answer by spending a relaxing hour at this historic fish hatchery. After crossing the bridge over the Metolius—with the obligatory mid-bridge stop when your jaw drops at the sight of the Metolius' oh-my-god bluuuuue—you'll park and begin by strolling the hatchery's manicured grounds. There's an informative kiosk that details the hatchery's historic beginnings (with the story of the wizard). There's a huge variety of trees throughout the grounds, each with a helpful label identifying the different kinds. Then you'll come to the typical ponds full of fingerlings…and this is where the fun starts. There are machines that dispense fish food for 25 cents a handful—be sure to bring lots of quarters. It's fun to stir-up a feeding frenzy by chucking the whole handful in at once! Past the fingerling ponds is a large pond packed with full-sized lunkers. These lunkers have escaped from the rearing ponds and have grown to massive size in the protective pond, all with the help of the nearby fish-food machines and generous visitors. A little-known secret is that some resident Bald eagles have lived around the hatchery for years—look around on the tree tops near the lunker pond and you may see one or more.

From the hatchery riverside trails head both upstream and down along the crystalline Metolius. Thus, you can learn about the fish, feed the fish…then take a soothing riverside walk along the incomparable Metolius.

Ooh-la-la Blue!

Metolius Bridge

D
R
I
V
E

From Sisters take Hwy 20 west for 10 miles. Just past MP 91 turn right onto FS 14, signed to Camp Sherman. In 3 miles veer right, then go 7 miles more to the signed left turn to the hatchery (passing the "Head" after 1.0 miles).

➤ **Drivetime from Bend: 45 mins**

Family feeding frenzy

HIKE: The Metolius River Trail goes for miles along the river, but an especially great 2.5-mile section heads upstream from the hatchery along the west bank. This section is the locals' favorite because it stays near the river with no private property, detours, roads, nor campgrounds—just goliath orange Ponderosas and unfettered Metolius charm! This 2.5-mile stretch ends at Canyon Creek Campground, but a good turnaround point is at the two-mile mark where an 80-foot-long spring gushes gorgeously into the deep blue river! After the hike, make sure you walk out onto the Wizard bridge to get another good eyeful of the bluuuuue before you leave. This aquamarine river trench is the pro photographer's favorite spot on the Metolius' short (30 mile) run to Lake Billy Chinook.

Bring Quarters!!

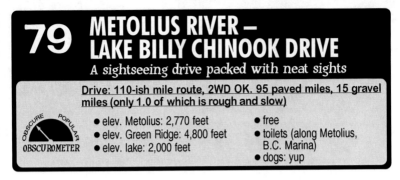

79 METOLIUS RIVER – LAKE BILLY CHINOOK DRIVE

A sightseeing drive packed with neat sights

Drive: 110-ish mile route, 2WD OK. 95 paved miles, 15 gravel
miles (only 1.0 of which is rough and slow)

OBSCUROMETER

- elev. Metolius: 2,770 feet
- elev. Green Ridge: 4,800 feet
- elev. lake: 2,000 feet
- free
- toilets (along Metolius, B.C. Marina)
- dogs: yup

This is a fascinating loop driving route encompassing Sisters, the Metolius River, and Green Ridge and its lookout... all before winding thru the juniper/ sagebrush plains to Lake Billy Chinook and Cove Palisades State Park...then completing the loop via Hwy 97.

The most obvious highlight of the route is the startling transition from the vivid greenery and Ponderosa forest of the Metolius River to the stark juniper/ sagebrush plains and basalt cliffs of Cove Palisades. Along the way there are a heaping handful of interesting stopping points—the Head of the Metolius, Camp Sherman Store,

Green Ridge Lookout

Wizard Falls Hatchery...up Green Ridge to see the lookout's grand vista...then down to Billy Chinook's Balanced Rocks and Deschutes Formation strata, the Crooked River Petroglyph, the Cove's Palisades, and finally the basalt-hemmed bridges across both Deschutes and Crooked River arms of Lake Billy Chinook. Finishing the drive you'll ascend out of Cove Palisades to take Hwy 97 back to Bend.

This is a brilliant drive in the spring when the temps are cooler and the high country is yet to open up. Any 2WD car can make this route—there's only one bumpy mile in the 15 miles of gravel.

Balanced Rocks

THE DRIVE: 2-4 hours

You should have a decent map to do this rive, or at least good detailed printouts from Google Maps. A Gazetteer will work, but the Sisters Ranger District map is better. You can do the drive either direction, but the route listed here goes clockwise with the Metolius first.

Descending to Lake Billy Chinook

From Bend head to Sisters on Hwy 20. Pass thru Sisters and in 9 miles turn right at signs for the Metolius. Go 4 miles (staying right) to the first stop, Head of the Metolius (entry 77). Pass the Head by 2 miles and swing left to visit the historic Camp Sherman Store and stock-up on food and drinks (and to see how the Metolius has changed in just 2 miles!) Continue north for 4.2 more miles to the turn for Wizard Falls Hatchery and its wonder-bridge (entry 78).

From Wizard Falls Hatchery head 2.2 miles north and just past Pioneer Ford turn onto FS 1490. Climb this gravel road 6 miles (the 1.5 miles in the middle are ROUGH and SLOW, but 2WD passable). Level out and arrive at the FS 1140 junction signed "Billy Chin.15 miles".

For a side-trip here to see the ridgetop Green Point lookout, go right on FS 1140 for 1.5 miles, stay right then right again on FS 600 for another mile to the lookout's green gate at FS 650 (if it's open you can drive in, otherwise make the short walk.)

Now, back at the 1490/1140 junction stay on 1140 to the right to Billy Chin. In the next 9.5 miles there are two junctions and the road becomes FS 1170, but stay straight all the way until a T-intersection with FS 64. At this junction turn left for only 100 yards to find the Balanced Rocks roadside pull-off (entry 87). Turn back from the Balanced Rocks, re-gain pavement and head 12 miles to the bridge over the Deschutes arm of the lake. From the bridge it's a couple

Crooked River Petroglyph

miles to the little right-side parking area to see the Crooked River petroglyph with the good view of the Palisades towering overhead. Cross over the Crooked River, turn up at the marina and ascend to the rim. For another good side trip head left on the rim drive. There are 3-4 viewpoint parking areas the first 3 miles and if you go 5 miles you'll get to the Dam overlook and its interesting VisCtr building with a view up the Metolius arm – worth a look! From the rim drive head back south and zigzag 5 miles thru Culver to Hwy 97 for the 35-miles back to Bend.

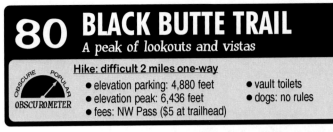

Hike: difficult 2 miles one-way

OBSCURE — POPULAR
OBSCUROMETER

- elevation parking: 4,880 feet
- elevation peak: 6,436 feet
- fees: NW Pass ($5 at trailhead)
- vault toilets
- dogs: no rules

A lone, proud sentinel standing aloof to the east of his High Cascade relatives, wise old Black Butte was often mistaken by pioneer geologists for a young cinder cone because of its conical symmetry. But no—paleomagnetic dating surprised scientists by revealing a million-year-old composite volcano! Black Butte, feet planted in the bed of the ancient Metolius River, watched all the surrounding peaks arise as perfect volcanic cones like his own, only to be ravaged by Ice-Age glaciers into their current craggy forms. Not Black Butte—he stands in the rain shadow of the Cascade peaks, never himself suffering an Ice-Age glacier. Surprised he is though, when looking

down he sees that the Metolius River has found its way underneath him, reappearing as a gushing spring on his northern flank.

It's hard to find a better place to appreciate Central Oregon geography than atop 6,436- foot Black Butte. The 2-mile trail is fairly steep and sustained (gaining 1,600 feet), but the summit rewards are worth every high-altitude gasp! You'll see peaks from Broken Top to WA's Mt. Adams. You'll look up to see the staffed lookout tower (built 1995), across the summit you'll find the antique1924 Cupola lookout cabin, and along the way some debris from the 84-foot 1934 tower (collapsed in a winter storm, Dec. 2001). Make sure to bring a map and binoculars. Look for Suttle Lake and Hoodoo Ski Area. How 'bout Smith's Monkey Face/Burma Rd or far to the SE, atop the lumpy Newberry Caldera rim, Paulina Peak. Straight down to the north look for the Head of the Metolius and its distinctive meadow. Then, over on the south side, look down to Black Butte Ranch where the Metolius' waters originate in the swamp. Plan for about an hour at the top—it's that good!

D R I V E

From Sisters take Hwy 20 west for 5.4 miles. Turn right onto FS 11—Indian Ford Camp. Go 3.7 miles then turn left onto gravel FS 1110 and follow it 5 winding miles to the road-end trailhead.

◆ Drivetime from Bend: 45 mins

Cupola lookout

Jefferson

Harley

HIKE: Straightforward 2-mile climb with no options. Just 30 steps into the trail look up through the trees to see the lookout tower on the summit.

Author's favorite

WHATEVER WHATEVER WHATEVER WHATEVER WHATEVER WHATEVER WHATEVER WHATEVER WHATEVER WHATEVER

Paleomagnetic Dating: Molten rocks often contain iron-oxide indicators which align to the earth's magnetic field at the time of their solidification. The earth last reversed its polarity 780,000 years ago—from pointing south to pointing north. Black Butte's oxides surprisingly point south, indicating its ancient age. All oxides in the other High Cascade peaks point north!

WHATEVER WHATEVER WHATEVER WHATEVER WHATEVER WHATEVER WHATEVER WHATEVER WHATEVER WHATEVER

OBSCURE POPULAR
OBSCUROMETER

- Open: 9-5pm, 365 days
- fees: $3 donation suggested
- flush toilets
- dogs: leash only

Petersen Rock Garden is a quirky testament to one man's passion for Central Oregon's rocks. Rasmus Petersen collected and sculpted his backyard into 4-acre wonderland throughout the 1930's and 40's, just for the hell of it. Word got out though about this local oddity and people wanted to come see....and soon ole' Rasmus'

hobby and pastime unwittingly became an international tourist destination! It garnered plenty of media acclaim back in the day for its dazzling castles of obsidian, bridges of petrified wood, and walkways of wonderstone—all intertwined with ponds and canals full of lily pads and bullfrogs. The garden harkens back to the day when roadside tourist attractions were all the rage in the post-WWII boom times. But, whereas many of the so-called "tourist attractions" were long on the hucksterism and short on the "wow", people have come to Petersen's for ages to ponder the unbelievable individual effort it must have taken to create this wonderland of rocky oddity.

Nowadays, 60-70 years later, the place is still exactly the same, and definitely one-of-a-kind! Peacocks in full plumage and odd-colored roosters strut amongst a carved Statue of Liberty and an American Flag mosaic. The sampling of melted-lava tree molds is rare—you'll never see a better collection than these! Inside the museum you'll find all sorts of bizarre rocks on display, and maybe the 2nd best display of unique cut and polished Thunder Eggs anywhere in the world (outside of Richardson's [90]).

Lilies, ladies, and Liberty

D R I V E

From Bend take Hwy 97 north 6.3 miles. At Petersen signs turn left onto Gift Rd then immediately right. Go 1.0 miles then left onto Young Rd. Go straight 1.0 miles, crossing the intersection, then right onto 77th St for .5 miles to the signed entrance.

◆ **Drivetime from Bend: 11 mins**

Come for a visit when you're not in a hurry – a grey day is perfect. The only person who won't like a visit to Petersen's is the rare person born without a funny bone…or maybe someone who's had their curiosity surgically removed. Petersen's isn't a schlocky "tourist attraction"… it's more of a history reminder of a time before boomtown recreational-mecca Central Oregon. A reminder of when all the mill-town families wanted to relax on their days off, not get a sweaty "workout" like we do now—their job was their workout! Petersen's came before Mt Bachelor and a Cascade Lakes Highway. Before A Newberry Natl Monument and Lavalands Visitor Center. Before a Smith Rock State Park. Before a legion of destination resorts. Before land-use planning and Urban Growth Boundaries. Even before the last two states were admitted to our Union!! Get it?? Petersen's is old and cool, despite being surpassed by the hoopla derby. Come see.

Count the stars!

Peacock

WHATEVER WHATEVER WHATEVER WHATEVER WHATEVER WHATEVER WHATEVER WHATEVER WHATEVER WHATEVER

Count the stars on the flag mosaic. Alaska was admitted in 1958, Hawaii in 1959. Remember "Hawaii 5-0"? The "5-0" represents the 50th state. "Book 'em, Danno!"

WHATEVER WHATEVER WHATEVER WHATEVER WHATEVER WHATEVER WHATEVER WHATEVER WHATEVER WHATEVER

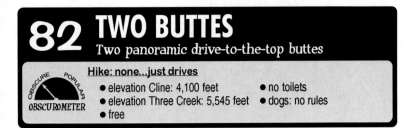

82 TWO BUTTES
Two panoramic drive-to-the-top buttes

Hike: none...just drives

OBSCUROMETER

- elevation Cline: 4,100 feet
- elevation Three Creek: 5,545 feet
- free
- no toilets
- dogs: no rules

Cline Buttes:

The Cline Buttes, rising immediately west of Redmond, provide the perfect panorama-postcard view of the entire Three Sisters country as well as everything east between Madras and Newberry Caldera. Surprisingly, few people outside of old-timers and Redmondites know that you can make an easy drive to the top for the epic vista. It's totally worth it! The Cascade volcanoes line up for a sweeping row-call from Bachelor to Mt Adams. The only photographic dilemma you'll face will be choosing which gnarled Juniper to use for your foreground framing...but you can spend a happy hour up here figuring it all out.

Sadly, the Cline Buttes seem to host a weekly low-IQ contest—whoever can trample the most virgin soil and old-growth juniper with their ATV while strewing beer cans and shooting shotguns WINS!! No brains req'd for entry, just a hell-bent disregard for the land. Mornings are nice and quiet and photogenic atop Cline...happy hour is sad once the ATVs roar.

Things to spot: Three Creek Butte pokes up in the area between Broken Top and South Sister. Just above Bend's Aubrey Butte you'll see the top of Lava Butte. Newberry's Paulina Peak is situated directly over Pilot Butte.

DRIVE: In Redmond take Hwy 126 west towards Sisters for 4 miles. Cross the Deschutes and turn right and up onto the Cline Falls Hwy towards Eagle Crest. Drive south 4.0 miles and just past MP 4 turn right onto a gravel road heading thru an open gate over a half-cattle guard (#67555).

(To get here via Bend's "back" way, head towards Sisters and after crossing the Deschutes River take the first right—Cook Ave—which becomes the Cline Falls Hwy. Go 6.4 miles [there are no mileposts heading north] with

Cline Butte view

Three Creek Butte

the Buttes rising ahead and when you get near the Buttes [past the ranches] slow down and look for the cattle-guard entrance.)

Once over the cattle guard stay immediately right and ascend this 2WD gravel road 2.5 miles. The peak itself is gated and fenced, so you'll have to turn around just before the peak. There is a 4WD spur just before the gate that gives you the supreme view, as well as leading over to the east side where you can look down past all the thoughtless rubbish to Redmond/Smith/Ochocos.

(Hey wait…just prior to this publication [5/2010], it seems that the Prineville BLM has cleaned up the extensive rubbish at the Redmond overlook and installed some new no-ATV signs. Thanks BLM!!)

Three Creek Butte:

Three Creek Butte is the highest spot anywhere north of Tam MacArthur Rim that you can drive to. At 5,545 feet it's higher than both McKenzie (5,324) and Santiam (4,711) passes. Thus, this little-known former lookout site is actually the highest spot you can easily drive to between Tam MacArthur and Mt Hood's Timberline Resort.

Three Creek view

The epic views extend from the jagged crown of Broken Top all the way to Mt Hood… with the Three Sisters front and center. Looking east you see from Madras south to Lava Butte. Look towards Bend and you may make out the trio of smokestacks of the REI Old Mill building. Far to the east, past Prineville you'll see the curved hump of Lookout Mtn (94) with the triangle point of the Ochoco's Pilot Butte to its right.

The top of this butte is a fantastic place to spend a night car-camping. There a perfectly flat 7' by 7' cement pad from the old lookout that just fits a tent. The Cascades sunset will undoubtedly dazzle, but the real zing is seeing the entire Central Oregon plain sparkle with lights from Madras to Bend. Come dawn you've then got the Three Sisters framed out your tent flap…really nice!

DRIVE: Check the blog to see where the butte is located. **Don't attempt to drive here without a map and a 4WD vehicle.** The roads in the area are poorly-marked at best, and at worst a total confusing nightmare if you get on the wrong one or turned around. Get a Sisters Ranger District map from either a FS office or at "Bend Map and Blueprint" before attempting the drive up Three Creek Butte.

Here are some tips to use with a map: Head up FS 17 from Sisters and at MP 13.5 turn left onto FS 1628 for 1.7 miles. Turn right onto FS 600 for .5 miles then left onto FS 620 for a rough .4 miles then left again for a short distance until a distinct 4-way intersection. Go right here and ascend a 4WD rocky .7 miles to the top.

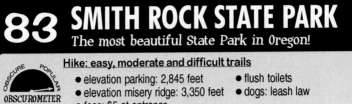

Hike: easy, moderate and difficult trails

OBSCURE ● POPULAR
OBSCUROMETER

- elevation parking: 2,845 feet
- elevation misery ridge: 3,350 feet
- fees: $5 at entrance
- flush toilets
- dogs: leash law

Smith Rock State Park features an epic panorama of unexpected beauty—colorful 700-foot walls rising directly above the meandering Crooked River. Millions of people pass by the road signs every year on Hwy 97, not knowing that someplace truly exceptional lurks just over the ridge just past the dull-sounding park name. A better name might have been "Odin's Lair" or "Eye-candy Cliffs State Park"...but oh well, Smith Rock it is. This park has a greater world-wide recognition than anywhere else in Central Oregon due to its rock-climbing credentials. The park once hosted the world's toughest rock-climb and now still proves a testing ground for the world's elite climbers...right here in our own back yard.

But the park isn't just for climbers—it has something for everyone, and nobody can gaze upon Smith's dazzling orange/yellow skyscraping cliffs in sparkling morning light without feeling a sense of awe. Nature's majesty is writ LARGE at Smith....so pack up a lunch, pack the hiking boots, and pack plenty of mega-pixels for your visit.

Whether you're a sight-seeing picnicker, a rock climber, a hiker, a Mtn-biker, a photographer, a bird-watcher, or an equestrian... there's something spectacular to do at Smith Rock.

A mapboard at the park's entrance/parking area details all the trails that are open for hiking, biking, and horses. If you plan to rock climb, Mtn Bike, or ride a horse...it'd be best to consult a sport-specific guidebook for much better details that the park's signs can provide.

Hiking: There are easy photogenic trails on the bluff or down along the Crooked River. The one standout hiking destination that's a must-see is Monkey Face. Monkey Face is a

Climbers on Morning Glory

D
R
I
V
E

From Bend take Hwy 97 north for 21 miles past Redmond. About 3.5 miles north of Redmond you come to Terrebonne. At the yellow traffic light turn right onto B Ave. Go .5 miles then left onto First St at a sign for Smith Rock. Go 2 miles more and look for the small entrance sign marking the left turn into the park.

➡ **Drivetime from Bend: 26 mins**

detached 350-foot pillar capped by the incredible likeness of a monkey's face. This is no squint-and-hope-you-see-it type of likeness...this is like the Planet of the Apes guy got frozen into stone! The premier way to see Monkey Face and the entire scope of Smith's wondrous rocks is to hike the Misery Ridge/Monkey Face/ River loop, but if you're not up for a hillside named Misery, then you can simply walk around the flat river trail for an out and back to see the Face.

Asterisk Pass

Mt. Jefferson

Misery/Monkey/River Trail: **This trail is definitely one of the most scenic hikes in Oregon!** It's a 4-mile Mod/Diff loop from the parking lot. This trail features the grandeur of Smith's Rocks, cliff-top views of <u>All</u> the Cascades, a look into the Monkey's mouth from above, then a steep descent past the Monkey's base to the river trail where you'll then make the easy loop along the river and past all the rock-climbing areas.

From the rim head down and across the footbridge. Go straight to begin the .75 mile "most difficult" climb to Misery Ridge. Once atop, head right. At the first glimpse of the Monkey's head the trail turns right for a steep .5-mile descent. At the Monkey's base go sharply right down to the riverside trail. Now head left for an easy 2-mile cruise back to the footbridge.

Burma Rd/Monkey Face loop trail: This is a locals' favorite hike because it's a bit longer and tougher, and it also avoids the majority of the crowded/

Monkey Face

touristy parts of the park. Alas, it's also difficult to succinctly describe. Check the blog for Google maps and a good description.

Camping: There is walk-in tent camping right at the park, but for car/RV camping you'll need to find BLM's Skull Hollow campground about a 10-minute drive around the "backside" from the park (leave park and go left for 2 miles. Left for .7, then left again onto Lone Pine Rd for 4 miles).

84 GRAY BUTTE LOOP TRAIL
An unconventional loop to a remarkable view

Hike: difficult 4.5-mile loop scramble

OBSCUROMETER

- elevation trailhead: 3,700 feet
- elevation peak: 5,100 feet
- free
- no toilets (at Skull Hollow)
- dogs: no rules

Road access open only 4/1-9/28

Here's a never-before-published hiking loop that's sure to please eager (and gung-ho) springtime hikers who are a bit tired of Smith Rock and the usual array of springtime-availability trails. (On the other hand, if you've yet to exhaust Smith Rock, don't bother with this one yet...of course Smith's trails rock!)

This is more of a "route" than a trail, since it takes an unconventional approach to bagging Gray Butte's peak and then making a loop out of the affair. To make this happen you plod up Gray Butte's cell-tower service road to the peak then plummet down the west side on the bootleg ATV track before picking up the "Gray Butte Trail" which contours you around the south side of the Butte back to your starting point.

Here's the main reason to do this unorthodox loop – the peak of Gray Butte is kick-ass!! It rises to 5,108 feet and can be seen from most anywhere in north-Central Oregon. What this means is that, on a clear spring day, you'll be able to see EVERYWHERE from Gray Butte's peak. No joke...the Ochocos east, the entirety of the Cascades to the West, Smith Rock looking itty-bitty below, Prineville, Madras, Bend out yonder, etc etc. Sharp eyes may spot the COI irrigation canal and even the canyon of the Metolius. A truly superb springtime vista point! Henceforth, every time you'll spy Gray Butte from other Cascades vantages, you'll say, "Yup, done that".

HIKE: **Note: If the road up to the upper Cole trailhead is closed (Oct-March), you could still walk up the Cole trail from near the cattle guard, but it adds 2 miles each way.**

From the upper parking start up the Gray Butte service road from where the Cole trail crosses—this will be the end of the loop also. Go around the gate then a steady steep 2 miles to the peak's cell towers, the view improving every step. Topping out at the towers, look down to spot the rough track that descends down angling left. After lunch and a long look-round, head north over the top onto the rocky ATV-type track as it starts its rough .5-mile plunge downwards—it's super steep, sure, but neither too loose nor too bad. As the slope eases you'll come under a powerline, and conveniently, this is where the single-track Gray Butte trail crosses. Go left on the trail for an easy mile, through a gate, then a mile more back to the car.

In Terrebonne on Hwy 97 turn east onto Smith Rock Way at the flashing light. Follow it for 4.8 miles (don't turn towards Smith Rock itself). At Lone Pine Rd turn left and go 4 miles to the signed left turn for Skull Hollow/ Gray Butte Trailhead. Turning left onto the gravel you'll see the popular (with rock climbers) campground on the left. Keep straight for 1.1 miles then turn left over the cattle guard onto unsigned FS 5720. Head up this steep road 1.6 miles, go through the wire gate, up the hill and right 200 yards until you see a little "Cole trail" sign. Park near the Cole sign anywhere off the road.

◆ **Drivetime from Bend: 40 mins**

Gray Butte as seen from Grizzly Mountain's 4-mile 2WD access road

Mt Washington

McKenzie Pass

Three Sisters

Park

Skull Hollow

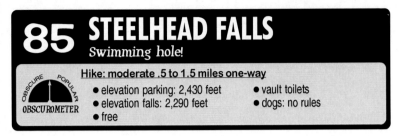

85 STEELHEAD FALLS
Swimming hole!

Hike: moderate .5 to 1.5 miles one-way

OBSCUROMETER

- elevation parking: 2,430 feet
- elevation falls: 2,290 feet
- free
- vault toilets
- dogs: no rules

The mighty Deschutes River is 252 miles long from its headwaters near Mt Bachelor to its confluence with the Columbia River in the Gorge. This is the best swimming hole on the entire river!!!!!!!!!

Steelhead Falls is a 15-ish foot drop along the river and below the falls is a huge, deep, placid swimming hole. Hot August day perfection!! Better yet are the 15-25 foot rocks that line the trailside bank, making the perfect springboard for the young and young-at-heart. Where else can you huck into the ever-chilly Deschutes? Nowhere!

Deschutes Formation

JUMP!

D
R
I
V
E

Complex directions, but it only takes about 15 minutes from Terrebonne. From Bend take Hwy 97 north 22 miles to Terrebonne. Pass small Terrebonne and a half-mile to the north turn left onto Lower Bridge Rd (signed Crooked River Ranch). In 2 miles turn right onto NW 43rd then 1.8 miles to a T. Go left on Chinook Rd for 1.0 miles then left into Badger Rd. Follow Badger for 1.6 miles to its end at Quail Rd. Turn right for 1.0 miles then left onto River Rd for the final gravel mile descending to the trailhead.

➤ **Drivetime from Bend: 40 mins**

To sweeten the scene at the falls you've got towering striped canyon walls where the river has eroded its way down through the **Deschutes Formation (see entry 86).**

The trail to the falls is a steepish half-mile, and you can explore downstream at least a mile farther via a fishermen's trail along the bank. Go on a 100° day to jump, play, sun, and swig with the locals, or go anytime else year-round for remarkable scenery and solitude.

Whitey
Hucks it!

WHATEVER WHATEVER WHATEVER WHATEVER WHATEVER WHATEVER WHATEVER WHATEVER WHATEVER WHATEVER

The masonry walls left of the falls are the remains of a 1922 fish ladder built to help the fish in low flow years. Round Butte Damn, built around 1964, wiped out virtually all the namesake Steelhead—but sharp eyes may still see a jumper in the fall.

WHATEVER WHATEVER WHATEVER WHATEVER WHATEVER WHATEVER WHATEVER WHATEVER WHATEVER WHATEVER

86 ALDER SPRINGS TRAIL
A High Desert Shangri-la

Hike: moderate 1.5-mile or 3-mile one-way

OBSCURE — POPULAR
OBSCUROMETER

- elevation parking: 2,600 feet
- elevation springs: 2,240 feet
- elevation confluence: 2,100 feet
- **CLOSED 12/1 thru 4/1**

- free
- no toilets
- dogs: no rules

Closed 12/1 – 4/1...and <u>bring flip-flops</u> for creek crossings.

On the Alder Springs trail you'll descend from a dry juniper 'n' sagebrush plateau down into the much-lusher canyon of Whychus Creek. This hike's destination, Alder Springs, is a canyon-bottom mini-meadow where numerous ice-cold springs gurgle to life for a quick 100-yard journey to the Whychus. This trail's dull moniker, "Alder Springs Trail" hardly captures the essence of the scene down here. Since the Whychus has been re-named from its former "Squaw"... maybe a better name for this trail would be "Oasis on the Whychus".

Deschutes Formation

The Whychus Crossing

On the other hand, why do that? Few people other than in-the-know Sisters-ites (Sisterns?) come to visit, leaving the parking area wonderfully lonely most of the time.

Rainbow Rock presiding over the Confluence

To add to the charm of the canyon-bottom surroundings, on the way down you'll be descending through the stratified layers of "The Deschutes Formation." The canyon walls here look like a micro Grand Canyon—super neat! The Deschutes Formation is a 7-million year-old layering of volcanic ash and debris flows interbedded with river sediments – the same colored banding that make up Billy Chinook's more-famed palisades (entry 87).

Once down to Whychus Creek the trail demands that you de-shoe for a foot-deep slosh though the 12-foot-wide Whychus Creek to reach the spring-laden Ponderosa-studded meadow.

D
R
I
V
E

Directions To Alder springs are somewhat complex. From Bend take Hwy 20 west towards Sisters for 10.5 miles. At MP 8 turn right onto Fryrear Rd. Go 5.5 miles to the intersection with Hwy 126/ Holmes Rd. Cross Hwy126 onto Holmes Rd and follow it to MP 7. <u>Exactly</u> at MP 7 turn left onto gravel FS 6360. In 150 yards go straight past the Alder Springs signboard, then 4 bumpy miles (watch odometer) to the Alder Springs sign. Turn right for .7 miles of rough road to trailhead.

From Sisters take Hwy126 east 5 miles then turn onto Holmes Rd. **From Redmond** take Hwy126 west 13 miles to Holmes Rd.

➡ **Drivetime from Bend: 40 mins**

Trail's end Joy

The ice-cold springs are perfect for chilling drinks, so be sure to bring some cans (and maybe bring a bag to carry out a bit of litter from the less-considerate.)

The meadow is the end of the official 1.5-mile BLM trail...but not the end for you. An unofficial, but well-traveled, path keeps heading downstream for another 1.5 miles to the confluence of Whychus Creek and the Deschutes River. The confluence is spectacular! A jutting prow of colorfully layered rock—oft-called Rainbow Rock—presides over the meeting of the rivers while a massive stand of Ponderosas scent the air. If there's such place as a High Desert Shangri-la, then this is it! If you've made the journey down to this confluence on a hot sunny day, then Mother Nature demands you strip off your sweaty clothes for a dip in her co-mingled rivers. To urge you on she's provided perfect river-smoothed boulders under the Ponderosas to serve as drying racks for warmed buns. Yummy!

HIKE: The trail begins and quickly passes the Old Bridge junction (only a so-so side excursion). Keep straight along the rim and begin dropping a mile into Whychus Canyon. As the descent steepens listen and notice Alder Springs on your left while the bizarre hoodoo pillars stand guard up and right (they're pretty neat to explore!). The trail then bonks into Whychus Creek where you'll break out the flip-flops to cross creek to the meadow.

The path downstream stays on the left bank for the 1.5-miles to the confluence. Once there strip, dip, bask, smile laugh, kiss...and then head back the way you came.

Ridge Hoodoos

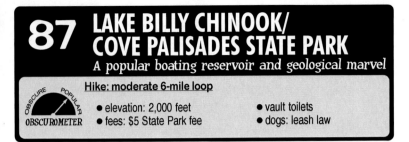

87 LAKE BILLY CHINOOK/ COVE PALISADES STATE PARK

A popular boating reservoir and geological marvel

Hike: moderate 6-mile loop

OBSCUROMETER

- elevation: 2,000 feet
- fees: $5 State Park fee
- vault toilets
- dogs: leash law

Lake Billy Chinook is a man-made oasis in the desert, a reservoir created by the 1964 Round Butte dam stifling the flows of three rivers—the Deschutes, the Crooked, and the Metolius. Everyone wonders "Who's Billy?" Turns out he was a celebrated Indian guide on John Fremont's 1843 Oregon expedition.

Rim Drive Viewpoint

For the most part Lake Billy Chinook/Cove Palisades is now a summertime redneck heaven where speed boats, fishing boats, house boats, jet skis, and wave runners all highlight the drinkin', campin', and fishin'. No MENSA convention has ever been scheduled at Billy Chinook in the summertime, and if you know what MENSA is, then you might want to avoid this place in the summer too!

OK, but now let's say it's the off-season and most of the boobs, boats, and bikinis are at home watching the fishing channel...is Billy Chinook worth a look??

YES, emphatically yes! The rampant geology of the three river canyons is stunning! The reservoir's sheer basalt walls showcase a smorgasbord of columnar designs while the namesake "palisades" dis-

LAKE BILLY CHINOOK

The reservoir behind Round Butte Dam was named Lake Billy Chinook by the Warm Springs Confederated Tribes as a tribute to the tribesman who served as guide and scout to Captain John C. Fremont on his exploration of the Oregon country in 1843.

play the layer-cake sediments of the Deschutes Formation. A leisurely drive will yield plenty of oohs and ahhhs for geology lovers.

Along the drive, on the "pass" between the Crooked and Deschutes River arms, you'll find the **Crooked River Petroglyph**—one of the most distinctive local Indian rock carvings ever found. As you'll see from the 9-second trail, the petroglyph has some serious *Gangatbama Idwacha*!

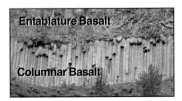
Entablature Basalt
Columnar Basalt

Next up on the excursion list is a hike on the **Tam-A-Lau** trail. This trail makes a 6-mile semi-loop (600 feet

D
R
I
V
E

Take Hwy 97 north towards Madras. After Terrebonne you'll cross the Crooked River bridge and go up and over Juniper Hill. On the down slope, at MP 106 turn left at signs for Cove Palisades. Go 5 miles of signed zigzags to enter the park.

Just before dropping into the Billy Chinook's canyon you can take a right onto the rim drive to some viewpoints and 5 miles to the interesting Round Butte Dam overlook/VisCtr, which sports a view up the Metolius arm.

➤ **Drivetime from Bend: 45 mins**

vertical) up to the plateau top then around and down. You'll get great views of the Island, the Cascades, and the Deschutes Formation. A trailhead mapboard describes how much of the surrounding lava flowed into the Crooked's canyon after the three river canyons already existed...and this new bunch of flows actually formed the Island and flowed upstream into both the Deschutes and the Metolius arms. This trail is better and more interesting than you'd think—try it!

Farther west, up the Metolius Arm towards Perry South camp, are the "famed" but generally little-known **Balanced Rocks**. The rocks appear on the cover of Steve Lent's *Central*

Hey, this one fell! ➤

Balanced Rocks

Oregon Place names Vol II. , as well as being featured in a *Homeward Bound* movie scene (see Appendix 5). Anybody who likes either rocks or Central OR oddities <u>needs</u> to see them. Remarkably, and sadly, one of

Petroglyph

the best rocks lost its balance between *Bend Overall*'s two editions (see blog for pix).

To find the Balanced Rocks drive 12 miles past the Deschutes Crossing bridge. At 10 miles you'll drop into Fly Canyon...and as you rise out of it the road turns to gravel at FS 1170. Just past FS 1170 pull off onto the righthand unsigned viewpoint/ trailhead... and then walk just a minute to overlook these wonders. If the road begins down towards the Metolius Arm, you've gone too far.

HIKE: The Tam-a-Lau trailhead is 4 miles from the Marina, at the Upper Deschutes Day Use entrance. Park in "Small Car" parking and walk

up the road, or park at the far end to walk further. The trail is a semi-loop. It's a steep one-mile to the top then a flat 4-mile tour around the plateau with excellent views all around. A trailhead sign details the route.

The Tam-a-lau Trail
Total Trail Length: 6 miles
Distance to Top of Rim: 1 mile
Total Elevation Gain: 600 ft.
PLEASE STAY ON TRAIL

88 RIMROCK SPRINGS TRAIL
A High Desert wildlife oasis

<u>Hike: easy 1.5-mile loop</u>

OBSCURE POPULAR
OBSCUROMETER

- elevation: 3,100 feet
- free
- vault toilets
- dogs: no rules

"Oh give me a home where the buffalo roam, and…"

Grab your binoculars and prepare to sing along as you stroll through this mellow chock-full'o'wildlife High Desert wetland oasis. An easy 1.5-mile loop trail begins with a half-mile paved wheelchair/stroller section leading to the first viewing platform down over the extensive marsh. Ducks quack, hawks soar, beavers slap, birds chirp…and the deer and antelope play. Seldom is heard a discouraging word from the birdwatchers who flock to Rimrock Springs. Past the first viewpoint the trail becomes dirt, but still very easy-going. It quickly leads to the second view-platform where curious folk can search around to find a cluster of beaver-felled junipers and some gnawed-into yet still standing rarities. To find the beaver's work take a faint path down and right about 100 yards. This may be one of the few places in the High Desert where ducks and beavers actually get along with each other!

Backtracking from the second viewpoint, the trail then slopes up to the area's highpoint on the rim. When the skies are not cloudy all day, the vista sweeps from Mt Bachelor to Mt Hood. Unlike the dramatic scenery of Smith Rock, this place is low-key, non-dramatic… and rarely has any visitors. This is a place for a quiet, reflective stroll where you can keep your eyes peeled fer some critters.

*Paved path to
first viewpoint*

D
R
I
V
E

Rimrock Springs are located on Hwy 26 between Madras and Prineville. The area is easily missed an often not signed at all. From Madras go south on Hwy 97 and quickly turn left onto Hwy 26. Go 9 miles, and at a rise in the landscape (with a hump on the left), slow down to make a left turn into the oft-unsigned parking lot.

From Terrebonne or Smith Rock check directions in entry 83 to Skull Hollow camp. Pass the camp until the next junction and then go left on Hwy 26 for 4.5 miles to the entrance on the right (just over the top of the hill).

➡ **Drivetime from Bend: 45 mins**

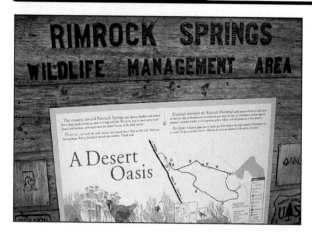

Beaver-chewed Juniper

"Home On the Range" was written in 1871 by Dr. Brewster Hisely about his Kansas home.

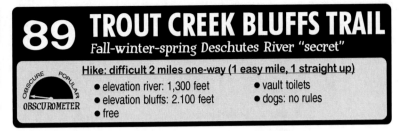

89 TROUT CREEK BLUFFS TRAIL
Fall-winter-spring Deschutes River "secret"

OBSCUROMETER (OBSCURE / POPULAR)

<u>Hike: difficult 2 miles one-way (1 easy mile, 1 straight up)</u>

- elevation river: 1,300 feet
- elevation bluffs: 2,100 feet
- free
- vault toilets
- dogs: no rules

The beauty here will surprise you! This cliff band, while unknown to the masses, is a favorite of the select few who know of its existence. To put it bluntly, this is probably the most dramatic example of columnar basalt in Central Oregon. Complementing the basalt's superb structure is the fact that it faces directly west, thus catching the "magic light" of a Cascades dusk…bathing the columns in a fiery orange glow. A total must-see for any Central Oregon photographer!!

This is an early-spring/late-autumn type of place. It's <u>way too hot</u> in the summer…best to go when the Cascades are snow-bound!

Here's why you haven't seen a photo of these bluffs yet: they're virtually unknown outside of the rock-climbing community, and they're a pain in the ass to get to. But quality climbers know perfect cracks and columns when they see them….and some of them have worked arduously for years to establish climbing routes on these bluffs, as well as building an access path that scales the steep 700-ish feet from the Deschutes. A major article in *Climbing Magazine* (spring '08) let the "cat out of the bag"…but these bluffs are still virtually unknown to anyone except hard-core crack climbers. Bless their taped-up fingers and hearts because now you can ramble an easy mile along the scenic Deschutes and then climb their ac-

Trout Creek Bluff

D R I V E

The trailhead is 15.5 miles from Madras (22-ish minutes). On the north end of Madras turn right onto Hwy 97 at the McDonalds. Go 2.5 miles then left onto Cora Rd. Go 4 miles then stay straight/left onto another road for 4 more miles to Gateway "town". In Gateway cross the RR tracks then take a right onto Clemens (signed to Trout Creek). Now it's 2 more paved miles then 3 washboard gravel miles to the Deschutes where you'll turn left and go to the far edge of the campground to the trailhead parking. Riverside camping at the Trout Creek campground is about $10.

➡ **Drivetime from Bend: 65 mins**

cess path up to this surprisingly unique and beautiful spot. You may wonder, "What's the big deal?" as you walk the Deschutes with the bluff up ahead, but once you see the glowing west face and then begin climbing closer, you'll fetch out your camera! Finally, after the steep scramble-path up, attaining the corner of the

Mt. Jefferson

curved/chopped hexes, you'll turn and see the storied Deschutes River as you've never seen it—glinting in the afternoon sun as it seems to flow directly from Mt Jefferson. Wow.

HIKE: (Check blog for Google map.) Best timing is afternoon. Head one mile upstream along the easy double-track Deschutes River trail. Up

Female climber

ahead the rocky knob atop the hill with the curved columns is your goal, but the trail heads up the west face, not the steep hill you see from the trail. So, pass the river island and then pass a barb wire gate...and just 200 yards (2 minutes) past this gate look for the path that angles up and left (often marked with a rock-stack cairn). Head up this path for a relentless and difficult .8 miles. Once you attain the cliff band, a super-rough rock-hop-jump "route" leads along the base of the cliffs (you MUST jump from rock to rock). Return the way you came up.

www.RichardsonRockRanch.com

OBSCURE · POPULAR
OBSCUROMETER

- open 7am-5pm 365 days
- phone: 541-475-2680
- free

- flush toilets
- dogs: only at digs, not at rock shop/office

Let me get personal here for a moment. I'm no rock-hound, yet I've tried to find neat rocks at many of the supposed Ochoco "rock-hounding sites." I've been disappointed at most every site, due to their difficulties and confusing-ness. But not at Richardson's. I LOVE this place, I love the attitude, I love the fun...and I love the ease of finding truly amazing Thundereggs! I've personally opened-up hundreds of just-cut Thundereggs in the 7 years that I've known of the Ranch's existence...and I've loved the true thrill of opening up every single one. The Richardson's run the nicest operation in the friendliest manner...and you'll get both a thrill and a keepsake for the cheapest price anywhere. An excursion to Richardson's is pure bang-for-the-buck. If you've put off visiting Richardson's, then take my advice and stop dallying. What if the Thundereggs run out?? Who's gonna kick themselves then? I know you've got space on your kitchen window sill for your very-own self-dug Thunderegg....get going!! Say hi to Norma, Bonnie, Johnnie, and John Jr. for me.

Indian legend has it that angry spirits bombed each other with Thundereggs. Check the Richardson's website for the best explanation as to how these little balls of wonder were formed 60-odd million years ago. Richardson's specializes in these tennis-ball sized agate filled "bombs" which have held the distinction of Oregon's State Rock since 1965. This low-key ranch caters to everyone, whether you're a rock-hounding collector, a Central OR explorer, or a family with curious kids. This is no snobby showroom gig—the

D
R
I
V
E

From Bend take Hwy 97 north for 40 miles to Madras. Go through Madras and at the north side of town head right on Hwy 97 towards The Dalles (straight is Hwy 26 to Portland). Go 11 miles and watch for signs for Richardson's at MP 81. Turn right, go 1.8 miles, then right again onto gravel for the last mile to the ranch.

➡ **Drivetime from Bend:** **60 mins**

Richardsons' humor keeps this "mom & pop" operation fun and playful—amazingly open every single day for the past 35 years!

There are two great reasons for a visit:

First, the rock shop's displays of polished rocks, geodes, fossils, spheres and Thundereggs are dazzling. You could easily spend an hour or two just browsing the shop looking at oddities from the world over…and don't miss the chance to try to pick up the yellow hunk of glass! There are fossils, ammonites, geodes, petrified wood, and spheres galore. Outside the shop are heaps of exotic rock, heaps of already-dug Thundereggs, and a flock of bizarre chickens pecking about. Even if you don't want to get dirty digging your own rocks, the rock shop is way worth the visit all by itself!

Rock foxes with $15 of just-cut eggs

Second, you can dig for your own unique egg. Norma will loan you a pick, bucket, and a map so you can drive the 6 miles out to the various egg beds. Once you're out there it's fairly easy pickins—just dig a bit in the "loosened" beds and you'll find an egg-carton full! Each egg costs about fifty cents and the shop will cut it in half for about another buck. Wow, everyone gets a one-of-a-kind souvenir for only about $1.50—that's bang for the buck! If you don't want to spend an hour or two drivin' and diggin', then simply pick one off the shop's pile and have it cut.

Summers at Richardson's Ranch are busy and fun and sometimes hectic on holidays—digging and cutting going non-stop. Around November the wet roads to the egg-beds are closed down until April. The shop stays open but egg-cutting is more sporadic in the off-season when kids who run the rock-saws are off in school. Call before you go in the winter if you have questions.

91 CROOKED RIVER CANYON DRIVE
Scenic canyon drive with optional hike

Hike: moderate 1.5-mile one-way hike

OBSCURE POPULAR
OBSCUROMETER

- elevation river: 3,000 feet
- drive: 60-mile loop from Bend with 23 miles of scenic canyon

The Crooked River canyon drive is a scenic delight featuring a meandering river walled-in by towering layer-cake basalt cliffs. Formerly a loop drive from Prineville to Bend was a pain in the ass because of long stretches of washboard dirt needed to make a loop out of the excursion. No more though. The entire drive from Prineville to Alfalfa to Bend is now paved.

The riverside drive is famously scenic from MP 6 to MP 20. The road hugs the eastern bank of the swervy Crooked River with basalt ramparts towering over the road's every crook. The road winds along at river level for the most part, but occasionally it leaves the river to contour along the cliff faces, yielding some excellent canyon photo-ops. Coming from Prineville the drama of the canyon begins near MP 6 and goes non-stop until climbing up the Bowman Dam to Prineville Reservoir at MP 20. Along the reservoir here are some roadside stops and boat-ramp access. Continuing 3 miles past the Reservoir you'll turn right at MP 23 to get on the road back west via Alfalfa.

For HIKERS there's a scenic trail that ascends 500 vertical feet up to Chimney Rock. It begins at a signed trailhead at MP 16.5 (Chimney Rock campground). This moderate trail snakes 1.5 miles up a juniper 'n' sage canyon before angling across a plateau to visit the canyon's most prominent knob.

Chimney Rock

CHIMNEY ROCK
Recreation Site

**D
R
I
V
E**

To access the Crooked River canyon from Prineville, turn south from the center of town onto Main St (Hwy 27) signed towards Bowman Dam (not towards Prineville Res.) The canyon proper begins around MP 6.

Coming from Bend (35 min. drive), head east on Hwy 26 from the Forum (27th St) for 2.3 miles and turn left onto Alfalfa Market Rd. In 1.0 miles turn right and then zigzag 15 miles through Alfalfa until you hit a 4-way stop in the Millican OHV Area. Continue straight through the stop on Reservoir Rd for 7.5 miles until it hits Prineville Res Rd. Go left here to tour the canyon from south to north (this is MP 23 measured from Prineville).

If you're the least bit athletic then the trail is well worth the effort. It gets you out of the car and lets you really take a long look at the fabulous basalt layering, the crookedly flowing river, all the while breathing the charismatic desert scents under the ever-blue skies. Very nice!

Your shadow

The view from Chimney Rock

For Campers there are 8 established campgrounds along the river. Each one is first-come, first-served at $8 per night. This is a real nice place to do a springtime camp trip when most other spots are still snowed-under. Camping is also free Nov thru March!

92 PRINEVILLE RES-JUNIPER HILLS-MAURY MTNS LOOP DRIVE

A sightseeing drive with a few interesting stops

Prineville Reservoir North Bank Road open: 4/15 - 11/15

OBSCUROMETER

- elevation Prineville: 2,900 feet
- elevation Maury Mtn top: 5,600 feet

Prineville Res (site 18)

This is an "Oregon Outback" loop drive either from Bend or Prineville, involving many miles of well-maintained gravel roads. The best time is in Late-May/ early June when the reservoir is full, the temperature not oven-like, and so many other places still snowed-in. Note: Prineville Reservoir's North Bank Rd **re-opens** April 15th each Spring… but at that time the Maury's will still be snowed-in. The road over the Maury Mtns usually clears near the first of June, depending on snowfall.

Bring a map…either the Prineville Ranger District, the cheap Central OR Rockhounding Map, or the Oregon Gazetteer.

The highlights of this Outback tour are many:

1st: Seeing the upper reaches of Prineville Reservoir along the reservoir's North Bank Rd.

2nd: A stop into the "town" of Post, the geographic

Juniper Hills Preserve
Please help us protect Oregon's native plants and wildlife.

center of Oregon… where you can stock-up on road-trip supplies, have a beer in the tavern, and post a postcard from the Post Office in Post.

3rd: Take a short easy walk to see the lone out-of-place painted hill that The Nature Conservancy purchased in order to turn into a Preserve.

4th: Take the gravel roads that climb into and through the Maury Mtn range… just to see what's up there…and make a loop out of the excursion.

5th: to finish the loop back to Prineville you'll go through the Crooked River Canyon (91)…or to get back to Bend you'll connect with Hwy 20 at Brothers and pass Dry River Gorge (8) and the Badlands Wilderness (7) on the way home.

This description begins in downtown Prineville (from Bend the best way to Prineville is via the Powell Butte Hwy 2 miles east of The Forum shopping center on Hwy 20.)

On the east side of Prineville on Hwy 26 turn right onto Combs Flat Rd at signs for "Prineville Res/ Paulina." Go 1.2 miles and turn left at the signs for the reservoir. Go 16 miles to the reservoir, staying left towards Jasper Point. Just before Jasper Point turn left onto the not-well-marked North Bank Rd signed "Caution: Unimproved Rd". The North Bank Rd wiggles 6 miles along the reservoir, passing 35 signed and designated free camp spots. Stop into the "Cattle Guard" camp to see the strange Skeleton Rock across the waters...where half the basalt stands straight up and half points directly at you. Jim Witty once wrote about a buried treasure atop Skeleton Rock (pg 221 of *Meet Me in the Badlands*). Another good stop along the Res is at camp spot #18 where there's a jumping/swim-

Post's post

ming rock. As you finish the NB Rd look for pointy Pilot Butte up ahead with the cell towers...then junction with Hwy 380 at MP 16.5.

Turning east on Hwy 380 go 9 miles to Post. Continuing, head east to see the Juniper Hills Preserve at MP 36. Along the way you'll pass, at MP 30, the signed FS 17 that heads up and over the Maury Mtns...but first go see the Hills. At MP 36.1 is a left-side one-car spot marked with a small Nature conservancy sign...with the painted hill obviously ahead. A half-mile walk gets you up-close with the hill, but please don't tread on the sensitive "painted" clay, as footprints mar the hill for a long time (...take only pix and LEAVE NO FOOTPRINTS!)

Now backtrack to MP 30 and turn onto FS 17 (Pine Crk Rd.) Set odometer. Head straight thru the first junction and climb an easy and beautiful Ponderosa-riffic 9 miles to the pass, and then 1.0 more miles to the T-junction with FS 16. A left here goes 4-miles to see Antelope Reservoir (not too scenic, but what the hell? Res camping is $8.) To fin-

Maury Mtns Antelope Reservoir

ish the loop though turn right onto FS 16 and go 7 miles to FS 1640 junction (signed to Bear Creek.) Go left on FS 1640 for 5 miles to the next T junction at Bear Creek Rd. At this point, to return to Prineville via the Crooked River, turn right for about 15 miles to FS 27, then right again to head north thru the Crooked Canyon and back.

To go back to Bend go left on Bear Creek for 3 miles then right onto Pringle Flat Rd for 7 miles more of gravel and then 7 paved into Brothers on Hwy 20. A right turn will take you 43 miles back to Bend.

93 STEIN'S PILLAR TRAIL
An iconic geologic oddity

Hike: moderate 2-mile one-way (700-foot vertical gain)

OBSCUROMETER

- elevation parking: 4,300 feet
- elevation pillar: 4,100 feet
- free
- no toilets
- dogs: no rules

Stein's Pillar is a 44 million year-old Central Oregon icon that has amazed everyone who's seen it. This free-standing pillar is reminiscent of Smith Rock's Monkey Face, but Stein's Pillar is *hard* to describe. It stands *erect,* a proud *member* of the rhyolite

family, *poking* skyward about 350 feet above the *wooded* hillside. Certainly Enoch Steen, the 1860 "discoverer" of the pillar is turning in his grave, ever since his name was misspelled in an outrage of historic *fallacy*.

You can either simply drive up to a viewpoint to see this odd monstrosity from below...or you can hike a moderate 2-mile trail that traipses you through a nice Ponderosa/Juniper forest until delivering you to the very base of the monolith. The roadside viewpoint may yield the best photo-

Scramble viewpoint

Roadside view

From Redmond take Hwy 126 east to Prineville. Head east through Prineville and 8 miles out of town, just past the Ochoco Reservoir at MP 28, turn left onto Mill Creek Rd. Go 5 miles to the Brennan/Mill Creek split and continue straight onto gravel for 1.9 miles then right onto signed FS 500 for 2 uphill miles to the signed trailhead (note: the roadside viewpoint is 1.3 miles past the trailhead turn, and it's worth visiting first).

> ➡ **Drivetime from Bend: 1 hour**

ops, but taking the trail to the behemoth's base is super worth it. The base of the rock, where a pioneer scrawled his 1889 moniker and the first-ascent 1950 climbers set up their gear, features a little cave-like overlook that's sure to thrill height-lovers, while scaring the begeezus out of height 'phobes!

For an extra view-scramble, either before or after visiting the pillar's base, stop at the pre-pillar rocky viewpoint. If you're an athletic scrambler with little fear of heights...then up the rock you go to the BEST viewpoint of the whole shebang! Be warned, the drop-off and exposure are scary, but the extraordinary view is...!!!

FYI: Brennan Palisades, signed where the road to Stein's turns to gravel, are hardly impressive after seeing the pillar's enormity. But if you're interested in rocks heaps and some minor hoodoo formations then go up road FS 3370 for .75 miles and turn left at (possibly) unsigned FS 100 for .4 miles more.

HIKE: The signed trail has no complications, except that the highpoint is half way in, meaning that you'll have to gain the altitude twice.

Looking up from the base

94 LOOKOUT MTN LOOP TRAIL
A great Ochocos loop with mining ruins

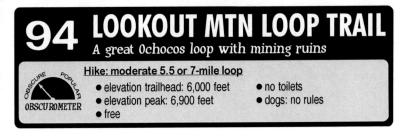

Hike: moderate 5.5 or 7-mile loop

OBSCURE · POPULAR
OBSCUROMETER

- elevation trailhead: 6,000 feet
- elevation peak: 6,900 feet
- free
- no toilets
- dogs: no rules

Lookout Mountain is a prominent 6,926-foot ridgeline running north-south in the central Ochoco Mountains. This former lookout site has a nice network of loop trails accessing its summit, enabling different loop options. A "secret" bonus to this hike is that the trails begin near the defunct yet explorable Mother Lode/ Independent Mine ghost town (see next entry). Thus, an excursion to Lookout Mtn is big bang-for-the-buck, especially if you visit in June when the Ochocos are green, the wildflowers are out, and vast expanses of this trail are festooned with giant-leaved Skunk Cabbage! All this while the Cascades are still snowed-in.

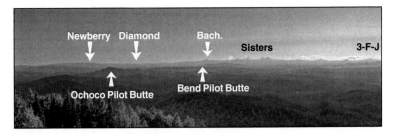

Newberry   Diamond   Bach.   Sisters   3-F-J

Ochoco Pilot Butte   Bend Pilot Butte

The loop trail itself is fairly mellow, as it only gains 900 feet in 4 rambling miles of climbing, but since you're at 6,000 to 7,000 feet, there still may be some heavy breathing. At the ridgetop you find a stone corral that surrounded the lookout site and sweeping vistas of a forever of Oregon. To the west you'll see an impressive line-up of Cascades volcanoes from Diamond Peak to the tip of WA's Mt Adams. Look for pointy Gray Butte (84) in the front right of 3-F Jack with Black Butte (80) to the left. To the left of Mt Bachelor Diamond Peak huddles with Maiden Peak with the double hump of Waldo Lake's Twins (30) to the right and Lava Butte in the foreground. Pilot Butte is just a wee bump down and left of Bachelor. Hope you brought both map and binocs!

Heading down just a few hundred yards from the lookout you'll find a rustic log snow shelter complete with a wood-burning stove...as well as views east over Big Summit Prairie. Bring matches and some spare paper if you want to fire up a lunchtime blaze in the rusty stove. Be sure to

Snow shelter

D
R
I
V
E

From Prineville head east on Hwy 26 and just past MP 34 veer right at signs for Walton Lake onto paved FS 23. Go 8 miles and just past the Ranger Station (MP 8), turn right onto paved FS 42 and follow it 6.5 miles to the clearly signed "Independent Mine" right turn. Head up this steep gravel road for 1.0 miles to the road-end trailhead.

▶ **Drivetime from Bend:** **90 mins**

scout around for the odd stump-chair that got "nailed" by the shelter's builders in 1989.

Mother Lode Mine/ Independent Mine ghost town. A super-interesting adjunct to this hike is a quarter-mile extra trip over to see the explorable ruins of the Mother Lode Mine. A 3-story building still stands with lots of arcane mining paraphernalia both inside and out. These relics are located a 5-minute walk from the trailhead, heading over the berm/fenced roadway. The Independent Mine ghost town is back down the access road at the Baneberry trail sign—see next entry for details.

HIKE: At the road-end trailhead are 3 trails. Basically trail 808 makes a 7-mile loop and trail 808a spurs off on the downhill leg to beeline back to the trailhead for a shorter 5.5-mile loop. The best loop is the 5.5-mile, but you could come and do a different variation every year.

The route described here is up 808 and down 808a, going clockwise.

Mother Lode Mine ruins

Heading up 808 it's an easy rambling 4 miles to the summit's open slopes. Just before the summit is a junction with the faint trail 807—stay straight and up. You'll finally attain the ridge and then it's just a couple minutes to the lookout site 4-way junction. Go left for the view (trail 804 is the 7-mile trail down to Ochoco R.S.) Stay right on the loop for a couple minutes over to the rustic snow shelter. Past the snow shelter just .3 miles is the signed "Lookout Tie" trail 808a heading down a surprisingly quick 1.2 miles to the trailhead.

WHATEVER WHATEVER WHATEVER WHATEVER WHATEVER WHATEVER WHATEVER WHATEVER WHATEVER WHATEVER

I want to end this entry by giving thanks to William Sullivan and his series of "100 Hikes" guidebooks. If you don't already know of them, you should—they are super-detailed and super-mapped. I want to give credit where credit is due. Without his book I wouldn't have known of this way-better trailhead for a Lookout Mtn hike than the Ranger Station's 7-mile one-way slog. Thanks Bill!

WHATEVER WHATEVER WHATEVER WHATEVER WHATEVER WHATEVER WHATEVER WHATEVER WHATEVER WHATEVER

Hike: short exploratory walks

OBSCUROMETER

- elevation: 4,800 feet
- free
- no toilets
- dogs: no rules

The Ochoco Mountains between Lookout Mtn and Big Summit Prairie once supported a thriving mining industry. Most of these mining operations were after the mineral cinnabar, which then was processed into mercury. Nowadays there are a handful of mining ruins, open for exploration, clustered together off of FS 42. Examining the ruins at each location is fairly simple, most sites only requiring a short walk to see the remains. The Ochoco Nat'l Forest did extensive clean-up at some of these sites, and they have been left "as is" because they are deemed "safe", in terms of hazardous material exposure. Toxic levels of mercury were cleaned up, so unless you eat a bucket-full of mine tailings, you'll probably be in no danger just walking and looking. Of course attempting to climb on any of the rickety structures is just dumb and will surely result in both gangrene and impalement. Just snoop, don't climb! If you are curious as to all the details of the mining history, stop in at the Bowman Museum in downtown Prineville to see their historical literature.

Mother Lode Mine

The best ruins and a mini ghost town are at the farthest west (nearest) site—the Independent/Mother Lode mines. But if you see these ruins first, then all the others will pale in comparison. Thus, it's better to start at the farthest east sites and investigate your way back west to finish at the Independent Mine ghost town.

Independent Mine
Ghost Town

Independent/ Mother Lode Mines. These two close-by sites are on the access road for the Lookout Mtn trailhead. The signed turn is at MP 6.5 on FS 42. Go up the road .5 miles and you'll see the Independent ghost town down to the left. Park at the Baneberry trail sign and walk down hill to explore the extensive buildings. The Baneberry trail is not the

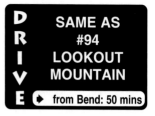

D
R
I
V
E

SAME AS
#94
LOOKOUT
MOUNTAIN

⬤ from Bend: 50 mins

route—you need to simply follow the old road down off the Baneberry. To see the 3-story mine building from the Mother Lode mine, pass Independent and drive to the road end. The two exceptional buildings are just 5 minutes ahead over the berm/ fenced roadway.

Amity Mine. This site is signed at MP 8.1, but there's no longer much to see. The building that once stood down below the sign has now toppled into a pile of planking. Check blog for an old photo of it.

Unnamed Site. These unsigned "hidden" ruins are off the south side of the road at MP 8.6, just before FS 200 takes off to the left (the Round Mtn access road). If you park at the beginning of FS 200 and walk across the FS 42 and down onto the abandoned road…it leads 5 minutes to some extensive ruins, including a wooden hopper structure up by FS 42.

Blue Ridge Mine. This site, the farthest east at MP 9, has a few areas to explore. The boarded-up bunkhouse by the road was the miners' quarters.

Blue Ridge Mine

100 yards north you'll find an angled 3-leveled sorting room open for exploration. Across FS 42 and west just 100 yards is a falling-down log cabin that's interesting for a peek.

<u>Drive: 6.2-mile gravel drive to top, last 1.5 miles 4WD-ish</u>

OBSCUROMETER

- elevation: 6,753 feet
- free
- no toilets
- dogs: no rules

Three Sisters

Black Butte

Round Mountain is Lookout Mtn's Ochoco neighbor peak. Lookout Mtn is now the hiking/biking mountain whereas Round Mtn is drive-able either by 4WD car or ATV. There is a trail that climbs to the top of Round Mtn from either side—either at Walton Lake or at the Independent Mine/ Lookout Mtn road. Either trail makes a 4-mile ascent…but it seems somewhat frustrating to make a long hike only to find trucks or ATVs sharing your vista at the top. Since both Lookout Mtn and Round Mtn sport almost identical views from almost identical heights, it then seems advisable to hike on the hiker's mountain and drive up the driveable mountain.

Round Mtn cell towers

Mile 1.5 from FS 42

D R I V E

From FS 42 the road is 6.2 miles to the summit, taking about 26 minutes from FS 42. The first 4.7 miles are 2WD-drive-able, but the final 1.5 miles are rougher, but only in terms of clearance, not traction (makeable in a 4WD low-clearance Aerostar minivan).

To find Round Mtn's road up follow the directions in entry 94. On FS 42, at the Lookout/ Indep. turn-off keep straight another 2 miles to FS 200 on the left. Turn onto this gravel road (only signed with a small "200"). Go 1.8 miles to the first junction. Stay right and up another 2.1 miles until a junction in an open skunk cabbage meadow (4-mile mark). You want the left fork marked with a "Road closed 1 mile ahead" sign (it isn't closed). Go left and up a rougher 2.2 more miles to the top (if you have a 2WD car you could still drive .5 miles above the "Unmaintained" sign park on the shoulder before a 100-yard rough gravel section, and then walk the road the final 1.7 miles.)

➧ **Drivetime: 1 hour, 45 mins from Bend**

Atop Round Mtn you'll find a few cell towers and the same WOW panoramic Cascades vista as atop Lookout Mtn (Diamond Peak to Mt Adams.) You'll also get a fantastic view east over the entire Big Summit Prairie. Along the way up you'll be cruise through some nice Ponderosa groves and, in the springtime, meadows of skunk cabbage and wildflowers. A Round Mtn drive makes a nice addition to a drive to explore the nearby Ochoco mining ruins (95) and a look-see at the Big Summit Prairie (97). The road to Round usually opens up in mid-June, so it coincides nicely with a visit to Big Summit Prairie. Another great time to make the trip is in mid-October when the plentiful Larch trees (tamaracks) along the road put on their showy yellow display.

Black Mtn Lookout

Big Summit Prairie

Round Mtn eastern view

97 BIG SUMMIT PRAIRIE/ LOOKOUT TREE
Spring wildflower explosion

Hike: short steep Black Mountain Lookout Tree

OBSCURE · POPULAR

OBSCUROMETER

- elevation: 4,500 feet
- free
- no toilets
- dogs: no rules

Big Summit Prairie is a vast acreage of open meadow plunked smack dab in the middle of the Ochoco Mountains. You gotta see it to believe it…these are no normal mountain meadows—these meadows are 10 miles long and 5 across…wow! The prairie itself is all private, but the road along the edge provides plenty of great views and photo-op stopping points. The main draw of Big Summit Prairie is its renowned springtime wildflower showcase. Plan a visit in mid-June and you'll see why the route gets nicknamed the "Butterfly Byway." In June you'll get vast expanses of yellow and purple flowers carpeting the middle of the meadows, and along the road there will be mini meadows every few hundred yards exploding into a rainbow of blooms. Adding to the attractiveness of the scene are groves of old-growth orange-barked Ponderosas all along the edge of the meadows. As a photographer you can't lose…except if you wait too long and miss the show! The wildflowers begin with the little ones in May, but mid-June is when the real fireworks burst in a grand finale.

Driving along the meadows edge on FS 42 you'll find little pull-offs here and there to get out and picnic or explore. There are some nice streamlets rushing into the meadows with springtime gusto. At the far east end of the prairie most people turn around at the bridged crossing of the Wild 'n' Scenic North Fork of the Crooked River (MP 20). This is a nice spot to look back at the colorful carpet with both Lookout Mtn and Round Mtn punctuating the western skyline.

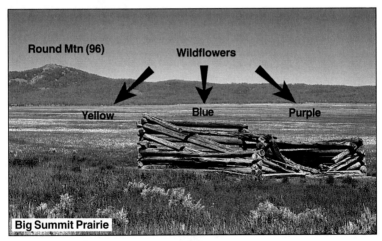

Round Mtn (96) — Wildflowers — Yellow — Blue — Purple

Big Summit Prairie

208

Follow directions to entry 94 Lookout Mtn, but stay straight on FS 42 for 3 more miles to the west edge of the Big Summit Prairie (MP 10). Note: at the closed Ochoco Ranger Station (at FS 42) you can see the Lookout cabin that was once located under the Lookout Tree.

FYI: you can make a great outback loop to Mitchell from the Lookout Tree via roads 3010 and 22. The route is 19 gravel miles from the Lookout Tree junction. The road is signed, fast and smooth (30 MPH), suitable for any car. The road comes out immediately east of Mitchell. It takes about 45 minutes from Lookout to Mitchell.

➡ **Drivetime from Bend: 93 mins**

Black Mtn Lookout Tree.

As an extra, you may want to make an additional foray to find the remnants of one of the oldest fire lookouts in the Ochocos. The rarely-seen Lookout Tree dilapidates before your very eyes...so hurry before it falls down (or gets removed). This lookout was the oldest type—just a ladder up a 100-foot tree with a platform to look out over the forests. Built circa 1920/30, it's surprisingly still mostly there! Please don't even think of trying to climb it...as you'll probably fall and die and then the Ochoco will have to tear it down and put a memorial plaque on the spot to honor your idiocy.

Circa 1920

Photo Courtesy of Bowman Museum

To find the tree head to the far end of the prairie on FS 42. At the Crooked River bridge, set your odometer and go left onto FS 30 towards Mitchell. Go 1.8 miles and at the junction with FS 3010 stay RIGHT for 2.8 miles more. At the 2.2-mile mark Black Mtn is the nondescript hill on the left. When you see the right-leaning orange Ponderosa on the right side of the widening road, pull over just before the tree and look up and left to see the lookout perched atop the highest Ponderosa. (If you get to another fork with a sign, you're .3 miles too far.) Climb the slope 5 minutes to the tree.

98 PAINTED HILLS
A must-see natural masterpiece!

Hike: various short hikes

OBSCURE — POPULAR

OBSCUROMETER

- elevation: 2,000 feet
- free
- vault toilets
- dogs: on leash

Visit in Spring or late Fall. Summer is too hot to enjoy!

Close-up

Oregon's Painted Hills are argu-ably the finest example of badlands coloration in the country. *Wait a minute, this is my guidebook and I don't need to write wishy-washy phrases like "arguably"...this is Central Oregon, a landscape of ex-clamations!!* Lemme start anew... OUR Painted Hills are the best in the country! The Painted Desert in Arizona's Petrified Natl Park comes close...and colored hills of Death Valley get more hype, but, nope, Or-egon wins. Our subtleties of color, shaping, striping, and sunset-facing-ness take the prize. If you haven't yet popped in for a look ...then **GO...this is an Oregon Must-See!** If you've been in Central Oregon for more than "a spell" and haven't made it out for a look at the Painted Hills then...??? If you've enjoyed any outing in this book or any of my writings about our landscape, then do it for me...go look at the Painted Hills. When I first saw the hills 20 years ago my jaw dropped so hard my toes still hurt. Go see!!! (But don't expect too much, as expectations often ruin everything. These hills are really dull humps of red-yellow, brown-black clay...so, big deal...just please, go look for yourself.)

Here's the history of this unique area: Mother Nature, just past the dawn of time and after pelting Noah with 40 days of rain, practiced her artistry all over the West before turning her attention to her intended masterpiece—Or-

D R I V E

On Hwy 26, about 47 miles east of Prineville, turn left at MP 62.5 at the Painted Hills sign then go 6 miles to the park entrance. The old-west town of Mitchell is 3 miles beyond the turn-off.

➧ **Drivetime from Bend: 100 mins**

egon. Once she had fashioned most of North America, but just before packing her bags for the two islands of New Zealand, she began molding the Pacific Coast. She swathed the coast and mountains with huge swipes of her G.B.I.V. brushes. **B**lue ocean and **I**ndigo lakes…**G**reen forest and mosses and leaves…and hey, for fun, how 'bout putting the bluest lake of all inside a crater! Then… maybe a spangle of **V**iolet flowers amongst the green springtime grasses. Whew, looks like no room for any R.O.Y. on the G.B.I.V. West Coast.

Painted Cove
Nature Trail

Painted Cove

Moving east, she knew she couldn't better her blue-green Cascades artistry, so she decided to dapple Eastern Oregon with shades of RedOrangeYellow. Here come **R**ed cinder cones, **O**range Ponderosas, and **Y**ellow flowers and grasses. While resting she mucked about with rocks for a spell making some red lichens and orange Smith Rocks. Only then did she set her mind to creating her masterpiece of R.O.Y. She took up her brush and painted the hills. She mixed the reds and oranges and yellows with a spot of black. She brushed with a delicacy she's never repeated. All she now asks in return is our delight and protection of her masterpiece.

HIKE: 1st) The Painted Hills Overlook Trail heads easily uphill from the first parking area. This is a must-do, as it's the easiest and best view of the colors and textures of the hills…and the Fabulous black streaking!

2nd) The Carroll Rim Overlook trail is the oft-overlooked trail that climbs .75 miles up the ridge opposite the Painted Hills. This trail is fairly easy after the initially steep 5-minute start, and it provides a 360° view of all things painted, plus offering interpretive brochures which detail the intriguing surrounding geology. Don't be lazy…go up the rim, especially near sunset with some beer/wine to help you enjoy the spectacle from the trail's-end bench.

3rd) The Painted Cove trail is a short easy must-see.

4th) The short Leaf Hill Trail is fascinating for some, drudgery for others. It's not scenic, but rather geologic and historic. But, just a half-mile past the Leaf Hill is the singular and lesser-known Red Hill, which offers the park's most up-close and intimate view of a vibrantly painted hill.

99 BLUE BASIN TRAILS
Otherworldly green-blue badlands canyon

Hike: easy .5-mile one-way or mod/diff 3-mile loop

OBSCUROMETER

- elevation trailhead: 2,150 feet
- elevation top: 2,850 feet
- free
- vault toilets
- dogs: leash

Picture Gorge Basalts
Painted Hill →
Blue Basin Upper Trail

The Blue Basin defies easy description. It also defies belief! To hear Tourism Oregon describe it you get, "a colorfully eroded badlands canyon in the sheep Rock Unit of the John Day Fossil Beds Nat'l Monument." To hear a geologist describe it you'd get an "a fossil-bearing strata of green-tinged volcanic ash claystone." Neither of those descriptions does a good job capturing the "Wow" factor of this small canyon. Here's the *Bend Overall* take: this is an otherworldly canyon colored with the oddest of green—a very unnatural green. It's as if a moon-green cheese crash-landed in an obscure corner of nowhere Oregon, spraying the green cheese up into odd corrugated pinnacles. This box canyon is like NOWHERE else in America—it's that weird. You gotta see it, as photos never do the place justice (especially these lame B&W pix). Blue Basin is a long drive from Bend and it wouldn't be in this guidebook unless it truly was drop-jaw phenomenal!

There are two ways to see Blue Basin. The most popular is the easy half-mile trail that winds into the heart of the canyon bottom. Along the way you'll follow a creek seemingly flowing with green clay…and also read/see displays about the amazing array of fossils that have emerged from the ash clays of this 40-million year-old former Eden-like savannah. Who'd believe that saber-toothed Nimravids once roamed this very spot?!

The other Blue Basin hiking option is to tour the upper rim via a steepish 3-mile loop. The loop is <u>very</u> worth it—seeing the canyon from above is stunning and you'll have little or no yapping tourists to accompany the wonders. Besides the obvious visuals on the loop you'll also pass through a heap of "banded ignimbrite" rocks that are quite peculiar in their own right (on the north side). If you do the upper loop, make sure to visit the heart of the canyon first—it'll give you fun info to ponder on the longer route.

Banded Ignimbrite

From Prineville head easy on Hwy 26. Mitchell is 40-odd miles (the only supply stop) and keep going another 32 miles on Hwy 26 to the signed turn at MP 98. Turn left onto Hwy 19 for 2 miles to Sheep Rock and the VisCtr. Blue Basin is 3 miles further north at MP 118.7. Also, be sure to drive 2.5 miles north of Blue Basin to see the stunning Cathedral Rock presiding over the John Day River!

As an extra, if you're in no hurry to head back west, consider making a loop drive back to Mitchell by heading north from Blue Basin then west to Spray and Service Creek before turning south on 207 back to Mitchell. This 70-mile route to Mitchell features stunning layer-cake geology, some scattered painted hillsides, and 40-mile drive along the banks of the rarely-seen John Day River. It's a great bonus drive!

➤ Drivetime from Bend: 2 hours

" No region in the world shows a more complete sequence of Tertiary land populations, both plant and animal than the John Day Basin".
—Ralph W. Chaney

Condon Visitor Center

Sheep Rock Unit. On the way to Blue Basin you pass colorfully-striped Sheep Rock and the adjacent air-conditioned Thomas Condon Visitor Center. This museum-like center is a **Must-See**—it's a veritable Paleontological fossil-rama! The fossils inside are simply phenomenal, as is the intriguing sights 'n' sounds presentation of the incredible 40 million-year historical record entombed in the local hillsides. The theater shows a fabulous 18-minute film detailing what makes the John Day area so unique in the world.

Picture Gorge. Picture Gorge basalts are the layer-cake basalt strata that you see atop Sheep Rock and beyond Blue Basin. Hwy 19 forks left at the entrance to Picture Gorge, and if you want to see some of the actual pictographs the gorge was named after, then drive south thru the gorge one mile and park on the left at the gorge's mouth. Some pictos are at river level just under the monument sign. Please be respectful!

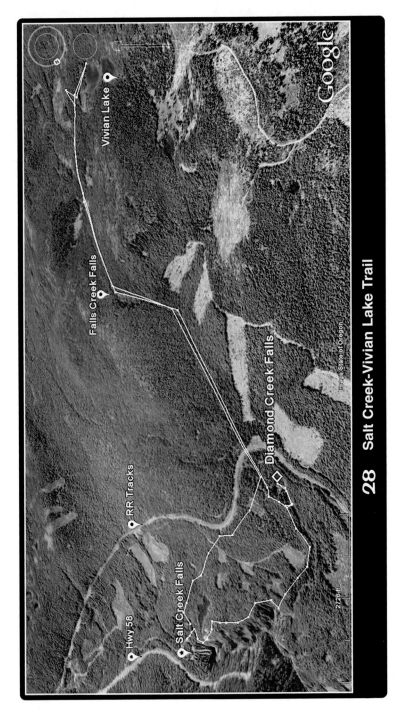

28 Salt Creek-Vivian Lake Trail

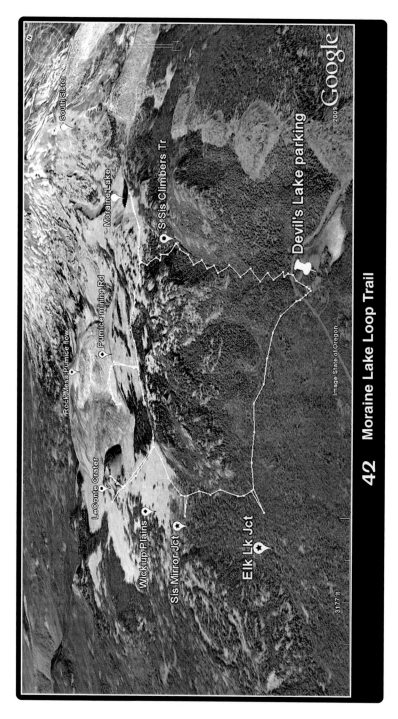

42   Moraine Lake Loop Trail

South Sister

Moraine Lake

S Sis Climbers Tr

Devil's Lake parking

Pumice mining Rd

Rock Mesa Pumice flow

LeConte Crater

Wickiup Plains

Sis Mirror Jct

Elk Lk Jct

Image State of Oregon

2009

3177 ft

215

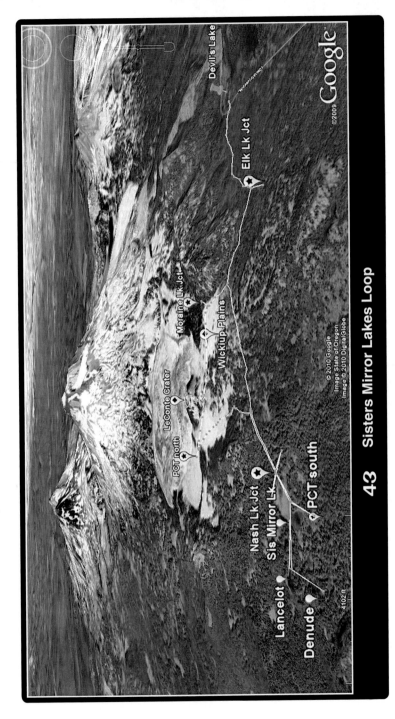

43   Sisters Mirror Lakes Loop

Broken Top's lake

Broken Hand

W.Rim Vwpt

The Prow

3 Creeks Lk

Li'l 3 Creeks Lk

Image State of Oregon

4270 ft

48 Tam MacArthur Rim Trail

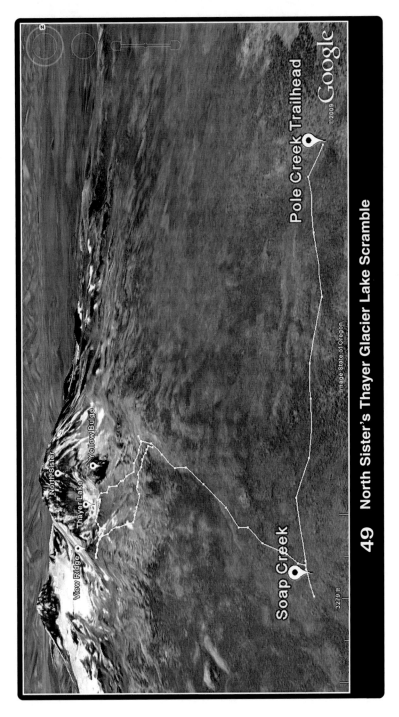

49   North Sister's Thayer Glacier Lake Scramble

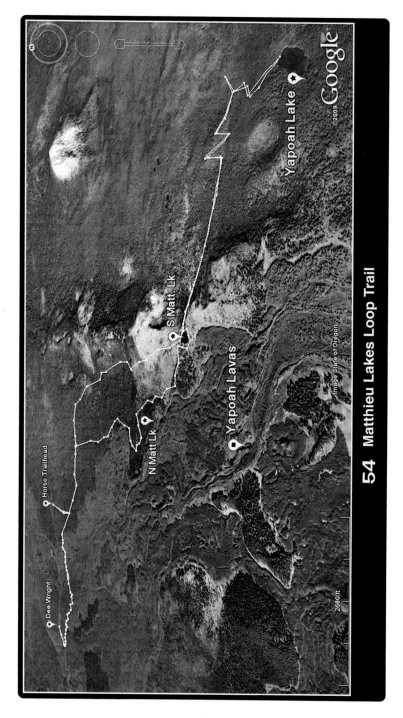

54 Matthieu Lakes Loop Trail

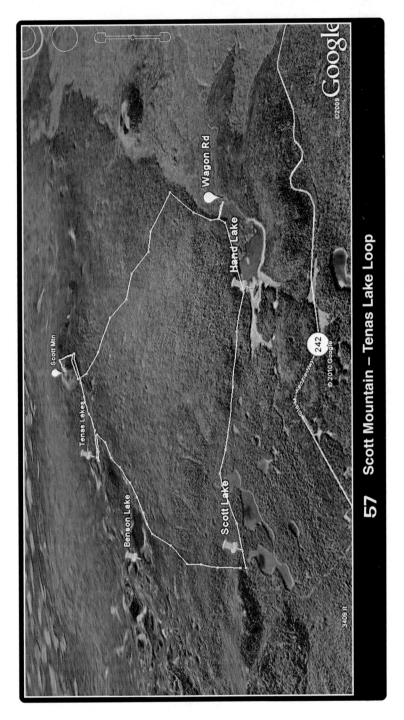

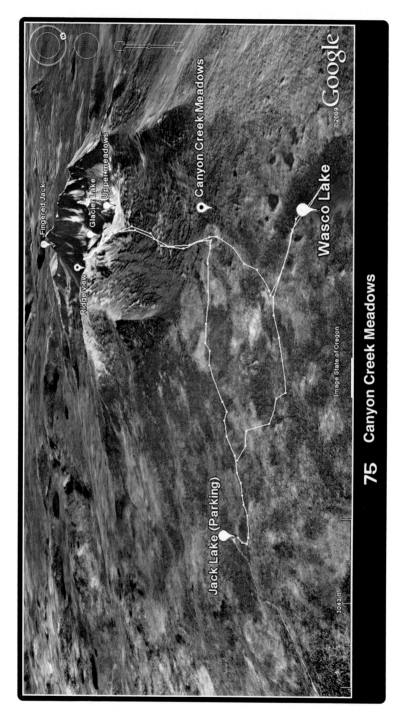

75　Canyon Creek Meadows

Identifying the conifers around Bend overall is fairly easy, but it's still a fun challenge and an impressive feat to know them all. There are only about a dozen major tree types, and unlike some other regions, each of our trees has recognizable characteristics for the everyman – no need for super-close scrutiny to tell this region's trees apart. Once you learn a few clues to help with the comparing and contrasting, the ID is a snap! The fun challenge around here is when the harsh growing conditions—lava flows, cinder hills, pumice fields—interact with variable rainfall and altitude to torment the trees into surprising forms.

This guide is meant to be a down 'n' dirty crash course in conifers. If my clues don't do the job, I recommend two excellent easy-to-use books: *Trees to Know in Oregon* by Ross and Jensen for O.S.U., and Falcon's *Western Trees* by Stuckey and Palmer.

To start off, here's a list of our native conifers broken down into three groups:

LONG-NEEDLED BUNCHES	SINGLE-NEEDLES ALONG TWIG	SCALE LEAVES
Ponderosa pine	Douglas-fir	Juniper
Lodgepole pine	Englemann spruce	Incense cedar
Western white pine	Mtn hemlock	Western redcedar
Whitebark pine	True fir	
	Larch (Tamarack)	

Now here's a cross-section diagram generalizing where the trees grow according to east/west orientation, rainfall, and altitude:

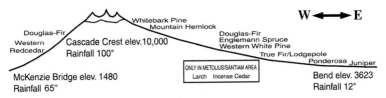

W ◄──► E

Whitebark Pine
Mountain Hemlock

Douglas-Fir
Western Redcedar

Cascade Crest elev.10,000
Rainfall 100"

Douglas-Fir
Englemann Spruce
Western White Pine
True Fir/Lodgepole
Ponderosa Juniper

ONLY IN METOLIUS/SANTIAM AREA
Larch Incense Cedar

McKenzie Bridge elev. 1480
Rainfall 65"

Bend elev. 3623
Rainfall 12"

STARTING THE IDENTIFICATION PROCESS: Begin with the pines because they are the easiest. The four pines all have longish needles bunched towards the end of the branch (like a brush), whereas the single-needle trees sport shorter needles all along the twig (like teddybear arms).

True fir, WW pine.

Pine, single-needle.

Pine Characteristics:

Ponderosa: Long needles in bunches of three. Large woody cones. Mature bark is orange, young bark is blackish. Elev. range 3,000-6,500 ft.

Lodgepole: Short needles in bunches of two. Small, 2-3 inch cones have a flattened side. Bark is gray, thin, and scaly. Elev. Range 3,000-8,000 ft.

Western white: Needles in bunches of five. Cones are 6-8 inches and shaped like bananas. Mature bark forms a squared "alligator-skin" pattern, young bark is gray and scaly. Elev. Range 4,000-7,000 ft.

Whitebark: Needles in bunches of five. Cones are egg-sized. Only grows at alpine treeline (6,000-8,000 ft) and is often short and contorted due to wind and snow.

Scale-leaf tree Characteristics:

Juniper: Desert tree—grows everywhere east of Bend. Sometimes contorted and short, other times tall and straight. Little blue berries. Foliage is somewhat bushy, whereas the cedars' foliage splays flatly.

Incense cedar: The "dry-side" cedar. Twigs splay flatly and angle sharply forward. Small duck-bill shaped cone. Not as droopy looking as the redcedar, nor is the vertical bark as stringy. Mostly grows in the Metolius River vicinity.

Western redcedar: The "wet-side" cedar. Droopy foliage. Small and plentiful rosebud-shaped cones. Very stringy vertical bark that can be peeled into long strips. Mostly grows at lower elevations on the west side of the passes.

Single-Needled Characteristics:

Now comes the hard part—*the single-needled trees are the trickiest ones. Learning these five will definitely separate the casual outdoorsman from the tree guru!*

- Douglas-fir
- Englemann spruce
- Mountain hemlock
- True fir
- Larch

First, a word about true firs. There are actually five firs in the area: white, silver, grand, noble, and subalpine. They give IDers fits because they interbreed and mix attributes, becoming unidentifiable. Thus, experts often just lump them all as "true firs". Stuckey and Palmer say, "It is fairly easy to know that a tree in question is a fir; if the question is, which fir, it isn't so easy." Ross and Jensen comment, "...several of our species interbreed, resulting in offspring that have characteristics of both parents."

If you want to really try to ID the true firs, you better get a real tree book and prepare for confusion.

By the way, Douglas-fir is not a true fir. It is a psuedo-hemlock with down-hanging cones and spiraled needles, but a stiff tip.

That said, these five trees all have branches covered with single needles. (The larch is a bit unique so I'll talk about it at the end). The first features to look for on these trees are the cones—this is how you distinguish a true fir from a mtn hemlock/ Englemann spruce/Douglas-fir. A true fir only has cones on its very top branches in the late summer/fall. Also, fir cones sit upright on the branches, whereas on the other trees the cones all hang downwards. And, most importantly, the cones of a true fir do not fall to the ground intact—they disintegrate into flakes while still on the branch. So, on the ground under a true fir you won't find a bunch of cones (like under a Doug/Engle/ Hem), but just some triangular flakes. The bark on true firs varies from ridged gray/ black to smoothish gray with blisters.

Upright cone & flakes.

Under a Doug/Engle/Hem you'll find millions of cones and you'll also see plentiful down-hanging cones throughout the trees, year-round. So, if there are cones on the ground, it's not a true fir, and the trick to IDing a Douglas-fir from a Mountain hemlock or Englemann spruce is to examine a cone, then verify the ID with a look at the bark, tip, or needles.

Mountain hemlock –

Cone: 2-3 inches, darkish color, scales are rounded and often bent down.

Bark: Dark gray, thick, deep vertical ridges and furrows. Needles are short—.75 inches.

Englemann spruce –

Cone: 2-3 inches, yellow-orange color, thin papery scales.

Bark: Thin, gray, and very flaky/scaly. Needles are 1-1.5 inches and sharp.

Hemlock
Englemann
Douglas

Douglas-fir –

Cone: 2-4 inches, unique and distinctive 3-pronged pitchfork-like "bracts". **Bark:** Dark gray or brown, thick, deep vertical ridges and furrows. Needles are long, 1.5 inches, and softish.

MORE TRICKS: The tips of hemlocks all droop over. This is unique—Doug/Eng/True/Larch tips all point straight up.

An Englemann's needles are sharp—grab a twig and you'll say "ouch!" The other trees have no-ouch needles.

Drooping hemlocks.

Now the **larch**, often called a tamarack. The larch is the only deciduous conifer—its needles turn bright yellow in autumn, fall off in the winter, and regrow a bright green color in the spring. One of the best places to get to know a larch is the Jack Creek area. The larch grows arrow-straight and tall, has dark, furrowed bark like a young ponderosa, and unique needles that grow in clusters off "pegs" along the twig.

GOOD PLACES TO EXAMINE TREES:

Tumalo Falls: Across the river from the top viewpoint, four trees gather at the falls – ponderosa, lodgepole, true fir, and an Englemann. Now look left to see a droopy-tipped hemlock.

Jack Creek area: Ponderosa, Douglas-fir, larch, Englemann spruce, incense cedar, true fir, and more! Head up to Jack Lake to see lodgepole, mtn hemlock, and a W. white pine (along the lakeshore).

Cultus Lake resort: Lots and lots.

KOKANEE SPAWN

Kokanee are smallish land-locked salmon which spend their entire lives in lakes. They're unlike anadromous salmon (Columbia River, etc) which hatch in rivers, live as adults in the ocean, then return to their natal river waters to spawn and die. Kokanee spawn and die either in their lake's tributary streams or along a gravelly shoreline.

The autumn spawning is fascinating because it's the only time you actually get to see hundreds of wild fish acting like wild fish (as opposed to a hatchery's horde of farmed fish). Not only do you get to see lots of fish crowding into the near-shore shallows of these spawning streams...the fish are also remarkably colorful! The heads of the Kokanee turn bright red while their bodies turn a deep green...and the males grow a gnarly hook-jaw called a kype that prepares them for their spawning-rights battles. You can watch hundreds of these colored fish chasing and splashing as they battle each other, all no more than 20 feet away in the eddies and pools of a crystal-clear stream—Wow! It's a wildlife spectacle that's super-easy to view when you know when to go...right in our own back yard!

Central Oregon has some of the Northwest's premier Kokanee lakes. In the summer the fish are relentlessly pursued by fishermen, but beginning in late September the spawning show is the ticket!

The Metolius River: The Kokanee head upstream from Lake Billy Chinook into the Metolius River beginning in mid-September. The fish love the section of the river just downstream from the Head of the Metolius, and in recent years OR Fish & Wildlife has re-habbed the stream to help out the Kokanee. You can take a peek from the Camp Sherman Store bridge, or better yet, from the river's edge adjacent to the "Riverside Tent-Camp" area (just downstream from The Head of the Metolius at the next dirt road). You can't see much from The Head—all the action is a mile downstream (check the blog for vids).

Odell Lake: This is the latest running spawn—from early October thru Thanksgiving. It's truly an awe-inspiring Oregon spectacle as <u>billions</u> of Bald Eagles migrate to Odell Lake to feast on the <u>gazillion</u> bright red Kokanee that literally choke Trapper Creek, the lake's SW shoreline, and the li'l spring-fed streamlet by the Shelter Cove Lodge. Check entry 26 for details and the blog for color pix and vids.

Suttle Lake: In late September the fish migrate from Suttle Lake up Link Creek towards Blue Lake. It's difficult to see too much because of private lands and brushy creek banks, but it's worth a stop 'n' look if you're a Kokanee fan. Suttle Lake is 13 miles west of Sisters and Link Creek is at the far western end of the lake.

Des Chutes Historical Museum, Bend

Downtown Bend at 129 NW Idaho (at Wall St) in the historic Reid School Bldg. $5 entrance fee. Phone 541-389-1813

Inside the museum you'll find a fascinating array of all-things-Bend. Neat displays of mid 1800's items, as well as more modern stuff like Mt Bachelor promos. The resource room has an invaluable selection of books and 100-year set of bound *Bend Bulletin* newspapers. These newspapers are a treasure! Come on a drizzly day and just open a random newspaper book and Bend's past will come alive—from astronauts training on our lava flows to the mills planning summer picnics to Mt Bachelor's grand opening…etc etc!! If you love Bend, a day spent with these old papers will make you love the town even more.

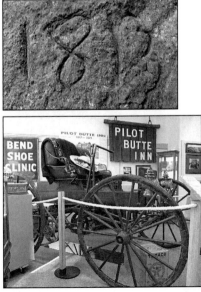

Bowman Museum, Prineville

Downtown Prineville at 246 N Main St (Hwy 26). FREE. Phone 541-447-3715

The Bowman Museum houses an interesting array of Crook County oddities. This is an old-school museum with shelves full of intriguing bric-a-brac. Guns, arrowheads, Thunder Eggs and what-nots...you will find something to tickle your curiosity. (For me the display of old-time mouse traps is priceless. Imagine a trap with a built-in wheel that the mouse, once trapped inside, runs on to propel the trap out of its hidden corner and into the living room!) Best of all is Steve Lent, the Asst Director who mans the front desk most days. Steve is a living encyclopedia of all things Central Oregon. If you've got an odd historical question bugging you, then Steve may be your answer—give him a call or just pop in to say hello.

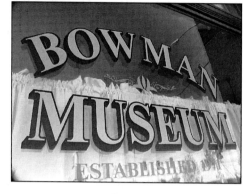

INSCRIPTIONS

Odd stuff painted on or carved into local rock.

Devil's Garden (41). On the roadside lavas just before Devil's Lake are a few remarkable red Indian pictographs. Down the slope at

Satan Creek's little creeklets you'll find a scad of more modern rock etchings from the 40s to today.

Crooked River Petroglyph (87). Directly under the namesake palisades resides a fabulous Indian petroglyph with its own parking lot and interpretive trail.

Stein's Pillar (93). Some numbskull had to carve his name into the pillar in what appears to be 1889. You'll see it where the trail ends at the pillar's base.

Dry River Gorge (8). An astounding array of modern rock-etch petroglyphs are just a 5-minute walk into the canyon...my favorite reading, "A mouse in the mouth of a cat is in no more danger than a man in the hand of a lawyer."

Des Chutes Historical Museum. The museum houses the earliest record of white man's exploration of Central Oregon—a rock carved with a date of 1813!!

Cougar Hot Spring (60). Beside the top pool is a 3-foot cougar carved into a rock. That's a dedicated soaker!!

Dee Wright (32). At the bottom of Dee's front staircase his name is immortalized in cement.

Crater Lake's Lady of the Woods (25).
A nude woman was carved into a boulder behind the lodge back in 1917.

Pictograph Cave (12). Excellent pictographs adorn a section of wall between the two cave tunnels.

Badlands mini Dry Canyon (7). On the mouth of the cave are some REALLY faded pictographs.

Bend Amateur Athletic Club. This little-known building next to the Historical Museum and across from the library sports 8 odd bas-reliefs on its upper corners. No tellin' what the Indians featured on the panels are up to.

Rocky Top (74). Look for the 1945 Lookout inscription.

Picture Gorge Pictographs (99). At the mouth of the gorge are some easy-to-find pictograph panels.

Central Oregon has hosted an amazing line-up of big Hollywood stars in 55 years of local filming. Check out this roster: Katharine Hepburn, Sally Field, Uma Thurman, and Jennifer Aniston… Kirk Douglas, John Wayne, Walter Matthau, John Travolta, Robert Mitchum, Kevin Costner, Liam Neeson, Pierce Brosnan, Art Carney, Don Knotts, Sal Mineo…and Slim Pickens. WOW!

In terms of locations there are three popular spots, each appearing in numerous films:

Smith Rock State Park: *The Indian Fighter, Tonka, Rooster Cogburn, Hot Lead & Cold Feet, Homeward Bound, Even Cowgirls Get the Blues, The Postman, Swordfish, Into the Wild, Management.*

Deschutes River: *The Indian Fighter, Rooster Cogburn, Hot Lead & Cold Feet, St. Helens, Up the Creek, Homeward Bound.*

Mt Bachelor: *The Way West, Rooster Cogburn, St. Helens, One Flew Over the Cuckoo's Nest.*

These films are ordered by their respective "BEND-ness". The times listed are as accurate as I could make them…but it seems that different copies of the same movie sometimes have different timings, so be a little flexible when trying to FF to a particular scene.

<u>Rooster Cogburn (1975)</u>. This John Wayne/Katharine Hepburn classic is the Bend movie-locations champion!! John Wayne plays, well, John Wayne…while Kate Hepburn plays the sidekick as the two both chase down and run from the bad guys.

The Bend action starts fast and furious with glimpses of Sparks Lake, South Sister, Broken Top, and Mt Bachelor all in the opening credits. The Fall River (32) is where the shoot-out happens at minute 7—note the shallow, moss-bottomed waters. At minute 17 the homestead is on Sparks Meadow, just past the current campground (39). Smith Rock begins its limelight at minute 30…and at minute 53 and 57 the scenes of "Kate's Saloon" were filmed at Smith's present-day RV parking lot. The actual "Kate's Saloon" was moved after the filming and now acts as a storage house next to the Juniper Junction ice cream/climbing shop.

Satan Creek and the Devil's Garden lava flow (41) are the stars of the movie from minutes 35-40, followed by Todd Lake (37) hosting a drunk John Wayne from min 50-57. Soon the movie moves to the Deschutes River (6) at minute 77 for the final 30 minutes. The Big Eddy rapids star at minute 94. Here the movie switches back and forth between the Deschutes and the Rogue River, and you'll recognize the Rogue for its bathtub-ring high-water marks on the riverside rocks, as well as the high cliffs.

<u>Up the Creek (1984)</u>. This is B-Movie comedy at its best/worst. *Up the Creek* was an attempt to glom onto the Oregon fame of *Animal House* by using both Otter and Flounder, while also mixing in the tits and ass of *Porky's* (using one of its stars). Whether the movie is watchable is questionable, but it does rate 4.5 stars on Amazon. The story is this: An annual collegiate rafting race on the Deschutes pits the geeks vs the frat boys vs the hot chicks vs the Marines. Needless to say it's all over-the-top wackiness, plus some bare boobs...all in our backyard!

Bend and the Deschutes are featured prominently throughout the movie. The very beginning of the flick shows the Reid School posing as Le Petomane University (our present day Historical Museum (Appendix 3). Le Petomane means "The farter" in French (Google it!)...leading to the joke of "Le P.U." university. Hahaha!

The gas pump scenes were shot at the Inn of the 7th Mtn, back when it sold gas. The subsequent bar scenes were inside the former Bend Woolen Mill bar. The Deschutes rafting starts at minute 38 and runs the rest of the movie. Five minutes before the end a raft goes over Class IV-V Dillon Falls.

FYI, I have no idea how they staged the final house-flood scene. If you know the details, please send me an email and I'll post the info on the blog. Also Youtube *Up the Creek* to see Cheap Trick's title-song 80's video.

St. Helens (1981). This is a sort of made-for-TV movie that dramatizes the 1980 eruption of Mt St Helens. It's a decent movie, well worth watching, that does a good job telling the real-life stories of both Harry Truman (the caretaker resident of the Mt St Helens Lodge) and David Johnston (a young USGS scientist) who both died in the eruption.

The Bend scenic action is non-stop throughout the entire movie, as Mt Bachelor stands in for Mt St Helens, Elk Lake and its Lodge (45) stand in for Harry Truman's Spirit Lake and Mt St Helens Lodge, and Lava Butte (14) acts as the eruption command center. There's extensive footage of Mt Bachelor, the Cascade Lakes Hwy, and aerial shots of the Three Sisters throughout the movie. Some harder-to-place scenes are the Deschutes at Bill Healy Bridge at minute 5, Devil's Lake/Garden at minute 11 (41), the Pine Tavern at minute 16, Benham Falls at minute 32 (6), and the Old Mill's trio of smokestacks at minute 104. Bend old-timers will recognize the bar scenes as inside the former Bend Woolen Mill bar. Real old-timers may also recognize the old Shevlin Park Aspen Hall at minute 60 (4).

The Indian Fighter (1955). This is probably the least known locally-filmed movie on this list, but it surprisingly features non-stop central Oregon action! For any fan of locally-filmed movies, this is a Must-See!! Kirk Douglas portrays a western scout who both fights with and against the Indians. Walter Matthau plays a role, as does the pre-*Gilligan's Island* "Skipper," Alan Hale. Extensive filming was done at the Head of the Metolius (77), Smith Rock (83), and the Deschutes River (6). Little-known is that a HUGE fort was built atop Benham Butte just west of Benham Falls, later taken down circa 1963 due to vandalism concerns (thanks to Les Joslin for the info!).

Here's the rundown of local spots: The movie

begins with a view from the Head of the Metolius with a large Indian camp placed in the foreground meadow. Kirk spies on an Indian girl skinny-dipping in the (38°!) Metolius waters and the next 20 minutes are in the area. Fort Benham then makes its first appearance. Minute 40 skips over to Smith Rock after a scene with the Skipper. Minute 43 moves to excitement on the Deschutes at Benham Fall (6). Minute 47 moves back to the Head of the Metolius where Kirk and the girl have a romantic roll in the river!! The battle at Fort Benham rages near minute 70. At minute 81 may be the first appearance of Monkey Face in a Hollywood film, shot from the west side of the Crooked River. And finally, as the credits roll, Kirk and his impish Indian princess skinny-dip together in the Deschutes, presumably near Benham Falls.

Homeward Bound (1993). This Disney adaptation of the book *The Incredible Journey* features a smorgasbord of iconic Central Oregon locations as three lost pets attempt to return to their home while dodging bears, porcupines, cougars, and police. This movie is really good...HONESTLY! Tears will flow.

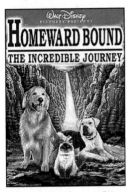

The Central Oregon action starts near minute 35 when Sassy the cat falls into Paulina Creek (19), which then becomes the Deschutes' Big Eddy rapids (6), then being swept over the McKenzie's Sahalie Falls (65), to finally end up in Tumalo Creek (4)—Whew, what an Incredible Journey! At minute 45 a cougar enters the fray at Smith Rock (83), but the scene quickly shifts to Billy Chinook's Balanced Rocks (87) where the big cat goes flying at Cline Falls! At minute 50 the posse troops across Sparks Lake meadows in front of South Sister (39). The waterfall at minute 55 surprisingly switches to the Columbia Gorge's Wahclella Falls (entry 13 in *Curious Gorge*). Then, back to Bend for a surprise appearance of Shevlin Park's Hixon Covered Bridge in minutes 60-66 (This covering on this bridge was actually constructed by the film crew in 1990 as payment for the use of Shevlin Park in the film [4]). Finally, nearing "home" the trio trots across in front of a Broken Top backdrop.

The Way West (1967). The Way West is a Big Hollywood star-studded gritty drama about a wagon train of pioneers crossing the Oregon Trail. Not only do you have Kirk Douglas, Robert Mitchum, and Richard Widmark...you've also got a 21-year-old Sally Field in her debut performance (playing the cutest li'l trollop the Oregon Trail ever saw!) And, not only is the movie actually Good and watchable, it features plenty of Mt Bachelor action! There's illicit sex leading to a gruesome hanging filmed adjacent to Todd Lake's access road with Bachelor as the backdrop (mins 59 to 72). Then the pioneers scale the treacherous scoria slopes of Mt Bach (minute 99). A traipse across Broken Top's Crater ditch plains leads the wagon train to the hellish dunes of Fort Rock's Christmas Valley, where, grasping defeat from the jaws of victory, Kirk's son is squashed into the sands. The movie ends at the Crooked River's sheer canyon (just north of the Hwy 97 bridge) where Kirk Douglas, on the brink of Willamette Valley success, plummets to a tragic death into the Crooked River. This movie is a MUST-SEE for Bendites!

Tonka (1958). This Disney western epic stars a young Indian who befriends a magnificent stallion named Tonka. The story moves on to Custer's Last Stand at Little Big Horn where most everyone dies...except the two stars! Most of the movie was filmed on the Warm Springs Reservation using the tribe members as extras, but significant portions were filmed in The Badlands as well as in the pre-State Park Smith Rock. Smith Rock is easily recognized in scenes at both minute 34 and 52. Much harder to recognize is the Little Dry Canyon near the Badlands Rock trailhead (entry 7). This rock-bound defile is featured as Tonka's capture pen between minutes 15 to 34. Sharp eyes will see the pictograph-adorned smoke-blackened cave as well as the water-basin tinajas at the head of the canyon.

Wow, who knew...a young Sal Mineo in the Badlands and a young Slim Pickens at Smith Rock??!!

Even Cowgirls get the Blues (1994). A wacky movie from two of the Pacific NW's wackiest creative-types. Gus Van Sant adapts Tom Robbins' novel, starring the angelic Uma Thurman as a girl with big thumbs and strange goings-on. This movie gets reviews like "Worst of all-time" and "completely unwatchable"...so you best be prepared with some seriously LOW expectations here.

The Central Oregon bits begin at minute 26 and last the rest of the movie. The main location is a private ranch on the west side of Smith Rock State Park (83). Big surprise though is Uma Thurman partying inside Hidden Forest Cave (11) at minute 53, and a quick glimpse of the Painted Hills (98) at minute 105. Little-known also is the voluptuous Heather Graham appearing in a quick scene with Monkey Face (83) prominently in the background – minute 83. What may be most surprising is that in an entire movie about sexy women, they never take their tops off but they do pull down their pants!

Hot Lead and Cold Feet(1978). This movie is a family-style Disney western where one actor plays three different roles in farcical shoot-'em up Disney style. Don Knotts co-stars as Don Knotts in one of his final roles. The Central Oregon action begins, of course, at Smith Rock before the opening credits are through. The next hour is mostly on Hollywood sets until the Big Race begins and the brothers take to the Deschutes at Big Eddy Rapids in canoe-kayaks (minute 57). At minute 65 the preacher attempts a drunken aid ascent at Smith Rock. Minute 68 is tight-rope walking over the roaring Deschutes just downstream of Dillon Falls (6). The action then moves to the low-water lower Deschutes canyon at an unknown locale.

Management (2008). The filming of this Jennifer Aniston romantic comedy was big news when the stars came to shoot in Madras the summer of 2007. Sadly, Madras isn't all too recognizable in the final cut, except to madras residents.

The first seconds of the movie shows Gray Butte (84) from Hwy 97, then a glimpse of Smith Rock, then a quick showing of the Crooked River Bridge…as Madras/Terrebonne stands in for Kingman AZ. Sonny's Motel on Hwy 97 in south Madras (north of BiMart) is the next stop at minute 15 when Jennifer literally offers-up her butt!! (OK J.A. fans…you can stay in that exact room to fulfill all your secret Jen fantasies…ask for room 217!) 5 movie minutes more and Jen's getting nasty in Sonny's laundry room (nope, you can't rent that room!)

That's the high point of the flick though, as Management takes this promising start and then dashes it into the pits of "dramedy" and decides to wallow in sappiness for the rest of the movie. At the very end, minute 84, there's 9 seconds more of recognizable Gray Butte/Bridge/Madras.

Swordfish (2001). This is a shoot-em-up thriller featuring John Travolta, a post-wolverine Hugh Jackman, and Halle Berry's boobs. The movie has nothing to do with Oregon except one scene at minute 63 where Travolta pilots a helicopter down to the west side of Smith Rock (83) along the Crooked River where he then blasts Senator bad guy.

Into the Wild (2008). During Chris McCandless' foray through the west before he took off on his fateful trip to Alaska…Mr Alexander Supertramp makes the briefest of visits to Central Oregon. At minute 38 Alexander quickly walks through the Belknap lavas atop McKenzie Pass (52). The scene abruptly shifts to the bridge in front of Mt Hood's Sahalie Falls (entry 84 in *Curious Gorge* guidebook) where he talks to his apple. Finally, Smith Rock gets the briefest glimpse as Alex shaves in a foreground sprinkler.

Seraphim Falls (2006). Big stars come to battle on the McKenzie River as Liam Neeson attempts to hunt Pierce Brosnan down to avenge the wrongful killin' of his wife. At the movie's start, minute 5, we join the chase as Pierce dunks into the McKenzie and hurls over Sahalie Falls (65). Then Liam, not intent on doing the spectacular loop hike, simply does a one-way along the McKenzie river trail between Sahalie and Koosah Falls while Pierce pulls a MacGyver to start a fire to warm up after his icy swim.

The Central Oregon scenes stop after 6 minutes of McKenzie footage, but the gritty action doesn't. This is a fairly good movie with a bizarre ending.

One Flew Over the Cuckoo's Nest (1975). This jack Nicholson masterpiece is largely regarded as one of the best movies of all time. Most all the filming was over in the Willamette Valley with a bonus excursion with the loonies out to the coast at Depot Bay. But,...the opening credit sequence surprisingly features Mt Bachelor as the backdrop as a car passes by on the Casc Lakes Hwy in front of Sparks Meadow.

For true Oregon trivia nuts, Gov. Tom McCall appears on a TV screen at minute 25.5.

The Apple Dumpling Gang (1975). This flick did shoot scenes in/near Bend...but the backdrops are all but unrecognizable. Don't watch it expecting to recognize much.

The Postman (1997). Kevin Costner's nearly-worthless overly-long saga about a post-apocalyptic future in which pretending to be a mailman somehow saves the country. This egregiously bad film sadly demeans Smith Rock's beauty with its idiocy. Sorry, but I couldn't bear to watch it again to tell where the scenes are. You're on your own with this turkey. Some people like this movie...I apologize if you're one of them. Which is better, Postman or Water World??

Honorable Mentions (cuz I haven't seen the movies):

The Crater Lake Monster. B-movie gem...Google it!

Sasquatch, the Legend of Bigfoot. Supposedly lots of Central Cascades scenes. Bigfoot fans LOVE it!

Love at Large. Supposedly features scenes filmed in Bend. Sorry, haven't seen it.

INDEX

Prime space for rent

But Wait! There's More!
also by Scott Cook:

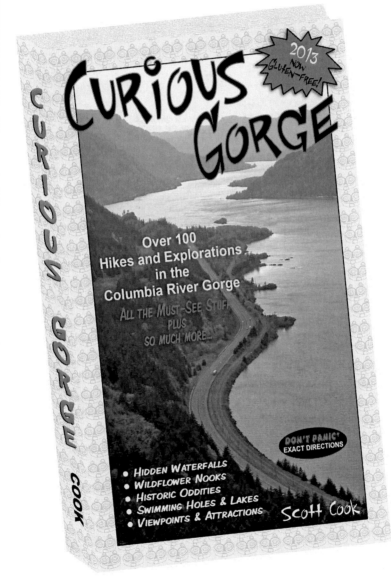

CURIOUS GORGE

2013 NOW GLUTEN-FREE!

Over 100
Hikes and Explorations
in the
Columbia River Gorge

ALL THE MUST-SEE STUFF
PLUS
SO MUCH MORE...

DON'T PANIC!
EXACT DIRECTIONS

- HIDDEN WATERFALLS
- WILDFLOWER NOOKS
- HISTORIC ODDITIES
- SWIMMING HOLES & LAKES
- VIEWPOINTS & ATTRACTIONS

Scott Cook